Bell P-39 Airacobra

BELL P-39 AIRACOBRA

Robert F. Dorr with Jerry C. Scutts

The Crowood Press

First published in 2000 by
The Crowood Press Ltd
Ramsbury, Marlborough
Wiltshire SN8 2HR

British Library Cataloguing-in-Publication Data
A catalogue record for this book is available from
the British Library.

ISBN 1 86126 348 1

Photograph previous page: Three P-39 Airacobras
photographed shortly before the United States'
entry into World War Two. (via David Ostrowski)

Typefaces used: Goudy (*text*),
Cheltenham (*headings*)

Typeset by Florence Production Ltd,
Stoodleigh, Devon

Printed and bound by Bookcraft, Bath

Acknowledgements

Any errors in this book are the fault of
the author. But gratitude is owed to many
people, including the following: amongst
P-39 pilots: Jerome Bachelor (Tonopah),
Lloyd P. Benjamin (4th Operational
Training Unit), Donald S. Bryan (328th
FS/352nd FG), Dino Cerutti (Victorville),
Gordon Graham (31st FG), George
Gunn (Victorville), Al 'Doc' Livingston
(16th FS, 23rd FG), Winton W. 'Bones'
Marshall (28th FS), Don McGee (36th
FS/8th FG), Howard 'Pete' Sheehan
(Mills Field), Evans G. Stephens (40th
FS/31st FG).

Thanks are also due to: Warren M.
Bodie, Clyde Gerdes, Bill Johnson,
Steve Mac Isaac, Sam McGowan, David
Ostrowski, Earl Otto, Tom Pittman,
Truman Partridge, Kevin Patrick, Norman
Taylor.

A special debt is owed to the Pima Air
and Space Museum where Ed Harrow,
Kirsten Tedesco, Stephanie Mitchell and
Scott Thompson are doing a superb job
of preserving aviation history. A special
debt is owed to the San Diego Aero-
space Museum where Ray Wagner and
A. J. Lutz are also doing a superb job.
Finally thanks to Aerospace Publishing
Limited.

Robert F. Dorr, Oakton, Virginia

Contents

Chapter One: 1941   7

Chapter Two: 1942   41

Chapter Three: 1943   75

Chapter Four: 1944   102

Chapter Five: 1945 Onward   118

Chapter Six: P-63 Kingcobra   133

Chapter Seven: Airacobra Survivors   145

Bibliography   156

Index   157

1941

Adventure, glamour, and a hint of brooding danger were all part of the Bell P-39 Airacobra story. That, at least, was the message in those colourful, slick magazines during the 'innocent' era when Europe was at war and Americans were blithely staying out of it.

'Pacemaker of Aviation Progress' was the name that Larry Bell's maturing aircraft company in Buffalo, New York, gave itself, and the commercial message was that flying a P-39 would assure excitement and victory. One advertisement told of '... the staccato bark of guns. A cannon's cough pierces the rhythmic whine of screaming motors. There's a flash of flame.' Any inferior aircraft fielded by the Axis powers that came up against a P-39 would be certain to go down in flames: the Airacobra, another advertisement proclaimed, 'always wins'. Decades later, A. M. 'Tex' Johnston, Bell's chief test pilot, would say that the Airacobra 'deserved to be considered a top-class fighter', and that it was 'under-rated'. Whether or not that is true will recur as an ongoing debate – and moreover an unresolved one – in the pages ahead.

Critical View

There was, of course, a different view. Despite all these accolades, pilots would still berate and defame the hapless Airacobra, which can perhaps lay claim to being the 'least liked' American fighter of World War II. One Army Air Forces (AAF) flyer training at Tonopah, Nevada, hated the plane's flying characteristics but loved its wide-track, tricycle landing gear – so in his imagination, instead of shooting down Messerschmitts or Mitsubishis, he fantasized about driving a P-39 down the highway all the way from Tonopah to Los Angeles where he planned to use the menacing 37mm nose cannon to hold up a grocery store.

When a British pilot first flew a P-39C on 6 July 1941, he declared he was 'dis-

mayed' by the 359mph (578km/h) top speed – even though this was comparable to the speed of many other fighters at the time. And it is no doubt significant that of the five principal fighters operated by the AAF in the war years (including the P-38 Lightning, the P-40 Warhawk, the P-47 Thunderbolt and the P-51 Mustang), the unloved, unlauded Bell P-39 Airacobra is the only one not to have a postwar pilots' reunion association.

In the narrative that follows, pilots are quoted on their opinion of the P-39 Airacobra, and it is interesting that except perhaps for Johnston, none of them puts it in the same league as the near-perfect fighting machine described in the glossy advertisements. Some put forward the conventional opinion – one that over the years has become accepted as the final truth concerning the Airacobra – that the Bell aircraft was a fine fighter that would have been among the best in the world if only it had been equipped to fly and fight at higher altitude. Others assert that, even

if its altitude capability had been enhanced, the P-39 was nonetheless hindered by its fundamental design and offered almost no potential for further development: basically, it was difficult to increase its fuel capacity.

In fact there was no practical way to squeeze more range or greater speed out of the basic airframe, because the system was flawed – namely, the long extension connecting the engine with the propeller created too many problems, for which there was never likely to be a solution. Many pilots questioned why the Army purchased the aircraft; even more, they wondered why it purchased 9,000 of them.

Chain of Command

Since the P-39 and the US Army are inextricably linked, it would be apposite to give here a brief explanation of the latter. In 1937, Air Corps officers were a small

The prototype P-39 (38-326), progenitor of all Airacobras to follow, poses at Wright Field around the time of its 6 April 1939 first flight. The P-39 had a radiator and oil cooler on its starboard side behind the exhaust outlets, and a three-bladed Curtiss-Wright propeller. The details of the cockpit design underwent numerous changes from the drawing board to the flight-line. via Dave Ostrowski

By 5 December 1939, the first aircraft was already flying in its revised configuration as the sole XP-39B (38-326). The decision to remove the turbosupercharger made it all but certain that the Airacobra would be useless against Messerschmitts and Mitsubishis at altitude. Apart from red-and-white tail stripes bordered by blue, the XP-39B was devoid of markings. via Dave Ostrowski

A YP-39 poses for the press. Aeroplane

Seen from the front, the Airacobra looked like a better fighter than most pilots gave it credit for being. This is a Bell Model 14 export Airacobra I at Buffalo, but this photo was used in a company advertisement to sing the praises of P-39s being built for the AAF. The wide-track landing gear made it possible to handle the Airacobra easily not just on taxi strips but, on rather frequent occasion, on roadways. via Bill Johnson

nucleus, some waiting for many years for even a modest promotion from first lieutenant to captain. The tiny air staff worked mostly in the State War Navy Building adjacent to the White House on 15th Street in Washington DC; the construction of a new building to house the War Department, and that included the Army, would not begin until 1941. Eventually, many of these staff officers would move into what became the world's largest office building, the Pentagon, completed in a northern Virginia swamp in 1943.

To forever confuse historians, the officers who flew American P-39s were members of the Army Air Corps, but after 21 June 1941, they were also members of the Army Air Forces (AAF). The people in the Army's flying arm were members of the Air Corps throughout the war (and until an independent US Air Force was created on 18 September 1947) but the planes, guns, bombs and bases belonged to the AAF – and contrary to the abbreviation used in umpteen history texts, it was indeed the 'AAF', the oft-published 'USAAF' being entirely incorrect. 'Army Air Forces' was always plural, and was never accompanied by a 'US' prefix.

The Army's leadership consisted of a handful of men who remained in uniform during the Great Depression, despite low pay and isolation from the struggling civilian world. They built a modest peacetime air force with the small number of dollars that Congress begrudgingly found for them. With little money and little interest in them on the part of press and public, these men achieved a tremendous amount of innovative work – in just a few years they went from an all-biplane to an all-monoplane fighter force – and they did it with their own preferences and prejudices. Air Corps boss Maj Gen Henry 'Hap' Arnold liked inline engines, and felt that fighter design work being performed by Bell was extremely promising.

With many achievements in which to take pride, and with some very sensible long-term decisions under their belts – for example, that in 1935 to proceed with a four-engined heavy bomber – Army officers could be forgiven for not realizing how completely unprepared for war they were. Neither Larry Bell nor Hap Arnold was well informed, for example, on what Willy Messerschmitt was doing, and so omitted to take any special notice in September 1935 when the prototype

Messerschmitt Bf 109 V1 took to the air. There would be 33,000 Bf 109s, more than any other wartime fighter, and right from the beginning the type would symbolize advanced technology and military preparedness.

Unready to Fight

To those most familiar with the P-39, then and now, the Bell pursuit ship symbolizes America's lack of preparedness for war – and this included a misguided assumption that a fighter manufactured in the USA was, by definition, superior to anything else in the sky. The P-39 was the first production aircraft to emerge from the Bell manufacturing firm following several years of fighter design studies, and it made an enormous contribution to the war, especially on the Eastern Front, even though it was never really in the same league as the Bf 109 or the A6M Zero.

Two views of a Bell model 14 Airacobra I ex-port ship in British markings at Bell's factory in Buffalo. These appear to be views of the same test ship, perhaps never actually delivered to the Royal Air Force, since it appears to have six exhaust stacks on each side of the fuselage rather than the twelve-piece exhaust stack characteristic of British Airacobras, found on the fuselage beneath the canopy. In any event, Britain quickly took a close look at the Airacobra and rejected it. via Bill Johnson

In heavy winter overcoats, Air Corps personnel examine an early Airacobra, apparently a P-39D, on the eve of the United States' entry into World War II. A press release of the time pointed to the '37mm. cannon in nose, tricycle landing gear, four machine guns in nose (covered over) and airscoop behind cabin.' The Airacobra is far from famous today, but as Pearl Harbor approached, most schoolboys in America were familiar with the sleek shape and unusual engine configuration of the fighter from Lawrence Bell's new company. Pima Air and Space Museum

The Airacobra was unique in many ways. The location of its engine, behind the pilot, was unorthodox, and it was also the first US Army single-seat fighter with tricycle landing gear: both of these design features were dictated – not chosen – by the desire to mount heavy armament in the nose; 1st Lt Winton W. 'Bones' Marshall, while flying the Airacobra at Las Vegas Army Airfield, Nevada, in 1944, remembered how the undercarriage worked:

The P-39 had an electric, motor-driven worm gear to raise and lower the landing gear. In the event of an electrical power failure, you had to make endless rotations by hand, of a landing gear crank, to get the gear down. On one occasion with electrical power failure, I had cranked my gear down but the landing gear would not lock in place. So I held the crank handle with all my might on landing to keep it from collapsing. As the aircraft slowed, the crank and the landing gear started to unwind. I tried to grab it again with my hand, but it was going too fast and hard to catch. As I immediately stopped the P-39 on the runway, the gear crank continued to unwind to within an inch of the propeller hitting the runway. My hand was black and blue for a week.

The unique armament and configuration of the Airacobra would later give rise to many myths, among them the notion that the cannon-armed Airacobra was a potent anti-armour weapon in Soviet hands; in fact, the cannon was never powerful enough to pierce the steel skin of a main battle tank.

Speaking of myths, the manufacturer's house organ, *The Bellringer*, was almost certainly wrong when it reported that on 8 January 1941 test pilot Andrew C. McDonough had flown an Airacobra in a dive at a speed of 620mph (997km/h). In fact the plane was neither as good nor as fast as some said, and by the time Japan attacked Pearl Harbor on 7 December 1941, the Royal Air Force had already tested the Airacobra, flown it operationally, equipped a squadron, found the aircraft 'unsuitable', and retired it.

The Under-rated P-39

Oddly enough, evidence abounds that the Airacobra was a far more respectable warplane than British or American pilots believed. Even the P-39's maximum speed

was perfectly acceptable – in some regimes it was faster than the Mitsubishi A6M Zero – and it was also more heavily armed than the North American P-51 Mustang. Furthermore the P-39 was undeniably manoeuvrable. Using the common term for the Messerschmitt Bf 109, a British evaluation document in 1941 reported that . . . 'the ME. 109 could not compete with the Airacobra in a turn, and even if the ME. 109 were behind at the start, the Airacobra should be able to out-manoeuvre and get on to the tail of the ME. 109 within two complete turns'.

The Bell pursuit ship was even included in a speech by Winston Churchill: he spoke of the war build-up, and promised that Britain would be getting more Spitfires and Airacobras – a curious choice since the most numerous fighter in the Royal Air Force, and an aircraft still very much in production, was then the Hawker Hurricane.

Design

No other fighter used in large numbers by any hostile force matched the Bell P-39 Airacobra for the unusual and unorthodox location of its engine. And as already mentioned, the Airacobra was also the first US Army single-seat fighter with tricycle landing gear, the undercarriage dictated by the requirement to mount heavy armament in the nose; this reflected the interest of all nations during the middle and late 1930s in developing fighter aircraft with good forward firepower.

Both the powerplant and the gun were sensible, and airmen were later to lament that they were not accompanied by a capability for effective combat at higher altitude. Even so, the most severe critics of the Airacobra would find plenty more to say about it, especially after it reached the hostile climes of the South Pacific. Throughout its service life, many considered the Airacobra to be a maintenance nightmare, largely owing to its complicated and not-too-reliable electrical system, its engine cooling problems, and the excessive vibrating fatigue with the long, geared propeller drive. Efforts to correct these faults were to produce mixed results over the period 1942–44 when the Airacobra was in combat in American hands; even more frustrating was the knowledge that some of the difficulties

Larry Bell's aircraft manufacturing company was prospering in the early 1940s, but he was a man of contradictions during his time at the helm. Although he had a true aviation pioneering spirit, much like other industry greats of his time, Bell absolutely hated to fly and could be talked into it only with the greatest reluctance. He was better at finances than aerodynamics – but no one ever doubted that he was in charge of *all* his company's operations. Bell

could have been addressed in the design phase, and never were.

As for the manufacturer, the Bell Aircraft Corporation was an outgrowth of a now commonplace phenomenon in the business world: the relocation of a manufacturing facility. The Consolidated Aircraft Corp. had been a long-time tenant of Buffalo, New York, but in 1935 the firm moved to San Diego, California, where it could continue development of its long-range flying boats. Left behind were key members of Consolidated management, and engineers associated with the company's single-engined fighters – and thus it was that Lawrence D. Bell, Robert J. Woods, O. L. Woodson and Roy Whiteman all ended their role as Consolidated executives, pooled their talents and resources, and formed Bell Aircraft, with Bell as president and Woods as chief design engineer.

It was the perfect time for this corporate team to come up with a next-generation warplane for the Army. In the mid-1930s, only newly equipped largely with monoplanes, the Army Air Corps was operating the Boeing P-26, Martin

---

Bell Model 3

Before any aircraft rolled out through the doors of the Buffalo factory in upstate New York, Larry Bell's engineering team had developed various paper concepts, the most important being the company Model 3 aircraft. Shortly after the company was launched in 1935, Bell proposed the design in response to US Army Air Corps specification X-609 issued in early 1937. The proposal was displayed in crude mock-up form at Buffalo on 24 May 1937.

Looked at with great interest by brass hats in Army uniforms, the Model 3 combined the sleek appearance of pre-war Greve or Thompson Trophy air racers with the tricycle gear, rear-mounted engine and automobile-style pilot doors of the later Airacobra. On the Model 3, the pilot's cockpit was located behind the trailing edge of the wing in the manner of the Curtiss XP-37. Unlike the Curtiss aircraft, the Bell design had tricycle landing gear: with the wing blocking vision in front of, and below the pilot, it would have been an extremely difficult aircraft to put down on a runway. Like the later Airacobra, it was designed for a 1,150hp Allison V-1710-C7 inline engine mounted in the fuselage behind the pilot and operated by a driveshaft extension running beneath the pilot's seat. Bell also offered rocket boosters to improve climb performance. The mock-up displayed provisions for a 25mm nose cannon with fifty rounds of ammunition, and two .50 cal (12.7mm) machine guns with 200 rounds each.

One veteran of the era remembers the inclination of Air Corps boss Maj Gen Henry 'Hap' Arnold:

He had a preference for inline liquid-cooled engines in fighters, as opposed to the old reliable Pratt and Whitney radial engines. This is one of the reasons why Alexander P. de Seversky [whose company became Republic and built the P-47 Thunderbolt] entered and won the Collier Trophy and the Harmon Trophy in the 1930s. It wasn't just that he loved racing: he wanted to prove that an aircraft equipped with radial engines had the speed, reliability and range to qualify as a fighter-escort. Another factor he advocated was survivability, because one hit in a liquid-cooled engine and it would be all over.

The battle raged on within the Army Air Corps for quite a few years. Seversky was a stubborn, outspoken, opinionated but brilliant man. He also had the knack for popularizing and simplifying arcane military concepts . . .

In the late 1930s, however, inline engines powered the proposals from Lockheed, Bell and Curtiss, and it was these that, in time, became the P-38, P-39 and P-40.

Bell's Model 3 would have been 27ft 10½in (8.5m) long with a wingspan of 35ft (10.7m) and height of 9ft 4½in (2.9m). Bell engineers laboured on the Model 3 concurrently with – rather than prior to – the design that became the familiar Airacobra. Once the Airacobra Model 4 had been accepted instead, this project was terminated. While it was still alive as a possibility, an Army officer visited the plant frequently to make key decisions: it is interesting to observe that he was a first lieutenant – today, the comparable job would probably be performed by a brigadier general.

B-10, Curtiss A-12 and Douglas O-36. The very first Northrop A-17s – those appealing progenitors of the better known Douglas Dauntless – were appearing in dive-bomber units, and the Seversky P-36 and Curtiss P-36 Mohawk fighters would soon join fighter squadrons.

The Army was on the verge of sinking an enormous chunk of its prestige and its Depression-era money into a new kind of aircraft, a four-engined heavy bomber being developed by Boeing. It was called the Flying Fortress, and it was more important to air officers than any fighter. But the time was ripe for a new-generation fighter, and that is exactly what the Army asked for in 1936 when it issued what would be known today as a request for proposals.

We tend to forget how much progress was made in the decade which saw the appearance of the P-26, the P-39 and P-51. By the time the United States entered World War II, virtually all front-line fighters – pursuit ships, in Army talk – were not only monoplanes but boasted cantilever wings and tail, i.e. flying surfaces which were unblemished by braces (an exception being the brace on the horizontal stabilizer of early Messerschmitt Bf 109s). Moreover, virtually every front-line fighter had some kind of air-blowing mechanism or supercharger to enhance engine performance at high altitude. (It must be remembered that aircraft engines must cope with thinner air at altitude, hence the variety of contraptions from the single-stage blower to the turbosupercharger to increase air availability.) The variable-pitch propeller, the self-sealing fuel tank, the modern radio, all were

Another view of the prototype P-39. via Dave Ostrowski

An early Airacobra poses for the press on a test flight. In this view the heavy cannon firing through the propeller spinner can be clearly seen. Aeroplane

finessed in the 1930s at the time when Bell was part of the story of American progress in fighter design.

Bell's chief engineer Woods and colleague Harland M. Poyer began with a false start, as they responded to Army Air Corps specification no. X-609 with the proposed Bell Model 3 pursuit ship. This, however, never reached the metal-cutting stage, and what amounted to something of a detour occurred, in part because the Army's specification was not very precise. Furthermore, the Bell engineers established certain goals of their own: good take-off and landing characteristics, excellent visibility, good ground-handling qualities, and in particular devastating firepower.

Armed with considerable new knowledge from their initial effort, in June 1936 they began working on a new fighter that would, in effect, be built around a cannon.

Cannon

In early 1935, these men had been present at a demonstration of the American Armament Corporation's T-9 37mm cannon (the manufacturer being a subsidiary of Oldsmobile, itself one of the companies of General Motors). Impressed by what they had seen, they instigated the design of a fighter which would include a T-9 cannon firing through the propeller hub. Bell was also working on the cannon-armed XFM-1 Airacuda twin-engined fighter: this became the company's first aircraft, although it was never rated a production contract.

In fact, while seeking to develop a high altitude interceptor, Bell never considered any other armament: right from the start he was wedded to the 37mm weapon. This gun had thirty rounds, except on YP-39 and P-39C where it had fifteen, and it became standard on all production models except the P-39D-1 and the export P-400 which employed a 20mm weapon instead, readily identified by the longer barrel extending from the propeller hub. Early Airacobras also had two .50 cal Colt nose machine guns with 270 rounds each, and four .30 cal Colt wing-mounted machine guns with 1,000 rounds per gun.

The decision to locate the cannon so that it fired through the propeller hub meant that the engine had to be mounted within the fuselage, directly above the rear half of the low-set monoplane wing, with the propeller driven by an extension shaft which passed beneath the cockpit floor. Early Airacobra pilots were fearful of the damage the driveshaft might inflict should it break loose or be damaged in combat, but in fact the arrangement proved as safe as any other, although one expert noted that it led to vibration as the aircraft got older.

With the engine situated far to the aft, a 10ft (3m) driveshaft was required to couple the engine and the propeller reduction gearing. The result was an aircraft fuselage that was rigid both literally and figuratively: engineers had few choices about where to put key features, and the orthodox, semi-monocoque aft fuselage was literally 'stiff'. The US Army gave Bell no choice about incorporating tricycle

landing gear – including a nose-wheel that added 128lb (58kg) to the preponderance of weight up front. Nor did the Army allow any choice regarding four .30 cal (8mm) Colt wing guns, which eventually remained standard until the P-39Q model, even though they involved a weight penalty that exceeded their benefit.

The Airacobra's retractable tricycle landing gear included a non-steering, self-castoring nose-wheel that retracted straight up and aft into the forward fuselage. The pilot raised or lowered the gear using a toggle switch in the cockpit. All wheels were constructed of magnesium alloy, and used tubed tires of three types: treaded for ice or snow-packed fields, flat contour for desert or sandy fields, and smooth contour for normal operations. Contrary to myth, the tricycle configuration was no less robust than a conventional undercarriage would have been. When 1st Lt George A. Ziendowski ran out of fuel on a routine flight in early 1942, he had no difficulty landing on Highway 501 near Latta, South Carolina, a secondary highway just 20ft (6m) wide.

Powerplant

The Allison V-1710 was an 1,100- to 1,300hp, liquid-cooled, twelve-cylinder V-type inline engine equipped with an integral single-stage, single-speed supercharger. Manufactured by the Allison Division of General Motors in Indianapolis, Ind., this engine evolved from a powerplant once used on US Navy lighter-than-air craft, known as blimps.

An early look at operational Airacobras. These two views show the 39th Pursuit Squadron 'Flying Cobras' working out in war games at Florence, South Carolina in November 1941. At the time these snapshots were taken, the Army's Capt J. C. Robertson wrote a notation lamenting that, 'We are still flying these.' Pima Air and Space Museum

This engine, like most inline power-plants, made use of a liquid cooling system employing Prestone (ethylene glycol, usually referred to as glycol for short). On the whole, the US Army still believed in the perceived advantages of a liquid-cooled engine over an air-cooled radial. A memo of the time spoke of '... Much closer tolerances (you can't hear pistons 'slap' in a liquid-cooled), higher compression ratios, and much better horsepower per pound . . .'. Each engine had a military designation with a number suffix (such as V-1710-35) and a manufacturer's designation with a letter-number suffix (such as V-1710-E4).

The V-1710 engine, which also propelled the Curtiss P-40 Hawk series, was generally well received in the field, although pilots and maintainers never quite forgave Bell for deleting the turbo-supercharger on the Airacobra and thus hindering its higher altitude performance. A 'secret' wartime report filed from hot-climate Henderson Field on Guadalcanal quoted both:

Reports on the Allison engine are very similar to reports elsewhere. Pilots like the Allison engines' 'guts' and ability to take punishment when necessary. All P-39 and P-40 pilots would like better altitude performance. Allison engine installation in the P-39 type airplane is preferred by the groundcrews because it is easier to maintain. The P-39 has a better daily 'status record' than either the P-40 or P-38.

Bell P-39 Airacobras at Selfridge army air base, Michigan, August 1941. The base was home to no fewer than five pursuit groups equipped with the Airacobra: the 31st, 49th, 50th, 52nd, and 58th. The first operational Airacobras were P-39Ds that went to the 31st Fighter Group and eventually were flown in combat by the group for a brief period. San Diego Aerospace Museum

'She looks like she's going 400mph just sitting on the parking apron.' That was the way people spoke in 1941 when Americans were about to go to war and P-39s equipped many of their fighter squadrons. The Airacobra really did look that way: except for the cooling intake behind the pilot, it had unbroken lines and was as sleek as any Messerschmitt. And as we see here, it was able to perform on rough surfaces too. Pima Air and Space Museum

Cockpit

The pilot of the P-39 Airacobra sat in a metal bucket-type, non-adjustable seat. A type B-11 Sutton safety harness was attached to the seat with a roller mechanism. Inertia-reel harnesses were not in use, and for some tasks the pilot had to release the four-way clasp to enable him to lean forward. Despite the numerous braces on the canopy, he enjoyed excellent visibility, especially for taxiing and ground handling. In the air, visibility was hindered to the rear quadrants, though few pilots ever cited this as a significant disadvantage.

With its unique aluminium auto-style doors on both sides of the cockpit, the Airacobra was easier to get into than it appeared, but the cockpit was cramped and space was at a premium. The cabin was designed to accommodate a pilot

The cockpit for the P-39 Airacobra was state-of-the-art for the era. The pilot sat between automobile-style doors (found on both sides of the aircraft). The drive tunnel for the propeller, readily visible here, was smaller than might be expected and not in any way an encumbrance. The pilot's seat, which is not seen in this photo, was relatively far back from the controls, and particularly from the instrument panel.
Warren Bodie

5ft 8in (1.7m) in height, and weighing no more than 200lb (91kg) with his parachute. The doors were fitted with positive locks and catches to prevent them from being sucked out at high speed. Each door had a roll-down type Plexiglas panel which could splinter if not wound fully up or down when closing the door. Improperly secured, the door had a tendency to fly off in high-speed dives, and pilots somehow ignored a latch retrofitted by Bell to prevent separation. Although the problem persisted throughout the Airacobra's career, ironically pilots also reported that the door was difficult to remove after a ditching at sea.

Development

In May 1937, Bell presented both the Model 3 and Model 4 pursuit proposals to the Army Air Corps' technical services office. Army officers rejected the Model 3 at this early juncture and it was never built, although many of its features would appear very much later in a Bell all-balsa fighting aircraft, the XP-77. The Model 4, however, was tabbed for further development.

The Airacobra concept was deemed sound enough to win, on 7 October 1937, an order for a single Bell XP-39 (Model 12) prototype. This progenitor of 8,000

Airacobras took off for the first time on 6 April 1939, flown by Lt James Taylor, a former dive-bomber pilot retired from the Navy. Ever after, the history of the Airacobra has been confused by numerous published sources stating that these early events – including rollout, delivery to Wright Field, Ohio, and first flight – took place a year earlier than they did: to reiterate once and for all, the first flight was in 1939, not 1938.

A day after that maiden voyage, pilot Taylor demonstrated the new aircraft for Army air boss Hap Arnold, although this flight was halted prematurely when the oil temperature shot up, causing the oil pressure to drop. However, Taylor managed another flight in the XP-39 on 22 April 1939, when he completed two flights totalling forty-seven minutes.

Twelve months later, following extensive evaluation by the US Army, twelve of the YP-39 pre-production version were ordered for a wider service test, plus a planned YP-39A that did not, however, materialize.

While the Army's early Airacobra development proceeded, the US Navy evaluated the Bell XFL-1 Airabonita, with tailwheel-type landing gear, strengthened fuselage and an arrester hook. First flown on 13 May 1940, the XFL-1 suffered from the beginning from weight and balance problems, and never showed any serious promise of becoming an operational, carrier-based fighter.

Following service evaluation of the XP-39, the National Advisory Committee for Aeronautics carried out a study of the prototype, recommending changes which included the provision of fairing doors for the mainwheel units, a lower-profile cockpit canopy, re-siting of the engine air intake and coolant radiators, and deletion of the turbocharger. The Airacobra prototype was modified to this configuration under the designation XP-39B. As a result, the decision was taken to delete the turbocharger from all future aircraft.

Turbocharger Issue

Of all the questions that revolve around the P-39 Airacobra, none is more tantalizing than the obvious: why did engineers delete from the aircraft design the very turbocharger which would have enabled it to fly and fight at altitude against Messerschmitts and Mitsubishis? Many

XP-39 (Bell Model 4)

The XP-39, the 'X' prefix signifying an experimental prototype, became the first aircraft in the Airacobra series. It came into being after Bell engineers examined several design concepts, all briefly at least identified by the Model 4 nomenclature. Once the company had settled on its final response to the Air Corps' 1937 specification X-609, the XP-39 progressed rapidly from drawing board to mock-up to actual aircraft, with minor changes in cockpit and fin design.

The prototype was powered by a 1,150-hp V-1710-17(E2) engine and was fitted with a B-5 turbosupercharger on the left side of its fuselage behind the exhaust stacks. This was the only Airacobra built with a second-stage turbosupercharger, and the decision to delete supercharging from the Airacobra was a critical one. Later it would be noted that at lower altitudes, the P-39 could handle itself against a Messerschmitt Bf 109 or Mitsubishi A6M2 Zero (albeit with difficulty). But without supercharging, the Airacobra was doomed to inadequate performance above 15,000ft (4,572m).

The XP-39 was therefore unique. This progenitor of the whole Airacobra series had a three-bladed Curtiss-Wright propeller, and a radiator and oil cooler on its starboard side behind the exhaust outlets; between roll-out and first flight it went through further minor changes, including the addition of braces on its cockpit. It had been rolled out of the factory as early as 3 December 1938, although Bell did not hold the unveiling ceremony until March 1939. The XP-39 completed its maiden flight on 6 April 1939, flown by Bell test pilot James Taylor – not at Buffalo but at Wright Field, Ohio, to which it had been shipped by land. Taylor kept his records in a diary written in pencil, and his entry for that

The Bell XP-39, or Company Model 4, poses at the factory on 3 December 1938, fully four months before its maiden flight at Wright Field, Ohio. This portrait seems designed to highlight the B-5 turbosupercharger on the left side of its fuselage which functioned perfectly on the prototype, but was dropped from production aeroplanes. The red-and-white tail stripes with blue border were standard Army Air Corps markings in the late 1930s. Bell via Truman Partridge

day consisted of just twenty-nine words: 'Flew airplane today. Everything went fine in the air. Experienced some oil cooler trouble. Also readjusted the idle setting getting 550rpm [revolutions per minute] to 2,600. Total flying time 20 minutes.'

This was a silvery and shiny aircraft. Indeed, the XP-39 looked much like the shiny metal children's toys of the era – left in natural metal finish with a dark anti-glare shield painted between the forward canopy and the propeller. Red and white American stripes appeared horizontally on the rudder in the style typical during the late 1930s. This aircraft became the XP-39B (see box on p. 20).

1 built.
XP-39 serial (1): 38-326.

Aerodynamics influence the shape of the 1940 Mercury convertible and the 1940-vintage P-39D Airacobra. Aircraft no. 33 of the 31st Pursuit Group at Selfridge Army Air Field, Michigan, wears standard pre-war olive-drab and insignia.
Pima Air and Space Museum

YP-39 (Model 12)

The YP-39, or manufacturer's Model 12, used the 'Y' prefix to indicate a service-test role. The aircraft was built and flown after the XP-39B (described separately, p. 20).

The 'YP' model incorporated design changes recommended by NACA (National Advisory Committee for Aeronautics) after the committee evaluated the XP-39 prototype. The first YP-39 (40-27) had its maiden flight on 13 September 1940, initially without armament installed. An order for thirteen of these proof-of-concept Airacobras was placed on 27 April 1939, and delivery – including one that had initially been planned as a YP-39A – was completed in December 1940.

Powerplant for the YP-39 was a 1,090-hp V-1710-37(E5) engine with Curtiss electric propeller. Armament consisted of two .30 cal (7.6mm) Colt guns with 500 rounds per gun, plus two .50 cal Colt synchronized machine guns with 200 rounds per gun, and the 37mm cannon with fifteen rounds (half the ammunition load for the cannon found on most Airacobras). The YP-39 was the first aircraft in the series to be flown with full armament.

The YP-39 flight-test programme included high-speed dives and spin work, and several of the thirteen airframes in this series underwent minor configuration changes as testing gathered pace. These aircraft contributed enormously to the production Airacobra that followed, but they never reached Army squadrons.

Rare in-flight view of a YP-39 flying near the factory, *circa* 1939. Bell via Truman Partridge

13 built.
YP-39 serials (13): 40-027/039.

YP-39A (Model 12)

This designation went to a planned service-test aircraft to have been converted from the YP-39. It would have had a V-1710-31(E2A) engine with the supercharger deleted. The project was cancelled and the aircraft intended for this modification was delivered as a YP-39.

---

wrong answers have been given, including the erroneous supposition that the P-39 was always meant for the air-to-ground combat role. It has also been suggested that officers of the Army's air staff in Washington were downright incompetent, or that sinister parties conspired to cripple the Airacobra as an air-to-air fighter. One aspect of the conspiracy theory is certainly true: Army officers were not paying much attention to the performance of the Bf 109 and the Zero.

Of course at that time Americans had not really studied the Bf 109 or the Zero. They would get their hands on a Zero remarkably early (in June 1942), but that was still a year away, and even then they would be slow to exploit the acquired knowledge. In fact – even if it means dwelling for a moment on the Japanese fighter – the information was available much earlier, thanks to American Col (later Maj Gen) Claire Chennault's pres-

ence in China. Dr M. P. Curphey, an aeronautical engineer for another American company in 1941, described it as follows:

Chinese reports were forwarded as soon as the Type 0 [the Zero] was encountered. That they were ignored had more to do with racial arrogance than the availability of the information. Please bear in mind, though, that most of the fighters the Chinese were encountering in 1939–40 were Ki-27 and A5M, which were not particularly outstanding aircraft and suited our bigotry. When the Zero became a 'fact' in our minds, flights of fancy on the part of Americans made it a copy of the Vought V-143 [it was nothing of the sort] and explained its long range with preposterous references to fanciful 'secret bases' in the Philippines. Only after mid-1942 did reality set in, though the reputation (vastly unwarranted) of the Zero as a super fighter had been enshrined in place of the stereotype of dim-witted Japanese copycats peering through coke-bottle glasses.

The Zero was able to clean the clock of most aircraft that got into a low-speed turning match. It was also capable of operating over a radius that exceeded any other single-engine fighter of the time. Lastly, it had during the first year of the war, pilots who not only had more hours than those of their opponents, but in the critical December 1941 to August 1942 period, combat experience in China.

Jiro Hirokoshi, the chief engineer on the aircraft, deemed it necessary to provide high control forces to prevent overstressing the extremely light construction required by the range specification. Put a flimsy wing on it, and then design the controls so that the pilot couldn't overstress it by high-speed manoeuvre, yet have them plenty powerful enough for low-speed manoeuvring. Not bad engineering, when you think of it. Remember, the aircraft the Japanese had been fighting in China were for the most part biplanes with low V-max and good manoeuvrability at those low speeds. Up against a I-153, the Zero could manage to

XFL-1 Airabonita (Model 5)

It was almost an Airacobra, if not quite, and it lingers as a curious footnote in history – and if things had gone differently it might have become a US Navy carrier-based fighter: this was the Bell XFL-1 Airabonita (Model 5), the result of a 1 January 1938 specification for a lightweight, carrier-based fighter to replace ageing biplanes.

The XFL-1 looked like an Airacobra with a tailwheel. In fact, its nose structure ahead of the pilot, although similar in appearance, was quite different, owing to the need for the entire structure to be stressed for aircraft carrier operations.

The Navy chose the XFL-1 for evaluation at a time when it was also looking at designs from Grumman and Vought-Sikorsky. It ordered one example on 8 November 1938, powered by a 1,150-hp Allison XV-1710-6 inline engine with a 10ft 4in (3.14m) Curtiss Electric three-blade propeller. As with the Airacobra, the engine was positioned behind the pilot, the first time this had been done on a naval fighter.

This undoubtedly contributed to the delays early in the programme. Having agreed to a $245,000 contract which included $125,000 for the airframe, Bell was at one point due to turn over the XFL-1 to the Navy's primary flight-test facility – Naval Air Station Anacostia, in Washington, DC – by August 1939. While design work was under way, and a full-scale mock-up was completed, there was debate about armament. Bell

The US Navy was really not interested in the XFL-1 Airabonita, Bell's one-off, carrier-based cousin of the P-39 Airacobra. The XFL-1 looked like an Airacobra with a tail-wheel (and no 37mm cannon in the nose), but in fact there were significant structural differences between the Army and Navy fighters. Bell

proposed a 37mm cannon, and the Navy countered with a requirement for a 23mm Madsen cannon, although neither was ever adopted.

From the earliest design stage, it was clear that the XFL-1 had a centre-of-gravity problem because of the engine location, but Bell engineer/pilot Robert J. Woods, in talks with the Navy, insisted on keeping the design intact rather than moving the wing further back on the fuselage.

The sole XFL-1 (bureau no. 1,588) was completed in April 1940 and delivered to Buffalo airport for flight-testing. The fighter made its first flight on 13 May 1940, only about a year after Airacobras were undergoing test-flying. The pilot was Bell's newly hired Brian Sparks, who had flown Boeing F4B biplane fighters in the Navy, and the flight was unintentional – a taxi test that resulted in the Airabonita becoming airborne. The flight went badly awry when flotation bags on the wings unintentionally deployed. Having put Larry Bell into a frenzy about the near-loss of the XFL-1, Sparks also encountered numerous technical problems on the second flight on 20 May. Sparks eventually completed seventeen flights before being badly injured in a different aircraft, and the test programme was taken over by pilot Robert M. Stanley who began flying the XFL-1 on 29 June 1940.

The XFL-1 finally reached Anacostia on 27 February 1941, but by then it was known mostly for its flaws. As predicted, the location of the Allison engine posed

The US Navy gave a full opportunity to the Bell XFL-1, that smaller-tailed, tail-wheel cousin of the Army's P-39 Airacobra. But the Navy was sold on air-cooled radial engines and did not, in any event, have strong reason to buy a fighter from a manufacturer it did not know. Kevin Patrick

XFL-1 Airabonita (Model 5) *continued*

centre-of-gravity problems, and the Navy rejected Bell's solution, which was to add ballast in the nose, raising the empty weight of 5,161lb (2,338kg). The Airabonita had a maximum weight of just 7,212lb (3,267kg) making it about 10 per cent lighter than a mission-equipped P-39 Airacobra.

The dimensions of the XFL-1 were as follows: wingspan 35ft (10.67m), fuselage length 29ft 9⅛ in (9.0m), height 12ft 9⅔ in (3.9m), wing area 232sq ft (21.55sq m). The wing, slightly smaller than that of the XP-39B, was designed to enable the aircraft to carry small bombs, part of a short-lived Navy scheme in which fighters would climb to higher altitude and drop projectiles on attacking warplanes.

Flight tests also showed the landing gear to be unreliable, and in December 1940 the Navy returned the Airabonita to Bell for

modifications. Under-wing radiators were complemented by a dorsal air scoop. The Airabonita was capable of a maximum speed of 307mph (494km/h) at sea level, or 322mph (518km/h) at 20,000ft (6,100m), and it had a maximum range of 1,072 miles (1,725km). But concerns about the basic design never went away, and in February 1941 the Navy decided not to proceed with the XFL-1. The competing design from Vought-Sikorsky was already being flight-tested, and it evolved into the brilliant Vought F4U Corsair. The specification that produced the XFL-1 also yielded the Grumman XF5F-1 Skyrocket (a twin-engine fighter which went nowhere) and the Grumman XF4F-3 Wildcat.

The XFL-1 was later used for non-flying armament tests, and destroyed. For many years afterwards, its remains were visible at the dump at Naval Air Station Patuxent River, Maryland.

XP-39B (possibly designated Bell Model 4B)

Flown on 25 November 1939, the XP-39B was the XP-39 prototype rebuilt with many changes. It was the first aircraft in the series to complete a maiden flight at the Buffalo factory. Its improved Allison engine was now designated V-1710-37(E5) and, most importantly, the turbosupercharger was deleted.

The changes to the XP-39B were made in stages. Many were put in place after NACA – at Langley Field, Virginia – conducted wind-tunnel tests on the prototype XP-39 and determined a need for numerous improvements. These included streamlining (and reducing the size of) the wheel doors, lowering and streamlining the canopy, moving the carburettor air scoop from the left side of the fuselage to behind the cockpit, and moving radiators from the fuselage sides to the central wing-root leading edges.

When engineers removed the turbosupercharger, they were making only one of many changes which defined the production Airacobra's configuration. But this particular step may have doomed the P-39 to 'also-ran' status among wartime fighters: in short, it drastically reduced the P-39's high-altitude performance, reflecting a now out-of-date doctrine which saw pursuit planes as low-altitude, close-support craft for the ground infantryman. Had it retained the turbosupercharger, the Airacobra clearly would have played a more important role in the air-to-air arena.

The XP-39B suffered a belly-landing during a demonstration at Wright Field, Ohio on 6 January 1940 at the hands of Army pilot Capt George E. Price, who refused an order by Larry Bell to bail out during an in-flight emergency. The aircraft survived and Capt Price later demonstrated it at Bolling Field in Washington, DC.

Frank Salisbury (left) and Larry Bell pose with the XP-39B Airacobra (38-326) at the factory on 20 November 1939.
Bell via Truman Partridge

(1) modified.
XP-39B serial (1): 38-326.

XP-39B

The XP-39B in its initial configuration at the Buffalo plant on 5 December 1939. Bell via Truman Partridge

Bell Airacobra Airplane built by Bell Aircraft Corp. Buffalo, N No. 4-064 Dec. 5, '39

On 18 December 1939, the XP-39B revs up in Buffalo. The aircraft received minor modifications after wind-tunnel tests. Bell via Truman Partridge

Pilot Homer Berry stands in the Buffalo snow in front of the XP-39B after its second modification, which has given the aircraft a new exhaust-pipe arrangement. Bell via Truman Partridge

XP-39B *continued*

The XP-39B after a third series of modifications to the aircraft, the most distinctive of which is a much smaller nose-wheel door. Note also the enlarged empennage surfaces. Not visible here is the final design for the carburettor intake scoop. Bell via Truman Partridge

The first major production version of the Airacobra was the P-39D. This example is standard. When the Army Air Forces took delivery of its first batch P-39Ds in April 1941, they were among the first American fighters to have self-sealing fuel tanks. The number of Airacobras accepted by the AAF leaped from thirteen in 1940 to 926 in 1941. via Dave Ostrowski

Clearly the product of a press release, this pair of photographs show a P-39 flying from Buffalo, NY, and the caption states it is 'the Army's newest fighter and rated the most formidable in the world'.

The clean lines of the Airacobra are evident from this side view of a P-39D ordered by the AAF in 1940. The lengthy pitot tube on the port wing is standard. Warren M. Bodie

manoeuvre yet had the V-max to engage or disengage at will.

The drop in manoeuvrability at speed, particularly the impossibility of rapid roll reversal, was critical to the tactics developed for use against the Zero. The F4F Wildcat, for example, was not a match for the A6M-21 in much of its envelope, but it could still manoeuvre easily in a dive whilst the Zero couldn't. As long as the Wildcat retained its energy, the Zero was at a disadvantage. Couple that with the utterly flimsy construction of the Zero, without self-sealing tanks, pilot armour versus the rugged construction of the US plane, and you had a much better match than the raw numbers would indicate. Of course, every pilot who ended up going against a Zero in a P-39 or P-400 Airacobra fighter knew that the other guy could fly and fight at much greater altitude.

So why no turbocharger? First, it should be noted that when the P-39 Airacobra was being designed, American turbosuperchargers were not considered reliable. Second, the National Advisory Committee for Aeronautics (NACA) noted that the original Airacobra design had numerous lift and drag problems. Wind-tunnel tests confirmed that in terms of aerodynamic performance, as one NASA official put it '. . . We have eliminated a

million and one [aerodynamic] problems by removal of the turbosupercharger.'

Army Thinking

In the 1930s, Army leaders saw bomber aviation as the primary force in the application of air power, and had relatively modest expectations for the performance of fighters. There was no thought that bombers would need fighter escort, nor was there any expectation that fighters would participate routinely in high altitude combat. Not only Bell, but Curtiss and Allison were forging ahead with engines and fighters that lacked supercharging, and no one seemed to find it remarkable. Allison, although a small company (it was then a division of General Motors), would not have manufactured the V-1710 engine without a turbocharger had officials not believed that they were on the proper course.

Ultimately, the Army revised its principal planning document (type specification 616), eliminated the turbocharger from the specification, and reduced the altitude at which it expected the P-39 to achieve certain performance goals. Some at Bell saw this as a good move solely for

financial reasons. There was no hesitation anywhere in the planning or development process.

The XP-39 would have been a worthy opponent of the Bf 109 or the Zero at any altitude, in any climate, on any day of the week. The same prototype airframe, bereft of the turbocharger and now designated XP-39B, was at best a mediocre fighter, though with many qualities at lower altitude. In the interest of reducing drag, cutting cost, and avoiding an unpredictable array of technical problems, Bell, Allison and the Army conspired to make the Airacobra less than it should have been. A few hundred miles away, Curtiss, Allison and the Army were doing the same thing with early P-40 Tomahawk fighters.

Airacobra Progress

NACA's wind-tunnel and flight tests of the XP-39 led to a dramatic overhaul of the first airframe. In a move that was unprecedented, engineers disassembled the prototype and rebuilt it from the inside out. They added a slightly altered fin, made structural changes, and increased the all-up weight by about 15 per

This P-39D Airacobra (41-6978) sits on the ramp with an early model 75US gallon (285ltr) fuel tank mounted to the centreline bomb shackles. Flight tests using this type of drop-tank were first conducted on an export P-400 (AP310). Pima Air and Space Museum

P-39C (Model 13)

The 'C model' Airacobra was almost identical to the XP-39B but for its engine. The P-39C differed from all other Airacobras in having its 37mm T9 cannon with just fifteen rounds of ammunition (half the load of other Airacobras) plus two .30 cal and two .50 cal guns all in the nose, and no wing-mounted weapons. This engine was the Allison V-1710-35(E4) rated at 1,150hp, and the aircraft was initially designated P-45.

Apart from its armament, the 'C model' was a production machine built to the standard of the XP-39B test ship with various revisions to the initial Airacobra design. But almost immediately, the Army decided that the P-39C was inadequately protected for its role as a ground-support aircraft and ordered substantial equipment changes, with the result that only twenty 'C models' were built.

The P-39C made its initial flight in January 1941. By March of the same year, all twenty P-39C fighters had been delivered to the 31st Pursuit Group at Selfridge Field, Michigan. Later, three of these aircraft went to the Royal Air Force in England, namely

40-2981 (DS173), 40-2983 (DS174) and 40-2984 (DS175). The first to arrive in the United Kingdom underwent a test flight on 6 July 1941, initially with an American pilot, Lt M. F. McNickle; British officers soon had their chance, however. But even after DS173 was sent to A & AEE Boscombe Down and DS174 joined the Air Fighter Development Unit (AFDU), British flyers were disappointed in the 359mph (577km/h) maximum speed attained during the flight. The aircraft used in this evaluation had tachometer problems and it was suggested at the time that the air speed might have been measured incorrectly. But a report dated November 1941 by an American representative in the UK said, 'To try to explain the loss of 33mph [53km/h] is impossible. It was later admitted by the Bell company [that] an airplane weighing more than a ton less than British Airacobras and highly polished was used for the publicity figure [of 392mph (631km/h)].'

20 built.
P-39C serials (20): 40-2971/2990.

Rarely has the streamlined, aerodynamic shape of the Airacobra been shown to better advantage than in this portrait of an early aircraft in the series, taken shortly after it was fitted with a nose cannon for tests in the autumn of 1940. When Bell distributed this photo along with a press release, the manufacturer of the Airacobra identified itself as the 'Pacemaker of Aviation Progress'. Bell

cent. At one point, the aircraft was rolled out of the Buffalo factory (on 5 December 1939) almost completely rebuilt but with armament not yet installed. Lacking the turbocharger and now sleeker in appearance, the new aircraft, designated XP-39B, looked great. But as late as January 1940 it still had no gun, which was installed only after a January mishap when its tricycle gear failed to extend on landing.

P-45 Fighter

At first designated P-45, the Bell Airacobra fighter was ordered into production with a contract dated 10 August 1939 and approved by the Army on 12 October; this was for 809 aircraft. Before the first of these was delivered, the generic designation reverted to P-39. The first twenty were completed to XP-39B standard but were designated P-39C (Model 13); sixty more had armament changes and emerged as the P-39D (Model 15).

The US Army ordered 369 P-39Ds in September 1940, and initial deliveries began seven months later. The first operational squadron was the 39th Pursuit Squadron 'Flying Cobras', 31st Pursuit

Group, at Selfridge Field, Michigan, soon followed by the 40th and 41st. (The 'Pursuit' appellation for squadrons and groups became 'Fighter' on 15 May 1942.)

Col Evans G. Stephens was one of the first dozen officers who went to Selfridge in July 1941. At this juncture, the 40th Fighter Squadron 'Red Devils' had just a single P-39D for the trial of new pilots, though others began to arrive quickly. The squadron also had BT-14, PT-17 and AT-6 trainers.

'Once the Airacobras arrived, we began to move around,' recalls Stephens. 'During the first week of September, the 40th

moved to Jackson, Mississippi for Louisiana manoeuvres. On the first of October we were at Bolling Field in Washington, DC. On 17 October, we moved to Augusta, Georgia, and on 16 November to Pope Field, North Carolina – all part of the war games that were taking place all over the South.'

Manoeuvres

At Bolling Field, the 40th FS flew low sweeps over the American capital to test the accuracy of civilian air observers

Specification – P-39 Airacobra	
Powerplant:	1,150hp Allison V-1710.
Weights:	Empty 6,300lb (2,835kg); loaded 7,650lb (3,465kg).
Dimensions:	Span 34ft (10.36m); length 30ft 2in (9.2m); height 11ft 10in (3.63m); wing area 213sq ft (19.8sq m).
Performance:	Max. speed 380mph at 11,000ft (612km/h at 3,400m); ceiling 35,000ft (10,700m); maximum range 1,466 miles (2,400km) with drop tanks.
Armament:	20mm Hispano-Suiza Mk 404 cannon with 60 rounds (RAF); or 37mm Oldsmobile T-1 cannon with 15 rounds (C), or 30 rounds (other models).

P-39D (Model 15)

The P-39D model began to reach the US Army in April 1941, and was identical to the XP-39B and P-39C but for different armament and a few minor internal changes. This first true production Airacobra had two .30 cal nose guns deleted and four .30 cal wing guns added. In addition, a centreline belly rack was added, the ammunition for the 37mm was increased to thirty rounds, and self-sealing fuel tanks and a fillet added to the vertical fin were also incorporated.

The 'D model' differed from all others in having a slightly smaller wing area of 213sq ft (19.7sq m) as compared with 213.2sq ft (19.8sq m) on all other models. An under-fuselage strongpoint enabled the carrying of a jettisonable fuel tank, a 300lb M31 bomb, or a 600lb M32 bomb. It is worth noting that the idea of a fighter carrying bombs was deemed somewhat unusual in the years before the US entry into World War II, and that this was one of the first times such an arrangement was introduced on the production line.

Several aircraft in the P-39D series were used to evaluate centreline fuel tanks, meeting an Army requirement to be able to ferry the fighter from the west coast to Hawaii. Real and mock-up tanks in sizes from 158 to 350 US gal (598 to 1,325 litres) were flown on about half a dozen 'D model' Airacobras.

429 built.
P-39D serials (429): 40-2991/3050, 41-6722/7052, 41-7057/7058, 41-7080/7115.

P-39D-1
The P-39D-1(Model 14A) was the Airacobra variant planned for delivery to Great Britain under lend-lease. It introduced a dorsal fillet to the vertical tail. The P-39D-1 was armed with a nose Hispano-Suiza Mk 404 (M1) 20mm nose cannon with sixty rounds. However, the 'D-1 model' used .30 cal wing guns in place of the British .303in weapons found on the P-400/Airacobra I.

186 built.
P-39D-1 serials (186): 41-28257/28406, 42-38220/38404, 41-38563.

P-39D-2
The P-39D-2 (Model 14A-1) Airacobra was also intended for lend-lease. Most D-1s and D-2s eventually went to the Soviet Union, with some reaching AAF units. The D-2 was powered by a 1,325-hp Allison V-1710-63 engine, and introduced minor changes. P-39D-2 models also employed a 20mm rather than a 37mm nose cannon. A number of these aircraft were modified to P-39D-3 standard (below) for reconnaissance duties.

It is likely that Airacobras armed with the 20mm weapon were considered inferior by US Army pilots. At one juncture, when some P-39s were moved from Canton Island to Guadalcanal while others remained on Canton Island (where no fighting was taking place), the 333rd Fighter Squadron with D-2 models was kept away from the combat zone, although a report noted that 'guns and cannons [are] working very satisfactorily.' Other Airacobras with 20mm guns did, of course, reach the fighting, among them reclaimed P-400 export models.

158 built.
P-39D-2 serials (158): 41-38405/38502.

P-39D-3
Twenty-six aircraft were modified from other P-39D configurations to P-39D-3 standard, establishing a standard for photo-recon conversions. The P-39D-3 reconnaissance ships had K-24 and K-25 aerial cameras in the aft fuselage, and armour added to protect oil and glycol coolers from groundfire.

P-39D-3 serials (26): 40-3025, 40-6730, 40-6767, 40-6773, 40-6780, 40-6791, 40-6818, 40-6965, 40-6985, 40-6990, 40-7002, 40-7011/7012, 40-7025, 40-7027, 40-7031, 40-7035, 40-7040, 40-7061/7062, 40-7065, 40-7068, 40-7073, 40-7075, 40-7094, 40-7097.

P-39D-4
The P-39D-4 variant emerged when eleven aircraft were modified for photo-reconnaissance duty.

P-39D-4 serials (11): 41-28281, 41-28288, 41-28340, 41-28367, 41-28370, 41-28375, 41-28400, 41-28402, 41-38296, 41-38301, 41-38315.

charged with reporting the movements of aircraft to message filter centres, part of a crude air defence system. Operating from grass parking areas at Bolling, the P-39D Airacobras also responded to simulated bombing raids, receiving credit for shooting down thirty attacking bombers. *The Washington Times-Herald* called the Bell fighters 'lethal as lightning and swift as thought'.

Still participating in the massive war games of the autumn of 1941, the 40th FS Airacobras continued south, though poor weather stranded several pilots at the Knoxville, Tennessee, municipal airport. Their brief stop coincided with a visit by Army Air Forces boss Maj Gen Henry H. 'Hap' Arnold, who had a chance to chat with the Airacobra pilots. Speaking of the pilots' attitude toward Arnold, the *Knoxville News-Sentinel* reported that 'It was easy to tell that they knew about him [and] worshipped him'.

On 18 October 1941 the *Augusta Herald* had as its headline 'Twenty Army Fighters arrive here for Manoeuvres'. The news story noted that 'the pilots, all commissioned officers averaging only twenty-three years of age . . . were . . . flying the new Bell Airacobra interceptor planes, the army's fastest and deadliest fighting ships.'

1st Lt Fred Dean, twenty-three years old and commander of the 40th FS, was depicted emerging from the car-style door of his P-39D cockpit at Augusta's Daniel Field, wearing a look that seems remarkably innocent when we consider what awaited these men just a few months in the future. When *Herald* photographer Frank Christian went up in a C-47 to photograph half-a-dozen 40th FS Airacobras flying over the Augusta canal, the newspaper reported innocuously that the fighters were 'protecting Augusta'.

Lt Gen D. C. Emmons, chief of the Army's Air Force Combat Command and boss of the manoeuvres, dropped in at Daniel Field to inspect the base and watch the Airacobras perform. Emmons and his entourage watched as Dean and the 'Red Devils' scrambled aloft to intercept a mock enemy threat. Soon afterward, however, a pair of B-17 Flying Fortresses participating in the war game managed to bomb Augusta 'heavily' while the Airacobras were patrolling elsewhere. A couple of days later, a miserable tropical storm in the region saved Augusta from further simulated bombing, usurping the job of the 40th FS.

The first operational Airacobras. These are P-39Cs with the production-style blunt spinner but not yet armed with nose cannons. The 39th Pursuit Squadron 'Flying Cobras' of the 31st Pursuit Group kept these new fighting machines in proud trim at Selfridge army air base in Michigan. via Dave Ostrowski

41-6786 was one of a batch of production P-39D fighters purchased by the US Army Air Corps on 13 September 1940. Here, the Airacobra is towed (by a treaded vehicle known as a Cletrack) through the snow in stateside exercises, while winter-garbed soldiers establish a temporary control facility during stateside manoeuvres.
via Dave Ostrowski

YP-39A, at a stateside base prior to the US entry into the war. Clyde Gerdes

Once the war games ended, it was time for the 40th FS to move on. Remembers Stephens, 'While the manoeuvres were taking place, a new airfield was being made ready at Fort Wayne, Indiana for the 31st Pursuit Group. The 40th FS arrived there on 6 December 1941.' The location was Baer Field. That Saturday was the last time Americans would know peace for a long while to come.

British Contract

Britain, of course, had long been at war. Britain's Airacobra purchase had been facilitated by a War Department authorization of 30 March 1940 which opened the door for such sales of most American-built warplanes. Bell had signed a $9 million contract with the French government on that date for delivery of 200 Airacobras to begin in October 1940, but because of the fall of France, those aircraft were of course never delivered (although Free French forces would employ Bell fighters later in the war). In late 1940, the initial French order was subsumed by the British purchase. The effective date of the British order was 30 April 1940.

In 1941, Bell turned out the first Airacobra Is ordered by the British Purchasing Commission which followed up on the unfulfilled French order. Great Britain signed contracts for 675 Model 14 fighters (initially dubbed the Caribou, and later known in US parlance as the P-400). These were like the P-39D, but with the 37mm T9 cannon replaced by an Hispano-Suiza Mk 404 (M1) 20mm cannon firing sixty rounds, and with the six .30 cal machine guns replaced by an equal number of .303in guns.

Rather incredibly, in the months that followed this arrangement, not a single British pilot flew the P-39. The first was Christopher Clarkson, who only began his evaluation of the aircraft on 30 December 1940. Years later in a letter to me, Clarkson spoke of the 'heavy responsibility' of paving the way for his countrymen. Production went ahead and plans for deliveries were forged, and most of this planning came to be, even though the Airacobra would prove both surprising and disappointing when it reached the British Isles.

It is worth noting that when Britain at last put in her order for the P-38 Lightning, she sought no fewer than 667 Lightning Is – and, once again, bought an American pursuit ship without turbosuperchargers.

British Cobras

The United Kingdom saw its first Airacobras – P-39C models – in July 1941; they were delivered by ship, and were assembled by a team from BOAC (British

Airacobra I fighters of the Royal Air Force. Some of these aircraft had faired exhaust stacks. All were
armed with 20mm guns instead of the 37mm cannon of the American aircraft. They were known as P-400s
in US Army jargon.

The British press were invited to view the RAF's new fighter.

The newsreel cameraman is framed by the nose gear. This shows the hoist position and the 20mm cannon shell ejection panel. Aeroplane

Fine view of the starboard exhausts and 'car' door of a 601 Squadron Airacobra I. Aeroplane

This Airacobra I of 601 Squadron is seen landing. Aeroplane

This tail shot of ♭♭♭♭ ⁺⁵ **Airacobra I shows the 601 Squadro** ♭♭♭♭♭♭ **~nd the rear fuselage pa.**

Aeroplane

P-400 (Model 14)

The P-400 (Model 14), variously also the Caribou or Airacobra I, was similar to P-39C/D models but had a nose Hispano-Suiza Mk 404 (M1) 20mm cannon with sixty rounds of ammunition. Also, the P-39D's six .30 cal machine guns were replaced by an equal number of Browning .303in guns. An identifying feature of this model was the rectangular field of exhaust stacks located behind and below the pilot, which had twelve stubs rather than the six on P-39 fighters. It is unknown whether initial plans called for the use of French armament on these aircraft.

The P-400 Airacobra came into being when France ordered 170 pursuit ships; the French order was placed on 30 March 1940 but was taken over by the British a month later. Initially, the Royal Air Force intended to call this aircraft the Caribou, but in due course it decided to stick with the Airacobra nickname. Britain's brief flirtation with the Airacobra, including its extremely brief employment of the type in combat, is described in the main text.

The initial French contract for 170 aircraft was followed by two British contracts for 205 and 300 aircraft respectively for a total of 675 P-400s.

675 built.
Serials: RAF aircraft: AH728/738; AP266/283; BW100-183; BX135/174.

Overseas Airways Corporation) at RAF Colerne. The first aircraft reached port on 3 July and was flying three days later. An Airacobra was delivered to the Air Fighting Development unit at Duxford on 30 July 1941 and was evaluated over a prolonged time – including comparisons with a captured Messerschmitt Bf 109E and with a Supermarine Spitfire VB. Not surprisingly, the Airacobra was competitive against both fighters in speed and manoeuvrability at low altitude, out-turning and out-diving the Bf 109E in every encounter. But the mock dogfights were all conducted at 15,000ft (4,500m) or lower, and British pilots found the Bell fighter 'utterly useless' above 20,000ft (6,000m).

The Bell company newspaper, *The Bellringer*, ran a two-page photo spread in December 1941 entitled 'Cobras Battle for Britain', with the subtitle '"Airacobra Best Fighter in the World," says the RAF'. In fact, nobody in the RAF uttered any such sentiment.

Pilots in the Royal Air Force immediately grasped the significance of the decision to delete the turbocharger, finding that the Airacobra had inadequate climb and high-altitude performance; in short, the fighter was simply unacceptable for the fighting conditions to be found in the European theatre of war. Only about eighty of the aircraft in the original order actually entered RAF service, and only with No. 601 Squadron, which gladly gave them up for Supermarine Spitfires in March 1942. As noted below, the British Airacobras flew one or two easy combat missions, essentially fighter sweeps to the coast of occupied France, in which little happened.

In late July 1942, after exposure to the feats and foibles of the P-39C model, British flyers began to receive the first genuine Model 14 Caribou/Airacobra I (or P-400) fighters, also at RAF Colerne. Workers assembled these aircraft – but not easily. Airacobras arrived dismantled in crates without having undergone any shakedown flying, and spare parts were largely lacking. Once a few were in the air, pilots found the Airacobra pleasurable enough to handle but were annoyed by shortcomings such as an unreliable compass, carbon dioxide vapours entering the cockpit when firing the guns, and limited gun accessibility during ground maintenance.

The first arrivals were sent on to A & AEE for tests (AH573/574, AH589, AH701). To meet RAF requirements for tests of flight performance and evaluation of differing exhaust pipes, aircraft AH573 was earmarked for an extended flight trials effort. Other uses of A & AEE Airacobras included studying general performance and gun heating (AH701), testing of the cooling system (by AH574, which was equipped with an automatic throttle), and studying carbon dioxide pollution (AH589).

In August of that year, No. 601 'City of London' Squadron began to exchange its Hawker Hurricane IICs for Airacobras. The squadron received both P-400s and P-39Ds at a time when the results of evaluation tests led to recommendations for no

fewer than twenty-five modifications to the basic airframe.

In October 1942, four Airacobras were declared operational, and ferried to RAF Manston. During 9–11 October, they ventured twice to the French coast. The compasses were still causing trouble, however, and after these actions the fighters were withdrawn for further study. The brief period of action was the subject of a report dated November 1941, from the US air attaché in London to the War Department in Washington:

Permission was granted to take the first four Airacobras to RAF Manston, and from there to go to [occupied] France for trial against any enemy that might possibly be encountered. On 9 October 1941, the first two Airacobra airplanes fired their guns at a small trawler and at some men standing on the docks in a harbour of a French town. The following day some invasion barges were fired upon by an Airacobra which went to the French coast alone. Five Airacobras crashed, and in each case the cause was determined as 100 per cent pilot error.

Britain eventually transferred some of these aircraft to Russia, and returned others to the AAF; 212 of the Airacobra Is originally ordered by the RAF were transferred to the USSR, although fifty-four of these were lost en route when the ships carrying them to Soviet ports were sunk. A few of these hapless aircraft, P-400s in Army Air Forces parlance, ended up in American livery on Guadalcanal.

In Soviet Hands

The Soviet Union would eventually fill out its Airacobra squadrons with primarily two models, the ex-British Model 14 Airacobra I, alias the P-400, and (subsequently) the lend-lease P-39D-2. Britain's decision not to use the Airacobra led to the Soviet Union receiving its first examples, even though the RAF compiled a litany of complaints about the type: unsatisfactory design, production defects, and no clear plan for the operational use of the aircraft. No less a figure than Winston Churchill assured Moscow's Josef Stalin

Bell's advertising during the wartime years (submitted to military censors before publication) emphasized patriotic themes and portrayed the P-39 Airacobra as one of the principal tools of the coming Allied victory. Bell

Night Landing of Cannon-Bearing Airacobra

...WHEN JOHNNY COMES Flying HOME

Above the clouds, through the screaming sounds of a night attack, comes the staccato bark of guns. A cannon's cough pierces the rhythmic whine of screaming motors. There's a flash of flame.

Then, Johnny Comes Flying Home.

Those few seconds flash back seven years to the start of the fighter plane that has since captured the imagination of men, everywhere. It's the story of blood, sweat, toil and tears through the years when Axis danger seemed a fairy story.

Johnny is flying a heavily armed Army Airacobra. It's generally considered the most deadly fighter plane on wings. With speed, fire power and maneuverability on his side—with motor aft and guns out front—a cannon firing through the nose—the odds are with Johnny. Much of Aviation's finest skill has been busy for years giving Johnny those odds.

And it's never too early to say that we are looking forward to the day when Johnny will really come flying home, to find his place in a new world of peacetime aviation.

Stepped up by the needs of war, we know America will have the benefits of the mass production of planes to carry on its commerce and travel in the skies.

But Johnny must have those future planes of peace...and when the time comes, we at Bell Aircraft will be doing our part not to let Johnny down. © Bell Aircraft Corporation, Buffalo, New York.

Airacobras for victory —

FUTURE PLANES FOR PEACE

BELL *Aircraft*

PACEMAKER OF AVIATION PROGRESS

that Britain would provide the USSR with 200 fighters, and the first Airacobras apparently began the trip to Russia on naval convoys in December 1941. Eventually, Britain was to send 212 Airacobra Is to its ally. At first, many were shipped simultaneously with export Hawker Hurricanes.

In a letter to Stalin, Churchill had shown enormous largesse:

In the first paragraph of your communication you used the word 'to sell'. We do not view the matter from this point of view, and never thought about payment. It would be better if any aid rendered to you by us could rest on that very same basis of fellowship on which has been erected the American legislation for lend-lease – that is, without formal monetary accounts.

Whatever the West may have thought or known about conditions in Stalin's Russia, military assistance of unqualified generosity marked Allied policy from the beginning, and the Airacobra was the touchstone of that policy.

Russian reports provide conflicting information as to when the British-supplied Airacobras – in effect, 'rejects' from the Royal Air Force – began to arrive at ports in the USSR. One report says that the first sixteen aircraft reached Archangelsk as early as 31 August 1942, and implies – but does not say – that they were Airacobra Is. It also states that between August 1941 and an early date in 1942, a dozen convoys brought fighters to Russian ports, including the Bell fighters from Britain. Almost immediately, the

Russian recipients are said to have believed that the British undervalued the aircraft, and to have rushed it into battle.

The Allied convoys which delivered the Airacobras over the treacherous northern route formed up in Reykjavik or Seidisfjord in Iceland. From there, they traversed the north-western part of the Atlantic to the Soviet ports of Murmansk, Archangelsk and Molotovsk (now Severodvinsk). This was a relatively short route, the distance from Reykjavik to Murmansk being just over 1,500 miles (2,400km), but it was fraught with peril: weather and ocean conditions were cruel, and German air and naval forces were within range. The best known of these convoys, PQ17, suffered horrendous losses.

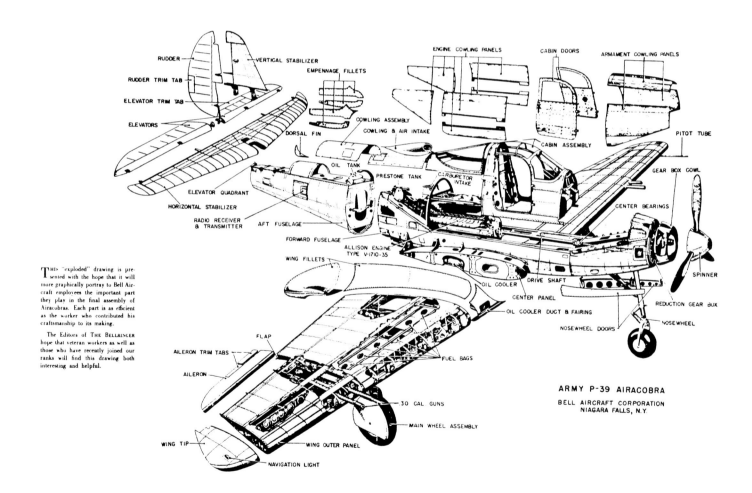

THIS "exploded" drawing is presented with the hope that it will more graphically portray to Bell Aircraft employees the important part they play in the final assembly of Airacobras. Each part is as efficient as the worker who contributed his craftsmanship to its making.

The Editors of THE BELLRINGER hope that veteran workers as well as those who have recently joined our ranks will find this drawing both interesting and helpful.

Exploded view of a P-39 from a Bell magazine, *The Bellringer.* BELL AIRCRAFT CORP. VIA EDMUND S. MAREK

This 'exploded' view of a P-39 from the Bell Aircraft house organ, The Bellringer, shows how the components of an Airacobra came together to become a complete aircraft. Bell

Russian shipments

The Russians claim that British reports indicate that fifty-four Airacobra I fighters were lost during sea transport; however, actual losses, they say, were more like twenty to twenty-five. Once off-loaded at ports in the Soviet Union, the newly arrived Airacobras then took several routes to operational units.

The Soviet Air Force (technically the Air Force of the Red Army, but usually known in the West as the VVS, for *Voyenno-Vozhdushniye Sily*, meaning Military Air Forces) already had great expertise at solving logistical problems – some of it, no doubt, simply the result of a long history of coping with difficult climate and geography. It was less well prepared to field a whole new generation of fighter pilots; but even as the Airacobras reached the frozen winter docks, the process of recruiting and retraining was well under way.

The first twenty Airacobra Is were on Soviet soil before the end of December 1941, and dozens more followed. The Airacobras craned off-ship at Murmansk were usually acquired by field army units and transferred either to air units of the Naval Air Force, located in the nearby region (the 2nd Guards Combined Aviation Regiment, the 78th Fighter Regiment), or were trans-shipped by railway to the Afrikand station and assigned to the 19th Guards Fighter Aviation.

The VVS was the largest and most important component of Moscow's aviation forces; it was commanded by Gen (later Marshal) Novikov, who was subordinate to the Red Army's general staff. On any organizational chart or 'wiring diagram', the VVS was divided into larger echelons, air divisions or air corps, and beneath these appeared the basic combat formation, the regiment. The numerical strength of an air regiment was thirty to

thirty-five aircraft, divided into tactical squadrons and flights. A fighter regiment usually boasted about 175 officers and men. Many VVS units, including regiments which operated a mixed bag of Soviet-built fighters and Airacobras, went through extended periods of the war far below planned operating strength.

By the time the Airacobra became part of the Soviet scene, the Russian High Command had already held the Wehrmacht short of Moscow, denying Adolf Hitler his prized goal of seizing the USSR capital. Ahead lay fighting, often in harsh wintry conditions, along a Soviet-German front which began near the top of this vast country (where Leningrad was under siege) to thousands of miles in the south and east (including the epic battle at Stalingrad). The Soviets had manufactured 8,000 aircraft during the six months prior to the German strike towards Moscow, but the bulk of the Russian industry was in the west and was overrun

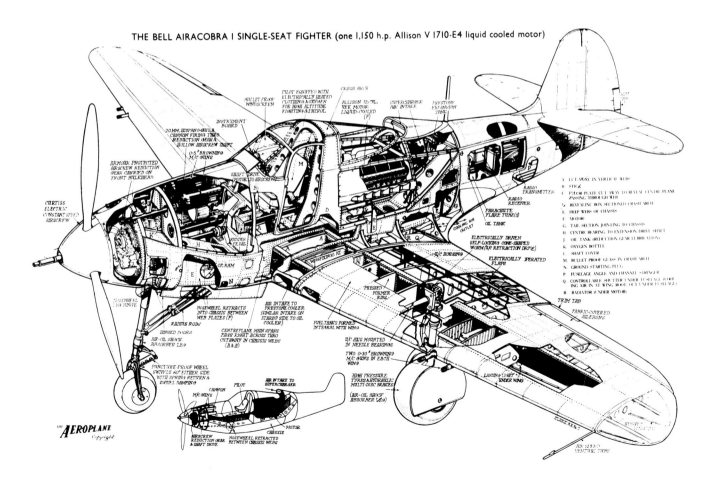

Frank Clark's cutaway of the Airacobra I, prepared for Aeroplane **magazine in the UK.** Aeroplane

At the time of the Japanese attack on Pearl Harbor on 7 December 1941 – here, showing the destruction of the battleship USS Arizona (BB-39) – the Army Air Forces had more than 900 Airacobras in inventory, but they were scattered among dozens of relatively small units. The P-40 Warhawk was slightly more numerous, while significant numbers of P-38 Lightnings, P-47 Thunderbolts, and P-51 Mustangs lay in the future. The Navy and Marine Corps together could boast only about 350 F4F Wildcats. US Navy

by advancing German forces. Aircraft production lagged to around 500 per month in late 1941, so the arriving Airacobras and other aircraft from abroad were not merely welcome, they were essential.

Airacobras that arrived by sea at Archangelsk and Molotovsk went on railway flatcars by direct line through Vologda, while those from Murmansk were shipped by the Kirov road to Belomorsk or to Volkhov. Not surprisingly, given the immediacy of the war with its enormous casualties, no one seems to have spent much time taking pictures

of these Airacobra deliveries, although photos would be priceless today. At the end of 1941, the Union of Soviet Socialist Republics could be forgiven for having other priorities.

Pacific Fight

There were no P-39s at Pearl Harbor when the Japanese attacked on 7 December 1941. A handful of P-35s and P-40s managed to get aloft to wage a largely ineffectual battle with the Japanese attackers.

Army lieutenants Kenneth Taylor and George Welch, both of whom would fly P-39s in the South Pacific later, managed to engage the Japanese in a pair of P-40s, Welch scoring four aerial victories.

On 12 December 1941, Col Claire Chennault's American Volunteer Group, the Flying Tigers, went into combat against the Japanese, flying from a base at Mingaladon, Burma – in a fighter developed by Curtiss, Allison and the Army without a turbocharger. Within days, the Curtiss P-40B/C Warhawk pilots of the AVG moved up to Kunming, China, to defend the Burma Road, and for the next six months would perform well against Japanese warplanes; the latter included Nakajima Ki-44 'Oscar' fighters (the Flying Tigers never fought the Zero). However, at least one historian has wondered if they might have performed better had they been issued Bell fighters.

Rick Mitchell, author of a P-39 monograph entitled *Airacobra Advantage*, points out that most aviation experts would automatically assume the P-40 to be superior to the P-39. However, he insists that, on the contrary:

> The truth is that no model of the P-40 during its entire service history was ever as fast as the

slowest P-39 variant. No P-40 was ever armed with the tremendous firepower or knockout punch carried by every P-39. Too many . . . make the mistake of comparing the P-39, America's earlier modern fighter plane, with much later World War II fighter designs, such as . . . the P-47 [and] the P-51.

So although the American Volunteer Group was a giant success, Mitchell believes the AVG record of aerial victories against the Japanese would have been even higher with Airacobras.

The outbreak of war caused many sudden uprootings. At Fort Wayne, Indiana, where the 31st FG lived with its Airacobras, there was much confusion.

'The 40th FS was assigned to proceed to Port Angeles, Washington,' remembers Col Evans G. Stephens. 'The air contingent with twenty-three P-39s departed on 8 December, and arrived at Port Angeles on 25 December. The trip was a "saga" involving weather, mishaps and lack of experience.' This was to become a familiar story, and at a time when most were celebrating Christmas and New Year, Americans were hearing one report after another of their forces being pounded on every front. The situation was not new to others in Europe and Asia – but for Americans, the end of 1941 marked the beginning of a dark period of difficulty and defeat.

A Bell YP-39 Airacobra, thought to be aircraft no. 40–27, on a test flight before the US entry into World War II. Bell

'Airacobra Fantasies'

So far as we know today, the Airacobra was never used to tow a signboard with a romantic message, or to harass campers on the Russian River in northern California, or to rob a supermarket in Los Angeles. These potential applications of Larry Bell's sleek fighter were the fantasies of bored US Army pilots at Tonopah, Nevada. Col Jerome Bachelor, retired, remembered that, for a brief time, the American pilots had little else to do but to dream up bizarre schemes:

There was this brief period after Pearl Harbor when we were in the war and nobody knew where we were going or what we were doing. We were in RTU [a replacement training unit] at Tonopah. All of us were fairly experienced – most of us had gone through flight training before 7 December 1941 – and we had these scruffy-looking P-39s. We were all itching to get into combat and they were keeping us there, in this one-horse town, while we waited for firm assignments. After a while we got tired of dogfighting each other and began talking about other things we might do with the Airacobra.

One of my wingmen was dating a girl named Elizabeth from nearby northern California. He actually built a wood and tarpaulin billboard with letters three feet high proclaiming 'I love you Elizabeth'. He was talking about attaching it to a P-39 and buzzing her house with it. He also had a scheme to make a low-level run over a beach she liked, where people camped out-of-doors in the winter. He was going to use his pursuit ship to proclaim his undying affection.

In those days it had not occurred to us to put the name of a wife or girl friend on the airplane itself. We did this later, although I never heard the term 'nose art' used until long after the war. Anyway, it's a good thing he never thought of painting the nose of his plane because he later married a girl named Harriet.

Bachelor fired the cannon and machine guns from a compass rose position on the ground one day, and was impressed with how much he enjoyed shooting while on the ground:

We were talking, and I was thinking about this grocery store in Pasadena [in the Los Angeles area] where I had grown up and where the proprietor had been mean to me and my mother. I got to thinking, since the P-39 handled so well on the ground, what if I taxi it out onto the highway – we had two-lane highways in California in those days – and 'drive' it the 400 miles [645km] down to my home town?

I would pull up in front of the market, point the nose of my P-39 at the front door, whip out a megaphone and announce, 'This is a hold-up! Put all your money in my airplane or I'll shoot this place to pieces!' I had visions of the guy I didn't like cowering in his shoes and apologizing, and then I was going to tell him it was just a joke. At least I thought I would tell him that. But I have to confess, I also had vivid fantasies of what it would be like to shoot up a building on the ground with that 37mm cannon.

Bachelor never carried out his fantasies. After a few weeks proving the axiom that military life requires one to 'hurry up and wait', he eventually received orders. He flew P-47 Thunderbolts in combat in the European War, F-80 Shooting Stars in Korea, and Kaman HH-43 helicopters in the Vietnam war. 'To this day, I still think of some of the crazy schemes we had for the P-39. I'm glad we were only fantasizing.'

The first P-39D model (40-2991) basks in the snow at the Bell plant in Buffalo. Bell

CHAPTER TWO

1942

For many Americans in uniform, the first days of the new war were strange, typified by somewhat tentative enterprise, and sometimes accompanied by moves in the wrong direction. Typical were the experiences of the 40th Fighter Squadron 'Red Devils', which took more than two weeks to fly its P-39D Airacobras from Fort Wayne, Indiana, to Port Angeles, Washington. On Christmas Day 1941, Col Evans G. Stephens remembers events very clearly:

The arrival at Port Angeles was very spectacular, with the 40th squadron in close formation at low altitude buzzing the town at about 11am when many of the people were at church. Some thought the invasion had started.

While the 40th squadron was at Port Angeles it was billeted at the County Fair grounds adjacent to the airfield. Submarine patrol flights were flown over the Strait of Juan de Fuca when weather would permit. We hit some redwood logs with gunfire, but didn't sink any. This was the first time that most of the pilots had fired a gun in the air. [In early 1942, rumours abounded of Japanese aircraft carriers off the west coast, or even of invasion forces ready to come ashore. Combat crews found themselves torn between defending against a phantom enemy at home and preparing for combat abroad.]

During the first week of January 1942, commanding officer Capt Fred Dean and his second-in-command 1st Lt S. M. Smith divided the squadron in half on paper, then Smith's half was selected to go to the Pacific area. On 18 January 1941, the squadron's supply and main-

tenance officers were sent to the San Francisco port of embarkation to obtain equipment and supplies to bring our 'half squadron' up to full mobility.

We left San Francisco around the first week in February and arrived in Australia in the first week in March. Upon arrival at Brisbane, the squadron was put in tents on the Ascot race track for the first night. Our maintenance personnel went to RAAF Station Ipswich to put the aircraft wings back on and flight-test each P-39 to make it combat ready. Then on 17 March 1942, the flight contingent left for Mt Gambier and gunnery training . . .

Meanwhile the 31st Fighter Group, to which the 40th had been assigned, headed for England. As we shall see, plans for the 31st FG to fly its Airacobras in combat never materialized – although the 39th Fighter Squadron 'Flying Cobras' was removed from the group, kept its P-39s, and went in the other direction. The men of the 39th preceded the 40th FS to Brisbane and then to the first operational base from which they would fly, Woodstock in northern Australia. Here

they received factory-new, export-model P-400 Airacobras.

On 20 April 1942, the 39th, 40th and 41st FS became part of the 35th Fighter Group that, in turn, was a component of the Fifth Air Force. At this juncture the 35th FG was still relatively new and untried; ultimately, however, it would become one of the premier combat formations in the Pacific.

Americans in P-39 Airacobras were already confronting Japanese fighters in the Aleutians, and they would soon face the enemy on New Guinea, and at Guadalcanal. Yet while Stephens and his fellow flyers were honing their skills for combat, the Army Air Forces (AAF) came to the conclusion that the Bell fighter should be employed primarily for training.

Instructional Tool

The Airacobra was already a mainstay at advanced flying schools, and the AAF decision meant that most pilots would

Bell's standard portrait of an Airacobra in flight, released by the manufacturer during and for years after the war, showed what appeared to be a P-39D model with the serial number obliterated. This was standard practice for a period during the war, intended to prevent enemies making judgments about aircraft production rates. In the case of this particular image, no copy with a readable serial number has ever surfaced. via M. J. Kasiuba

The 8th Pursuit Group (quickly renamed the 8th Fighter Group) went to the south-west Pacific in early 1942 with three squadrons of Airacobras: the 35th FS 'Black Panthers', 36th FS 'Flying Fiends' and 80th FS 'Headhunters'. After being on the scene for the defence of Darwin, the group moved up to Port Moresby, New Guinea, to confront a Japanese attempt to grab the world's fourth largest island.

only remember it for its performance as a trainer, and nothing else. When the war was over, pilots of the Army's four principal fighters – the P-38 Lightning, P-40 Warhawk, P-47 Thunderbolt and P-51 Mustang – all remembered flying the Airacobra in training but never as a combat aircraft, apart from a handful of men. To most, it was an interim aircraft that they flew on their way towards something else.

Typical was former Capt Al Livingston – inevitably 'Doc' to his friends – who later flew P-40 Warhawks with the 23rd Fighter Group in China and was among fighter pilots in Flying Class 42-H. (It was customary to identify a pilot class by the last two digits of its graduation calendar year, followed by a letter; this practice began with Class 40-A, and it created a permanent bond among all who earned their silver wings together.) When Livingston was sent to Sarasota, Fla., out of flight school to train in the P-39 Airacobra, he recalls: 'We thought we were going to be shipped out to the South Pacific where P-39s were being used.' Livingston heard mild criticism of the Airacobra:

We had a lot of people who talked about them stalling out and saying it wasn't a very good airplane. I didn't have any trouble with them. I would take one up to an altitude of about 12,000ft [3,657m], stall it out, put it into a spin, and then bring it out of a spin, all with little difficulty. At a reunion many years later, I asked an F-15 Eagle pilot what speed he landed it at. He said 105 knots. I said, 'You're not going to believe this, but in 1942 we were landing the Bell Airacobra at the same speed you use to land your fighter today.' We brought them in at 125mph [201km/h] on the approach, and we landed them at about 110mph [177km/h]. [Knots, or nautical miles per hour, replaced statute miles per hour in pilot jargon in the 1960s.]

Every other Army fighter landed at a lower speed. In a P-40 Warhawk, you would approach at 100mph [160km/h]. It would stall out at 85 to 90mph [136 to 144km/h]. The Airacobra was much faster coming in, but after you practised a couple of times and learned its stall speed, it wasn't difficult to land a P-39. You set it down on all three wheels in a three-point landing. We were trained to land fast and get off the main runway fast because airfields were always cluttered with traffic. In the P-39, you never touched the throttle from the moment you reached the runway until you turned off on the taxiway.

I had sixty-five to seventy hours in the P-39 at Sarasota. On one of my final flights, the right landing gear wouldn't come down. I called the tower and they reminded me of a manual procedure to bring the wheel down. I tried that and it didn't work. So they told me to raise the other two wheels to clean up the aircraft to try a belly landing, but the other two would not come up.

So I had to land the P-39 not on concrete or asphalt, but on the grass. I brought it in just as I would for a normal landing. When I hit the ground, the nose-wheel and left wheel folded up, and I slid along in a perfect belly landing.

The crew chief and I later agreed this was a mechanical problem, but it was not typical of the P-39. Normally, you had no trouble with the landing gear.

We had a cannon in the nose and two .30 calibre machine guns in each wing – no .50 cal guns – and we practised shooting at tow targets; we also practised strafing with the .30s and the cannon. We did some practice two and four-plane manoeuvres, and we also did a lot of solo flying. Several times I would fly from Sarasota, which is on the Gulf of Mexico side, all the way across to Palm Beach.

The P-39 was not a high altitude airplane, and I can't remember flying one over 15,000ft [4,572m]. It probably would have gone up to 20,000ft [6,096m], but not over that.

Decades later, Livingston lamented that he flew the Bell fighter only in training, and wished it had received more recognition: 'At the Air Force Academy [in Colorado Springs, Colorado], there is a sculpture honouring the fighters, and it has almost every type built. But there is none for the P-39.' The AAF 'and the rest of our government decided they weren't going to use the P-39 any more. So the Russians became the main user of the P-39.'

Second Opinion

James R. Hanson, another AAF pilot who flew the Airacobra stateside, had the following observations to make:

One of the principal reasons the Cobra obtained such a heinous reputation among RAF and AAF flyers was its uncanny tendency to flat-spin at the most unpredictable times. This characteristic, brought about by a critical centre-of-gravity envelope, resulted in the

Just weeks after Pearl Harbor, aviation cadet and future fighter pilot Clyde A. Curtin poses with a P-39 Airacobra at Myrtle Beach, South Carolina. Curtin would later fly P-39s at Ascension Island, then shift to the China-Burma-India theatre and the P-47 Thunderbolt; however, he would be better remembered as a Korean War air ace who downed five MiG-15s flying the F-86 Sabre. Clyde A. Curtin

The press image of the typical American fighter pilot. Aeroplane

especially after the narrow P-40 gear. We used to enter the pattern for landing in echelon at about 50ft [15m] altitude with the leader oblique looping, lowering the gear at the top for a 40 second pattern from break to touchdown. The gear took 28 seconds, being electric. It could be slipped safely with full flaps. Rat racing (individual combat) was really great because of its yo-yoing ability.

I believe the reason some P-39s flat spun was because of aft C.G. [centre of gravity]. Since there was only about a 3 per cent allowance in C.G. movement, it was critical, and you had to know where you stood weight and balance-wise before doing 'G' manoeuvres. Until you lost the weight of the ammo [after firing the guns], you should have a good airplane.

I always checked mine aerodynamically before doing aerobatics, by trimming for hands-off flight and climb power and then pulling the nose up about 10 degrees, releasing the stick, keeping the wings level with the rudder, and letting the ship oscillate back to level flight. In three oscillations it should return to level flight if the C.G. were in limits, and then you could do about anything you wanted. If the oscillations became worse instead of dampening out, you had to take it back in and find out if the ammo or the ballast was missing. This C.G. check actually works for most aircraft, although some, like the P-47, have neutral stability.

I only know of two of us who ever tumbled the Cobra deliberately. [Doing so inadvertently was a persistent fear of AAF pilots, especially after the AAF issued a cautionary message warning pilots that it had a tendency to tumble.] We didn't damage the aircraft because we had a system for locking up the controls beforehand, so they wouldn't thrash about. In preparation, we would get our elbows under the parachute straps, put both hands on the stick braced between the knees, and put our feet hard on the outboard side of the rudder pedals. Then we'd pull up to the vertical. When the speed dropped off to about 100mph [160km/h], we would apply smooth elevator pressure forward to start the tail-over-nose momentum. If you wanted to go over backwards for the entry it required a faster pull. It could be entered sideways with a kick of the rudder as well, but the entry didn't always result in a tumble. The tumble really was wild, and used up about 7,000 to 8,000ft [2,000 to 2,500m]. The key to losing a minimum of altitude was in keeping the controls from flopping about so that it would streamline itself and fall like a model airplane, ending up in a vertical dive. There was one peculiarity, though: if the controls were even moved at less than 250mph [400km/h], it would snap and spin.

death or injury of numerous young pilots who had not been thoroughly briefed on how to handle this tricky aircraft.

Most accidents occurred in stateside training when the P-39 was first introduced. Though proper checkouts eventually curtailed training losses, the Airacobra's reputation as a 'killer' was firmly implanted in the minds of all, especially those neophyte fighter pilots fresh out of school who found, to their chagrin, that they would fly the feared and fabled P-39. [Hanson's recollection that the reputation was entrenched

in fact differs sharply from the memories of other pilots.]

I'm glad I flew the Mustang in combat, but for real flying enjoyment it was the P-39. It felt like you strapped it on, rather than got into it. You sat high up over the wing and forward. The .50 calibre [12.7mm] machine-gun butts were right in the cockpit, one on each side of the instrument panel, and when you fired them, the cockpit smelled of cordite. The wings were a short 34ft [10m]. The take-offs and landings were a pure pleasure with the tricycle gear,

This nicely posed press shot clearly shows the reflector sight armoured screen and the rear of the instrument panel. Aeroplane

This P-39 Airacobra cracked up during war games prior to the entry of the United States into World War II. The location apparently is Wilmington, North Carolina, and the aircraft is attired in pre-war national insignia. Paul McDaniel

Lt Bob Powell, who went on to fly P-51 Mustangs with the 352nd Fighter Group in Europe, snapped these previously unpublished shots of a P-39 Airacobra at a training base in the United States while earning his pilot's wings. Bob Powell

1st Lt Bill Reynolds stands in front of his P-39D-1-BE (41-38297) of the 77th Fighter Squadron, 20th Fighter Group at Spartenburg Airport, South Carolina in July 1942. The squadron was on a TDY (temporary duty) stint at Spartenburg for ninety days. The 20th eventually built up an impressive combat record flying other fighters.
via Norman Taylor

Record-keeping was a shambles in early 1942, but squadron mates say that 1st Lt Robert Rutt was credited with four aerial victories. However, his claims do not appear on an aerial victory list assembled by US Army Air Forces. The aircraft is an export P-400 of the 80th FS 'Headhunters'; the location is Port Moresby. Note the distinctive extension for the nose 20mm Hispano cannon. Norman Taylor

XP-39E (Model 23)

First flown on 26 February 1942 (one source says 21 February), the experimental XP-39E or Model 14 was a highly modified P-39D airframe which had originally been meant to undergo a major powerplant change, to the Continental V-1430 engine. When this powerplant became unavailable, the 'E model' was flown with an Allison V-1710-47(E9) engine with two-stage supercharger driving an Aeroproducts propeller.

The XP-39E fuselage was lengthened 1¾ft (0.5m) to accommodate the longer -47. The 'E model' also had a slightly widened undercarriage. The XP-39E wing was larger than that of the standard P-39, the area enlarged by 22sq ft (2sq m) by increasing and slightly lengthening the root chord. Contrary to popular belief, the XP-39E did not have a laminar flow wing (which came later in the P-63 Kingcobra). It was distinguished in another respect, however: it was vastly overweight. At a maximum take-off weight of around 9,100lb (4,128kg), the 'E model' was, by a considerable margin, the heaviest Airacobra ever built.

Just three weeks after its maiden flight, the first XP-39E, dubbed the 'Green Hornet' by pilots, crashed while conducting spin tests on 26 March 1942. It was a dramatic moment. Test pilot Bob Stanley, who already had two emergency parachute jumps under his belt, pulled the wrong handle and jettisoned, rather than deploying, the drag chutes that were designed to bring the aircraft out of a spin. With no choice but to escape, Stanley opened the car-style door, and got out on the wing leading edge: he was observed sitting there for quite some time – in fact the XP-39E completed about a dozen more spins with him seated on the wing before he finally leaped clear and parachuted successfully.

The second aircraft flew on 4 April 1942. Minor differences in wing and empennage shape and area were introduced with each of the three XP-39Es. Flight performance was impressive in many respects, including a maximum speed of 393mph (632km/h) at 24,000ft (7,300m). Nevertheless, the XP-39E was a disappointment overall, and even though its engine was optimized for high altitude performance, Larry Bell found himself at one point recommending its production as 'an attack airplane against invasion forces'. The 'E models' did, however, contribute

The first of three XP-39E fighters (41-19501). The location of the carburettor intake scoop, flush against the rear of the cockpit, suggests that the two-stage Allison V-1710-47(E9) engine has not yet been installed. Bell via Truman Partridge

The second XP-39E (41-19502), viewed from an angle that emphasizes its squared-off wingtips. Bell via Truman Partridge

XP-39E (Model 23)

aerodynamic findings that were useful when Bell developed a new fighter, the P-63 Kingcobra.

It should be noted that the P-39E designation also applied to a planned production version of XP-39E. A contract for 4,000 initially identified as P-76 and P-76A fighters was cancelled.

Three built
XP-39E serials (3):
41-19501/19502;
42-71464

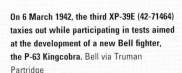

On 6 March 1942, the third XP-39E (42-71464) taxies out while participating in tests aimed at the development of a new Bell fighter, the P-63 Kingcobra. Bell via Truman Partridge

This airplane was a pleasure to fly as long as you flew it with precision. It required coordination and not kicking around, so this blew the combat performance, except for strafing type of work. Despite its reputation, I have a lot of good memories of flying this ship. I flew the 1944 Georgia, Tennessee, and California manoeuvres, and all of it at low altitude. We used it as a visual and photo recon fighter. I loved the Cobra, but it had to be treated with respect because its bite could be fatal.

Livingston went on to fly P-40 Warhawks in the China/Burma/India theatre in the 23rd FG under Lt Col Bruce Holloway.

Stateside Development

It should be noted that while thousands of stateside pilots were forming their opinions on the production Airacobra, Larry Bell and his growing company were doing their best to improve the aircraft and make it viable for the modern war in which the world was now immersed. The ultimate aircraft in the P-39 series was the

XP-39E (see box). After Bob Stanley's dramatic bailout from the prototype in March 1942, Larry Bell went to Maj Gen Echols, head of developmental work at Wright Field, and won approval to build a third XP-39E so that two ships would be available for tests.

Bell had high hopes for the 'E model', and pushed for a P-39E production contract. In a letter to Echols he noted that the XP-39E had reached 393mph (632km/h), although he did acknowledge that the new Airacobra had a maximum gross weight of over 9,000lb (4,000kg), which was substantially more than the AAF wanted; test pilot Stanley had complained that the XP-39E needed 50 per cent more runway for a standard take-off than did the P-39D. In his letter, Bell found plenty to praise – and yet he seemed curiously defensive:

The take-off, rate of climb and manoeuvrability with the present gross weight and the present propeller are not satisfactory. However, there is a new four-blade propeller about to be available that should retain and present high speed, and greatly improve the rate of climb and

take-off. The P-39E would have great value as an attack airplane against invasion forces. For low altitude work it could be used with a sea-level engine developing some 1,500 horsepower up to 3,000ft [900m]. For this it could be equipped with the 37mm cannon, six .50 cal guns (four free-firing) and a 500 to 1,000lb bomb. While its performance is approximately the same as the P-39M, it may have some specialized value of great importance in addition to its use for engine flight test.

It was odd, indeed, that at this juncture in the war an American leader was still talking of defending against invasion forces. The rumors of invasion persisted, however, and some of them focused on phantom enemies lurking off the east coast, rather than the west. In any event, the XP-39E was viewed as a 'lead sled' by some, and its testing moved in fits and starts, halted temporarily after the second ship suffered crankcase and engine-mount damage during a flight on 11 May 1942. In the end, the greatest contribution made by the XP-39E was as a test-bed for the engine that went into the next-generation Bell fighter, the XP-63 Kingcobra.

The three Bell XP-39E test ships provided pilots and engineers with data that influenced the design of the P-63 Kingcobra fighter. Bell

Other Developments

Although the basic P-39 Airacobra offered little in the way of growth potential, Bell never stopped trying to improve it, modify it, and make it applicable to additional missions. For instance, the manufacturer completed a mock-up of a proposed two-seat night interceptor, with an observer seated in a reclining position ahead of the pilot; this idea was never followed through, however. Also, Bell tested at least a dozen experimental external fuel tanks on the centreline, one of which was intended to enable the P-39 to fly the 2,400 miles (3,860km) from the California west coast to Hawaii – but none of the designs was adopted. The Airacobra was tested as a platform to drop air-to-air bombs for the purpose of destroying enemy aircraft at lower altitude, an idea that had also been mooted for the XFL-1 Airabonita – but no one was buying.

Even though the AAF decision to dispense with supercharging on the produc-

Bell's P-63 Kingcobra was an entirely new aeroplane which capitalized on the wing shape and taller tail tested on the XP-39E. On 27 June 1941, the US Army placed an order for two XP-63 prototypes to be powered by the 1,325hp Allison V-1710-47 liquid-cooled engine located behind the pilot and driven by an extension shaft. The first aircraft flew on 7 December 1942, but was lost in an accident a few weeks later.

The P-39F, G and J

The P-39F (Model 15B)

The P-39F Airacobra model began to appear in significant numbers in 1942, and differed from previous variants in that it boasted the new Aeroproducts 10ft 4in (3.18m) propeller, which was not so much an improvement, but a necessity.

The order issued on 13 September 1940 for the manufacture of 254 P-39Fs (of which 229 were eventually delivered) reflected the AAF's problem in obtaining propellers for its warplanes: Curtiss Electric propellers could no longer be delivered in sufficient quantities, and some aircraft were coming out of the factory door without any propeller at all. So the P-39F with a prop by a different manufacturer was essential. The P-39F also introduced other, minor improvements over the P-39D.

The powerplant of the 'F model' was the Allison V-1710E4, with a military power rating of 1,150hp at 3,000rpm. Among the 229 Fs, twenty-seven aircraft were converted for ground attack and tactical reconnaissance roles by AAF Field Modification Centers, and became P-39F-2 variants. Reports that at least one P-39F was rebuilt as the proof-of-concept ship for an Airacobra two-seat transition trainer are not supported by any existing documentation today.

P-39F Airacobra at the factory in 1942. Bell via Truman Partridge

229 P-39Fs built (of which twenty-seven were modified as P-39F-2)
P-39F serials (229): 41-7116/7344
P-39F-2 serials (27): 41-7123, 41-7177, 41-7182/7183, 41-7226, 41-7230, 41-7248, 41-7266, 41-7270/7272, 41-7278, 41-7294/7295, 41-7299, 41-7302/7303, 41-7305, 41-7309/7310, 41-7312, 41-7318, 41-7325/7326, 41-7332, 41-7334, 41-7339

P-39G (Model 26)

The P-39G designation was assigned at an early juncture to an aircraft intended to be identical to the P-39D-2 but with a different propeller. Before being cancelled, this designation initially applied to 1,800 fighter aircraft that were later produced as P-39K, L, M, and N models. The P-39H and P-39I designations were not assigned.

P-39J (Model 15B)

The term 'P-39J' identified twenty-five Airacobras that would have been the final P-39Fs but were delivered with an improved V-1710-59(E12) engine with automatic manifold pressure regulator. Like the P-39F, the rare 'J model' dispensed with a Curtiss Electric propeller in favour of the Aeroproducts 10ft 4in (3.18m) propeller.

Twenty-five built
P-39J serials (35): 41-7043/7056; 41-7059/7079

---

tive Airacobra was definitive, Bell continued to explore possibilities. A P-39 at the factory made test flights with a chunky, external turbocharger on the centreline: from the outside the gadget looked like a ramjet (of the kind that were tested on P-51 and P-80 fighters after the war), or perhaps a giant Hoover vacuum cleaner. Nevertheless it worked well, but the penalty imposed by its drag was greater than the increase in performance it afforded; even in level flight, it slowed the maximum speed of the Airacobra by some 41mph (65km/h).

The company worked closely with the AAF to test and evaluate the changes in the Airacobra that were adopted, sometimes even dictated. For example, to accommodate thick, bullet-resistant glass, a flat windscreen was tested on a P-39D-1, replacing the curved forward canopy that distinguished the YP-39 and P-39C models – and this feature became standard thereafter. When Bell turned to Aeroproducts as a second source for propellers for the Airacobra, the company's propeller was given thorough trials by a test ship – and adopted by several Airacobra variants. At least two Airacobras were bailed to Allison for engine development work.

To Tumble or Not To Tumble

AAF mishap statistics tell us that twenty-one Airacobras crashed in stateside mishaps in 1942, many of them caused by pilots failing to understand centre-of-gravity issues related to the location of the engine in the rear fuselage. Together with these accident figures that put the Airacobra in the middle range of US fighters where safety is concerned, the rumour was born that the Airacobra would tumble easily – going into a rotating manoeuvre that would take the pilot rapidly down to his death.

On 12 June 1942, this P-39F Airacobra (41-7323) made a visit to Lockheed Air Terminal in Burbank,
California, replete with a production version of the 175 US gallon (662ltr) centreline fuel tank.
Warren M. Bodie

**P-39D-1-BE Airacobra (41-28392) of the 77th Fighter Squadron, 20th Fighter Group at Spartenburg Airport,
South Carolina in July 1942.** via Norman Taylor

Bell P-39D Airacobra.
A well used P-39D, probably
a D-1 or D-2 lend-lease
version, with the 20mm
nose cannon. The 'D' model
was the first to have a small,
rounded, dorsal fillet at the
base of the vertical tail.
via David Ostrowski

No fewer than half-a-dozen Bell and Army test pilots took P-39s aloft and tried to duplicate the tumbling phenomenon. At Bell, test pilots Bob Stanley and Mark Heaney tested centre-of-gravity behaviour in spins using a P-39K (42-4395) modified to a P-39D-1 external configuration. At Wright Field, pilots attempted, without success, to induce the notorious tumble, using several P-39 airframes; at least eighty-six attempts were made to reproduce the so-called tumbling characteristics. None of the pilots could make the Airacobra tumble during these tests.

Aviation history is rich with tales of aircraft types that have been labelled deathtraps by their pilots, one well known example being the early B-26 Marauder medium bomber that was simply too hot for some to handle. The victim of verbal abuse that contained only an inkling of truth, the early B-26 became known as the 'widowmaker', and at the training base in Tampa, Florida, crews joked grimly about crashing 'one a day in Tampa Bay'. Similarly, the C-46 Commando transport gained a largely

unwarranted reputation as being prone to fires and explosions.

Although American pilots would speak of the Airacobra in negative tones ranging from mild disdain to outright hatred, especially in later years – and not withdrawing the comments of pilot Hanson, already quoted – it does not appear that the P-39 was ever-widely regarded as a dangerous aircraft to fly. The alleged tumbling received considerable attention throughout the AAF, but appears to have been largely a false alarm. As for the centre-of-gravity issues that arose with later and heavier Airacobras, they became well understood, and rarely prompted much concern amongst pilots.

Russian 'Cobras

The Airacobra seems to have consistently won praise in the Soviet Union whilst being heaped with disdain by American fliers at home and in the Pacific. Soviet combat operations in the Airacobra were carried out by the Soviet air force in

support of the Red Army. Intended primarily for close air support (including anti-tank work) but also employed in other roles including air-to-air combat, Airacobras equipped the 9th Guards Fighter Division and the 16th Guards Fighter Air Regiment. Indeed, it was only after the P-39 was supplied to the Russians that its true ability as a low-level attack aircraft was finally revealed. Fighting a far less sophisticated war, in a climate better suited to the Airacobra's engine cooling system, the Russians hailed it as one of the greatest weapons delivered under the wartime Lend-Lease programme. Employing it not as a fighter but as a close-support attack aircraft, the Russians managed to make the Airacobra extremely unpopular with Germany's Panzer columns.

The battered and largely rebuilt Soviet aircraft industry was back on its knees at the start of 1942 and was turning out 2,000 new combat aircraft per month by the end of the year, but the massive military aid from overseas allies – symbolized by the British Airacobras that began arriving in 1941, and the American-built P-39s

P-39 engine change by the 77th FS during temporary duty at Spartenburg, South Carolina, in July 1942.
via Norman Taylor

that came a year later – was important to the survival of the USSR. The VVS, or Soviet air arm, grew at a phenomenal rate in 1942, but while production of indigenous aircraft mounted rapidly, deliveries were augmented to an increased extent by supplies from outside, including those (unlike the British Airacobras) embraced by the Lend-Lease programme. As we shall see, the dubious British gift of Airacobras which were unwanted by Britons was followed by a steady stream of lend-lease American P-39s, or several variants.

Expanding Air Arm

The scale of outside assistance was quantified in a 1958 seminal volume *The Air Forces of the World* by William Green and John Fricker which provided the following numbers:

[N]o fewer than 14,984 US military aircraft were diverted to Russia, of which 14,187 reached their destination. Of these, 7,925 were safely delivered over the Alaskan-Siberian ferry route, 993 over the South Atlantic ferry route to Abadan, and the remainder were shipped to Murmansk, Archangelsk, or Abadan. The major types and the quantity of these supplied were as follows (the figures quoted in parentheses relate to the aircraft that actually arrived safely in Russian hands): 2,430 (2,091) Curtiss P-40s; 4,924 (4,743) Bell P-39N and P-39Q Airacobras [a figure which probably includes some P-39Ds but not the ex-RAF Airacobra Is]; 2,421 (2,400) Bell P-63A and P-63C Kingcobras; 3,125 (2,901) Douglas A-20C and A-20G Havocs; 870 (862) North American B-25C and B-25D Mitchells; 709 (707) Douglas C-47s; 94 (81) North American AT-6s; and 195 (186) Consolidated PBY-6A (and PBN) Catalinas. From Britain, Russian received Hawker Hurricanes, Supermarine Spitfires, De Havilland Mosquitos, and Armstrong-Whitworth Albemarles [as well as the Airacobra Is].

Abadan, of course, was in Persia (Iran), which was occupied by British and Soviet troops. British engineering troops expanded the ports, built roads and reconstructed the railway and airfield network, and Abadan became a principal stopover for aircraft en route to Russia. It also boasted a memorable 'graveyard' of wrecked aircraft, some nearly whole, some in bits and pieces, more than a hundred in all – including Bell fighters.

By late 1942, any German threat to Moscow lay in the past and the Russians were slogging through the terrible months of carnage at Stalingrad, which would culminate in the German 6th Army capitulating in February 1943. The Russians were beginning to operate better fighters of their own making, including the Lavochkin La-5 and Yakovlev Yak-3, soon to be joined by the superb Yak-9. It is not clear how many P-39 Airacobras participated in the battle of Stalingrad, where most action reports cite Soviet-built fight-

An ex-RAF Airacobra I, otherwise dubbed a P-400, following its delivery to the Soviet Union. This fighter belongs to the 19th Guards IAP which was the first Soviet unit to fly the Bell aircraft in combat. These men seem to be going over the instructions for loading the 20mm nose cannon on an aircraft that looks remarkably new. San Diego Aerospace Museum

ers. But by late 1942, Russians were making no secret of the pride they felt in achieving success while operating aircraft manufactured by their Western allies.

A glimpse of Airacobras at war on the Russian front – probably exaggerated – was provided by radio newsman Robert Magidoff on the NBC 'News Roundup' on 25 May 1942:

I spent the day with a Russian squadron flying exclusively modern American fighters. The squadron I visited has brought down eighty-six enemy planes since the outbreak of the war, twenty-nine of these laid down by flying Tommyhawks [a reference to the Curtiss Tomahawk], Kittyhawks, and Airacobras. 'Just look at these 'Cobras,' squadron leader Dimitro said to me, pointing at three fighters dashing

across a rain-soaked runway. It took them but 20 seconds to take off. They circled above the field twice and then disappeared behind the horizon, on their way to patrol the skies over Moscow.

'Yes, the Tommyhawk [sic] is a great plane,' said Dimitro, 'but the Kittyhawk is better, and the Airacobra better still. You ought to see it in action.'

The broadcaster went on to proclaim that the Airacobra would be 'the key to victory over Hitler in 1942'.

The delivery of British Airacobra I models to Russia via maritime convoy was completed by May 1942, according to one Moscow source, by July 1942 according to another. By then, of course, Russian forces were beleaguered all across the Eastern

front, even if the worst at Moscow and Stalingrad was behind them. The Russians liked the Airacobra, but they did not fail to note that the Western powers 'reserved for the USSR only "second-rate" military equipment . . . throughout the entire war'.

A handful of Airacobras appear to have been 'requisitioned' to serve as the personal conveyance of very senior officers who, in fact, rarely or never flew them in combat. Two of the Airacobra Is went to a Soviet developmental facility where they served as test ships for the remainder sent to combat units (the Russian term is 'experimental rabbits', or guinea pigs). One can readily imagine the adventurous spirit of the test pilots, provided with little or no understandable technical data and

Airacobra training formations in the United States during the war. via David Ostrowski

challenged to give the new and unfamiliar aircraft a thorough trial.

The Russians evaluated these two ships (AH628 and AH644) over a prolonged period beginning in May 1942, the test pilots directed to search for hidden flaws in the Bell fighter. They reported the same kind of engine problems that would plague the Italian air arm two years later: namely, they found that although the Allison engine was perfectly adequate most of the time, there were starting difficulties, and an undue sensitivity to impurities in aviation oil. It appears the Soviets may have tried minor modifications while evaluating these aircraft – but it also appears that Airacobras reached combat units almost exactly as they had come out of the factory.

Soviet pilots found the Airacobra inferior in performance to every other aircraft supplied by the West, including the Spitfire Vb which did not reach them until at least a year later. They did note, however, that the Airacobra seemed ideally suited to the character of military activities on the Soviet-German front. Here, the objective was not wide-ranging aerial supremacy, but aerial domination over carefully chosen sectors of the battlefield. Both the Luftwaffe and the Soviet air arm emphasized the need for dive-bombers and assault aircraft – warplanes meant to support ground troops at low altitude over the battlefield, or at medium altitude in the operational and tactical zone.

Thus, the Russians wanted fighters that could oppose attacking Luftwaffe formations and escort their own bombers, both duties being performed at relatively low altitude where the Airacobra's shortcomings were not evident. The Russians also wanted good manoeuvrability, ease of piloting, powerful armament, good visibil-

ity, and a practical design that was relatively easy to maintain. They were satisfied that the Airacobra was a rational solution for their needs on the Russian-German front.

Russian Processing

Most of the ex-British Airacobra I fighters ended up in the city of Ivanovo, where the 22nd Supply Aviation Regiment (22nd ZAP) was headquartered. In early 1942, this regiment became the replacement training unit for fighter aviation regiments (IAPs) of the Soviet air arm (the VVS) and was responsible for prepping troops on the imported Bell fighters. The 22nd ZAP at Ivanovo also assembled and test-flew all of the fighters that arrived via convoy from the West. Once deemed airworthy, the fighters were flown to the front. They

Fighting the Messerschmitt

To Americans, the Messerschmitt Bf 109 – called the Me 109 by everyone during the war – never seemed to inspire the awe or dread in which the Japanese Zero fighter was held. To the Russians, who fought it daily, the Bf 109 was a fighter to be respected, but not feared.

At RAF Colerne, the first P-39C to arrive in the United Kingdom was test-flown against other fighters, including a Bf 109E that had come into British hands. RAF pilots were impressed with the visibility afforded by the Airacobra – although the 'bubble' canopy so common on fighters later in the war was still a thing of the future – and found that the P-39 could out-turn the Bf 109E in almost any manoeuvring situation.

Powered by a 1,200hp (895kW) Daimler-Benz DB 601N V-12 inline engine, the Bf 109E tipped the scales at around 6,100lb (2,767kg) when configured for a combat mission, putting it in the same weight class as, albeit slightly lighter than, the Airacobra. The Messerschmitt was far more effective at altitude – indeed, it boasted a ceiling of 36,500ft (11,125m) – but the Airacobra was at least the equal of the German fighter when flying lower.

A Russian report credits the Airacobra with being able to sustain hits and keep flying. The heavy armament packed by the Airacobra was unquestionably superior to that of the German fighter, especially the later Bf 109F which dispensed with wing guns, but pilots on both sides always insisted that personal skill, training, team discipline and gunnery practice were more important than the size and caliber of the guns packed by the aircraft.

By the time a Bf 109 reached Wright Field for evaluation by American pilots, no effort was even made to compare it with the P-39 Airacobra. In the Caucasus, at Stalingrad, and along the Soviet Union's Kuban River, the Airacobra was battling the Bf 109 every day. But Americans were not likely to encounter the Messerschmitt in the Airacobra after a handful of battles in North Africa. As far as the AAF was concerned, there was little purpose in comparing the two any further.

were scattered from the northern to southern extremes of the main line of battle between Soviet and German forces, from Leningrad to Voronezh.

The job of training pilots was not easy. In the case of the Airacobra, Soviet officers decided to move carefully and deliberately. They had already experienced difficulty in adapting Hurricane and P-40C Tomahawk fighters to Soviet conditions, and they wanted to avoid mistakes; otherwise they could almost certainly have sent Airacobras into combat before May 1942. The 22nd ZAP had its first twenty Airacobras at the start of the year, and received considerable outside help from Moscow with managing acceptance and assembly of the fighters. Chief test pilot Capt Viktor Ye Golofastov exerted a tight discipline over the arrangements.

The assembly of the first ex-RAF Airacobra I fighters was under way by mid-January 1942, and test flights followed. Initially there wasn't a single American or British adviser on the scene, though later, an Englishman sent to assist with the assembly of Hurricanes, and who happened to be fluent in French, held frequent meetings with a Russian who spoke French but no English: they discussed not the Hurricane, but the Airacobra, of which that same Englishman had no experience. Russian VVS line personnel, tasked to cope with instructions in English, ran into almost comical periods of confusion, as when a landing light was confused with a flashlight; in the end, however, the Russians figured out how to put the Bell fighters together largely through improvisation, resourcefulness and common sense. It should also be noted that because air-to-ground action was so common on the Eastern Front, so too were engagements at lower altitude – and here the Airacobra was in its realm.

A Soviet report on an April 1942 test flight by VVS pilot Golofastov credits the Airacobra I with a ground-level speed of 306mph (493km/h), a maximum speed of 363mph (585km/h) at an altitude of 13,800ft (4,200m), and a rate of climb that would bring the aircraft to 16,400ft (5,000m) in 6.5 minutes. Golofastov's conclusion was that the fighter rejected by the RAF compared favourably with the best of Soviet-built fighters, such as the Yak-3 and MiG-3. One outcome of the test flights was the production of a technical guide to the Airacobra in Russian, for distribution to combat units.

Positive Outlook

So why did the Russians like the Airacobra so much if the British liked it so little? For one thing, the Airacobras were thoroughly 'broken in' by the time the Soviets got them, which meant that individual airframes were no longer burdened by their initial shortcomings. More importantly, the Soviets repeatedly emphasized that the Airacobra performed well in tests at the specific range of altitudes characteristic only on the Soviet-German front. The Russians themselves say that during the short testing period allocated to them they did not have sufficient time or talent to detect basic design flaws – that only later would they experience the Airacobra's tendency to go into a flat spin, the problems with the complex engine shaft, and the troublesome electrical system.

Pilots and maintenance crew from combat fighter regiments were sent to the 22nd ZAP for one or two months of training, then ferried the Airacobras to their units. During the training sessions there were mishaps, as on 10 July 1942 when one Airacobra I (AH669) was written off, and in November when two others (AH610, AH653) were lost. Altogether, the 22nd ZAP seems to have retained about a dozen Airacobras while cycling others on their way into battle.

The first VVS combat regiment to operate the Airacobra I was the 153rd IAP that had been in action at Leningrad and was reformed by the 22nd ZAP, beginning on 25 March 1942. The regiment completed type training by 10 June 1942, and departed for the Voronezh front. Contrary to popular belief, the Airacobra was not used solely for ground attack, either then or later, by its new Soviet operators.

First at Voronezh airfield, and soon afterwards at Lipetsk in the Voronezh area, the 153rd IAP engaged in considerable air-to-air fighting against the Luftwaffe: 259 aerial engagements in forty-five actions resulted in sixty-four German aircraft claimed, among them eighteen bombers (fifteen Ju 88s, one Fw 189, one He 111, and one Do 217), forty-five fighters (thirty-nine Bf 109Fs, one Bf 110, one Me 210 and four other aircraft), and one artillery spotter aircraft. In three months of combat with the ex-British Airacobras, the unit lost only three pilots and eight aircraft, plus one pilot and two aircraft claimed by non-combat causes. This was an extraordinarily laudable record, and one that is largely overlooked in Western literature.

In August and September 1942, an offshoot unit of the 153rd IAP notched up additional aerial victories, and after a brief respite, the regiment fought through to the end of the year. Thus the ex-British Airacobra I was on the scene at times when nothing less than the survival of the Soviet Union was at stake.

Airacobra Doubts

The positive attitude shown by many Russians towards the Airacobra is in direct contrast to the uncharitable attitude felt by many elsewhere; indeed, unkind comment about the aircraft will recur throughout this narrative. However, one rather surprising source of disrespect towards Bell's fighter was to be found in a letter to the factory dated 1 September 1942 by a company rep in the Pacific, who wrote:

> We frequently talk with the boys who have been in action against Zeros. Their big cry is, 'When in hell are the Brass Hats going to get wise to themselves and give us more H.P. [horsepower] motors?' In general they like the P-39, but its decided lack of power and performance is fast costing us . . . prestige. We owe a debt to those who fly our aircraft. They are our customers. They have our trust. We need to develop the P-39 so that when they use a product we have created, they will salute us and say, 'Yes, sir, I have the H.P. and the performance I need.' Again, I want to point to the fact that this is an expense for us, and that it is costing us prestige.

It was costing lives, too – although the Airacobra was able to extract blood at times. It appears that the first pilot to score an aerial victory in the Bell Airacobra was Lt Col Boyd 'Buzz' Wagner, whilst leading elements of the 8th Fighter Group. He was credited with shooting down two, and possibly three, Mitsubishi A6M Zero ('Zeke') fighters over Salamaua, New Guinea on 30 April 1942. Capt Daniel Roberts made two kills over Buna New Guinea on 26 August 1942, and two more soon afterwards. He would later be credited with fourteen victories altogether, four of them in Airacobras.

Did a Soviet pilot score earlier? The British Airacobra Is delivered to the

Soviet Union came via Allied convoys over the northern route throughout 1942, most arriving in Murmansk and Archangelsk, despite the rigours of convoy duty. One British source holds that no fewer than fifty-four Airacobras were lost while being transported by sea, though a more realistic figure may be twenty to twenty-five aircraft.

Most Airacobra I fighters (and possibly P-39D-2s, Ks and Ls, which began arriving in the Soviet Union in November and December 1942) went initially to the 22nd Supply Aviation Regiment (22nd ZAP), travelling from seaports on railway flatcars. The 22nd ZAP formed the training centre for Airacobra operations and other imported fighters, and ultimately

helped to create the aviation regiments that took these aircraft into battle.

Pacific Action

The Airacobra acquitted itself well in the south-west Pacific, but this happened only after a difficult start. As in most military campaigns, more Airacobras were lost to human foible and other non-combat causes than to Japanese gunfire.

In March, the 8th Pursuit Group (redesignated the 8th Fighter Group in May 1942) went to Australia, then moved north to New Guinea – the world's second largest island, and one towards which considerable Japanese attention was directed.

Indeed, one of the biggest blunders by the Japanese side was failing to seize New Guinea's principal town, Port Moresby – itself little more than a pier and a few tin warehouses – before the Allies could reinforce it. By the time the 8th FG and its Airacobras were facing navigational challenges to move north-east, the chance to take Moresby had passed.

Ever since, historians have insisted that the Japanese missed their chance. Their goal, always, was to seize enough of the South Pacific to negotiate from a position of strength and end the war in the Pacific, which always had second priority in American leaders' minds. As P-39 Airacobra pilots and others readily divined, the Japanese never had any

In February 1942 at Brisbane, Australia, armourers of the 39th Fighter Squadron/35th Fighter Group install 37mm ammunition in a P-39D-1-BE (41-38225). Norman Taylor

Sealed against the elements, this P-39 is unloaded after its long journey across the Pacific. Aeroplane

thought of invading San Francisco or occupying Washington.

The combat zone was a vast island chain – western New Guinea and the Solomons – with no cities, few resources, a primitive population that had no stake in the war, and horrendous weather. Every airfield in the South Pacific had to be developed using equipment and material brought in from outside, and every item needed to sustain an air war – from vehicles to clothing to food to spare parts – had to be shipped in from outside. Much of the war would be fought by fighters flying at the maximum distance they were capable of covering, a situation that initially favoured the Japanese who had longer-legged warplanes, and much of it would be fought in weather that was atrocious.

The American Airacobra pilots were young and inexperienced. Many in the 8th FG's three squadrons – the 35th FS 'Black Panthers', the 36th FS 'Flying Fiends', and (many weeks later) the 80th

FS 'Headhunters' – had never flown an aircraft in difficult circumstances. Many had as little as four to six hours of cockpit time in the Airacobra. To make matters worse, some were assigned to the export P-400 model, which had minor cockpit differences in addition to a smaller gun. These pilots were struggling – and it showed.

On 25 April, foul weather closed around six 35th FS Airacobras attempting the ferry trip from Woodstock, Australia to Port Moresby, New Guinea. The pilots lacked cross-country experience and navigation aids were non-existent, with the result that all six aircraft crashed and two of the pilots were killed. Then on 1 May exactly the same thing happened to the 36th FS: this meant that half-a-dozen Airacobras were lost in non-combat mishaps and one pilot was dead. 2nd Lt Bob Love lost his life when his wingtip caught on the ground and his Airacobra cartwheeled, catching fire and becoming a torch in motion; 2nd Lt

Arnold Swanberg managed to climb out of his sputtering, smoking 'Cobra, and lower himself gingerly to the ground.

Seven Mile Drome

P-39 Airacobras of the 35th and 36th FS were to be based at a strip called Seven Mile, north of Port Moresby, led by Lt Col Wagner, who made the leap from first lieutenant to lieutenant colonel in the span of just five months; he was sent by Fifth Fighter Command to whip things into shape. Wagner had established himself as the first US Army air ace of the war (with five aerial victories to his credit flying P-40s in the Philippines); he was also the architect of AAF fighter tactics in New Guinea.

It was a tough beginning. Of forty-one Airacobras that left Australia for the difficult journey to Seven Mile, only twenty-six arrived safely – though at least the airfield they arrived at was solidly built and ready for use. Officially dubbed

(This page and overleaf) P-39Ds in the south-west Pacific. Pima Air and Space Museum

Jackson Field, a name that no one ever used, Seven Mile boasted a 5,000ft (1,550m) surfaced runway that had been built with US funds before the war. At Port Moresby, all the airfields were named according to their distance from the port – thus Three Mile Drome, Seven Mile Drome, Twelve Mile Drome, and so on.

Throughout the war, Airacobra pilots and others on the Allied side took advantage of the Western Allies' seemingly limitless capacity to build, maintain, support and repair airfields, a mix of skills and resources the Japanese were never blessed with. Allied pilots never, for example, suffered the problem that plagued the Japanese whenever their airfields came under attack: not enough taxiways, with a good enough surface, to get warplanes into the air quickly.

Not that Seven Mile or any other friendly airfield was perfect. Before arrival, new pilots were warned that the runway was very narrow (which was more a problem for the Airacobra than the narrow-track Navy F4F Wildcat), and they were advised that they should clear straight ahead after landing and then taxi back on the dirt track parallel to the runway.

Immediately on arrival at Seven Mile, Wagner began stressing the need to take action, and also to avoid giving the Japanese any opportunity to discover the

valuable Airacobras on the ground. He wanted aircraft dispersed, and pilots alert; he also wanted to strike out.

Baptism of fire

He therefore set up a strafing mission against Lae and Alamaua, scheduled for 30 April 1942. This was the Airacobra's baptism of fire in the Pacific (Wagner's report is written in the passive, which for some strange reason is typical of fighter pilots):

On Friday 30 April, thirteen P-39Ds took off from Port Moresby on a ground-strafing mission against Lae airdrome, 180 miles [230km] north. Approach was made from Lae from 50 miles [80km] out to sea to avoid detection. When about 20 miles [30km] out, four planes were sent ahead to engage the Japanese security patrol over Lae drome. Top cover drew the

enemy security off to the east of the drome, and no resistance by air was encountered during the strafing. A line of thirteen to fifteen bombers were strafed on a sea approach in a three-three plane element. The planes in each element were disposed in echelon right.

Our strafing planes were then attacked from above by several Zero fighters. Belly tanks were dropped immediately and throttles opened. Our formation began to pull away from the Zeros when the last four P-39s in the formation engaged in combat with three Zeros. In the meantime more Zeros appeared, and it is estimated that there were twelve or thirteen altogether. The P-39s were hopelessly outnumbered, so the entire formation turned back and a terrific dogfight ensued. As a result of this low-altitude dogfight four Zeros and three P-39s were shot down. All P-39s going down had been hit in the cooling system as a glycol spray could be seen streaming out behind, while all the Zeros shot down went burning. All three

P-39 pilots were safe upon landing, either bailing out or crash-landing on the beach.

It now appears that a fourth pilot, Lt Edward Durand, was shot down and reached the ground alive, but was executed by the Japanese.

Wagner's actions against Lae and Salamaua were aimed at neutralizing the Japanese capability to fly reconnaissance over his own base. In tangling with the vaunted Zero, Wagner's Airacobra pilots discovered a secret that has rarely made it into the history books: below a certain altitude, the Airacobra was as good an air-to-air fighter as any aircraft in the world, the Zero included. There were other flaws in the Airacobra that were not yet apparent – for instance, none of the first-generation American fighters could match the Zero's combat radius, and none had as little potential for further development

---

Fighting the Zero

As early as 1941, Col Claire Chennault's Flying Tigers examined a Zero (Mitsubishi A6M2 Type 0 Model 21 Reisen, codenamed 'Hamp' by the Allies) that had fallen into the hands of the Nationalist Chinese, and sent reports about it back to Washington. And even before the Guadalcanal campaign, another Zero (also an A6M2) was found in the Aleutian Islands in June 1942. This captured war prize is often described as the 'first' Zero to fall into American hands and is sometimes called the 'Akutan Zero', after the island where it was retrieved.

During Japanese diversionary attacks on Dutch Harbor in the Aleutians on 4 June 1942, PO Tadayoshi Koga's Zero from the carrier *Ryujo* was hit by groundfire and forced to land in a remote area of Akutan Island. The aircraft landed with its gear down, settled in a marsh surface, and flipped on its back.

US Navy technicians concluded from studying this specimen that while the Zero enjoyed unparalleled manoeuvrability at speeds below 150mph (241km/h), aileron control became sluggish at 180mph (288km/h), and nearly immovable at 230mph (368km/h). They may have been optimistic in this determination, but when the Zero was examined and flight-tested, American officers knew that the Japanese fighter had superb manoeuvrability, long range, and respectable firepower, but provided inadequate armour and back-up systems for its pilot. Also, rather like the wood and bamboo houses in which many Japanese lived, the Zero could be transformed into a blazing torch if it could be hit and set afire.

But how much of this information reached American pilots in the Pacific? James Alexander was an intelligence officer with Thirteenth Air Force and sometimes briefed P-39 Airacobra pilots. He says:

> We felt we knew a lot about the Zero, but most of it came from our pilots' experiences. I was never aware of any flow of information concerning Japanese planes that had been captured and tested.
>
> In the P-39 vs Zero equation, we felt that the Zero was superior in every respect at higher altitude. It was faster and more manoeuvrable. But at medium or low altitude, we felt the P-39 had a chance so long as the pilot didn't get into a manoeuvring contest with his Japanese adversary. That was the one thing I stressed to them [the American pilots] over and over again: 'Defeat him in a dive but don't attempt to outmanoeuvre him,' I would advise. 'That Zero has a big wing shaped like a paddle, and ailerons the size of barn doors. If you're in a P-39 (and the same was true for the P-40), you get into a dogfight with him and he's going to kill you.' On the other hand, all of our aircraft were far sturdier than the Japanese, and would bring a pilot home after sustaining battle damage.

P-39 pilots who fought at New Guinea and Guadalcanal also said that they never had access to data about the Zero based on stateside test flights of the 'Akutan Zero'. By late 1942, however, other examples of the Japanese fighter were falling into Allied hands, and its characteristics became well known throughout the South Pacific.

---

as the P-39 – but in a low-level dogfight, the Bell fighter was a force to be reckoned with.

Wagner was especially displeased that the Airacobra had constant problems with its guns, particularly the wing-mounted .30 caliber machine guns and the nose-mounted 37mm cannon which were always jamming. Indeed, the twin .50 caliber machine guns which straddled the propeller hub on top of the nose were the only weapons that seemed reliable enough for sustained combat in difficult conditions. In a report to his superiors, Wagner compared the P-39 and P-40 by saying that the Airacobra was about 10 per cent better in every respect except manoeuvrability below 18,000ft (5,500m).

For better or worse, the Airacobra was the thin red line against the Japanese south of the Owen Stanley mountain range in New Guinea, together with a handful of Australian Warhawks. The P-40 Warhawks of the 49th FG were busy in the defence of north-west Australia, while the Airacobras of the 35th FG (together with the 8th FG's 80th FS) were still readying themselves for combat. As of 1 May 1942, only the 'Black Panthers' and the 'Flying Fiends' were in position to guard Port Moresby.

Ragged warriors

It was a thin line of defence. On an initial 40-minute Airacobra orientation flight in the combat zone on 27 April, 2nd Lt Don 'Fibber' McGee was 'going along just fine' when a faulty propeller splattered oil all over his windshield, blocking his vision. With 'just a little help from another pilot,' he landed blind.

At Seven Mile, McGee had a second such mishap on 30 April. Again leaking oil that blotted his windscreen, he collided on the taxiway with 2nd Lt Izzy Toubman's Airacobra. This minor scrape caused him to miss the first combat mission led by Wagner that day. But 36th FS acting commander 1st Lt Lewis 'Bill' Meng consoled him with the commitment that he could fly the first combat sortie the next day. Meng, incidentally, had only a single aerial victory to his own name, but pilots greatly admired his leadership.

1 May 1942

Rolling out at an early 4am, McGee was charged with leading the second element in a four-plane flight, behind flight leader 1st Lt Don Mainwaring and wingman 1st Lt Patrick Armstrong. McGee's own wingman never got airborne, grounded by one of those mechanical glitches which were to become so frequent. Thus three Airacobras instead of four climbed to 8,000ft (2,500m), looking for Japanese intruders who might be coming from Lae.

Their effort seemed fruitless. After two hours of 'boring holes in the sky', they descended to land, having seen no foe. Unexpectedly, Seven Mile was cloaked in fog. When Mainwaring went ahead and landed anyway, his undercarriage collapsed and his Airacobra spun around on flat ground, blocking the runway. The flight leader got on the radio and warned the two remaining P-39 pilots to delay their let-down. None of the men knew, yet, that a Japanese air attack was, indeed, coming their way.

Both low on fuel, McGee and Armstrong became separated as they broke out of the airfield pattern and climbed to 4,000ft (1,200m). That was when a voice boomed in McGee's earphones: 'Zeros, attacking our field!' The controller at Seven Mile sounded harried, but he couldn't have been as much as was McGee, who was now down to less than ten minutes' fuel and could see no Zeros, anywhere.

Abruptly, a single Mitsubishi fighter passed beneath McGee. Mindful of his fuel situation, he refrained from applying full power but descended towards the Zero and found himself gaining. He did not realize that more Japanese fighters were following him. 'I struggled with the gunsight and realized that I had not gotten a good enough briefing on the damned thing.' He fired several bursts and saw tracers fly out towards the Zero, but no sign of impact damage.

First blood

Nevertheless, the Mitsubishi rolled over, dropped into low-clinging fog, and exploded against the ground in a blast that was witnessed with relief by McGee and others. It was the first aerial victory for the 36th FS. 'It appeared that my bullets hit the pilot.' McGee then had to fight his way out of a storm of flying steel as other Zeros blazed away at him.

The American pilot avoided mortal damage, and soon the Zeros began to withdraw – again, the long distances from their bases limited the time they could spend over a target. As they did so, McGee went down into the fog, dropped his Airacobra onto the runway surface, and taxied into a spot of sunshine. He opened a window and gave a thumbs-up signal to waiting maintainers, but was unable to taxi his fighter to them: still on the runway, his prop halted, and he was out of fuel.

'Fibber' McGee would later be credited with two more Zero kills in the Airacobra before he switched to a new squadron and a new fighter (P-38 Lightning); in this he bagged two more Japanese aircraft, thereby gaining ace status. He later served in Europe as a P-51 Mustang pilot in the 357th FG and claimed his sixth aerial victory, a Messerschmitt Bf 109. Thinking of New Guinea, he remembers mostly the 'maintenance problems, lousy weather, vast distances, and thick jungle canopy'. There were stretches of little-explored rainforest in New Guinea where no Airacobra pilot 'would want to find himself on the ground, at any time, ever'.

Continuing struggle

The next day (2 May 1942), Airacobras took on fifteen Zeros, the American pilots finding themselves in the midst of a fight that had begun when the Japanese engaged Warhawks of Australia's No. 75 Squadron. Four Airacobra pilots scored aerial victories.

The Japanese struck back on 3 May with an attack on Port Moresby by a dozen Mitsubishi G4M ('Betty') bombers. The Airacobras engaged them and their Zero escort – but the crack Japanese pilots shot down 1st Lt Joseph Lovett, and in the days that followed, more than half-a-dozen Americans failed to return from their missions. There were extraordinary survival stories. Airacobra pilot 2nd Lt Michael

This South Pacific portrait of the P-400 Airacobra was 'passed by examiner' (censor), with the last three digits of the radio call number removed. It is difficult to know how those three digits would have assisted the Japanese, although they certainly had more trouble with the Airacobra than is generally recognized.
via Warren M. Bodie

Gilead ditched a P-39 in shallow water near a beach, walked ashore, and recruited local tribespeople who brought him overland to Port Moresby. He gave them a compass and his wallet, though kept hold of his .45 automatic and wristwatch.

As of mid-May, the two Airacobra squadrons boasted thirty-one confirmed victories against eight losses – though the figures are approximate. Fighting for their lives, the 35th and 36th FS pilots were little concerned with record-keeping. Lt John Mac Isaac, a Canadian-born Scotsman (see box), flew with the 35th FS and had two confirmed Zero kills, but they do not appear in postwar documents. The dangers inherent in fighter flying were illustrated when Mac Isaac was nearly killed in a fire and subsequent crash on a non-combat Airacobra sortie.

On 29 May 1942, seventeen P-39s and P-400s launched from Seven Mile to engage fifteen to eighteen Zeros near Hood Bay about 50 miles (80km) from Port Moresby. They threw themselves into a furious dogfight and claimed five kills. Lt Clifton Troxell, eventually to become an ace, scored his second aerial victory, and McGee recorded two Zero kills. 1st Lt Grover Gholson, who had already claimed one Zero in mid-month, latched behind another in this fracas and was about to shoot when it went into an abrupt climbing turn. Gholson stood his Airacobra on its tail and fired a couple of bursts that came close to his elusive prey – but then his P-39 trembled, stalled, and fell, out of control.

Gholson snapped the Airacobra level, but discovered tracers flying all around him: Zeros were bearing down on him with guns blazing. He released the door at his side and bailed out so quickly that he injured himself slightly on a protruding shard of metal; he delayed opening his chute until the air battle seemed distant. He reached friendlies on the ground and was back at Seven Mile ready to resume fighting within a month. He accomplished much of his trek through the jungle with the help of only a single native; unfortunately for him, he came down with not one, but three tropical ailments while hiking to safety.

The 35th FG was now becoming battle-ready, and the weary pilots at Seven Mile were joined in late May by the group's 39th FS 'Flying Cobras' and the 40th FS 'Red Devils'. 1st Lt Harvey Scandrett scored the first aerial victory for the 40th

John Mac Isaac

In his wartime logbook, John Mac Isaac treated the harsh conditions of the New Guinea campaign with relative disdain. His listing for a 21 March 1942 mission from Port Moresby in a P-39 contains the note 'Intercept (Zero)(15)'. Three days later on a P-39 mission he wrote, 'lost two boys on a raid.' During a layover in Melbourne, Australia, Mac Isaac wrote that he had been given a chance to make one flight piloting a 'Worldway', a reference to the Commonwealth CA-5 Wirraway II.

Col John A. Mac Isaac was born on 1 October 1919 in Nova Scotia, Canada – also the birthplace of Fifth Air Force commander Gen George C. Kenney. He became an aviation cadet seven months before the Japanese attack on Pearl Harbor. His military form 11 lists 'Twelve aerial missions, 36:40 combat hours (P-39), (P-40)'. A different source credits him with nineteen missions and 51:20 combat hours. He went to the South Pacific in January 1942, the darkest hour of America's involvement in the war.

Mac Isaac arrived in Melbourne on 1 February 1942. Given refresher training in the P-39 and P-40, he ended up in the 9th Fighter Squadron 'Iron Knights', 49th Fighter Group. The group was awarded a unit citation for flying in defence of Darwin.

In March 1942, as a second lieutenant, Mac Isaac went to Archer Field, Brisbane, Australia to join the 80th Fighter Squadron 'Headhunters'. Mac Isaac continued in combat until late April 1942 when an aircraft he was ferrying caught fire and crashed at the Australian base at Lowood, Queensland. Severely burned and hospitalized for several months, Mac Isaac asked to return to the 80th, but the squadron could not handle the healing of his burns because of its substandard living conditions, so he was instead

Capt John Mac Isaac was a P-39 pilot on New Guinea credited with two aerial victories and known as 'Johnny Zero' when he made a stateside war bond tour after being badly burned in an Airacobra crash. He eventually retired as a US Air Force colonel. Steve Mac Isaac

assigned as a transport pilot at Fifth Air Force headquarters. He later did a war-bond tour in the US.

News write-ups of the period credit Mac Isaac with shooting down two Japanese Mitsubishi A6M Zero (Zeke) fighters, plus one probably killed in the air and two destroyed on the ground. During his war bond tour, he was given the nickname 'Johnny Zero'. Mac Isaac remained in the Army, later the independent Air Force, and retired a colonel. He died in 1998. 'He was one of the few that never bad-mouthed the P-39,' says his son Steve, also an Air Force colonel.

FS when he took a Zero right over Seven Mile on 17 May 1942. Soon afterwards, 1st Lt Thomas J. Lynch took his Airacobra into a fray and claimed two Zero fighters as 'probable' kills; after Australian soldiers found the wreckage of the two, they were amended to 'confirmed'. Lynch's Airacobra was badly damaged, however, and limped home riddled with cannon and machine-gun fire.

On 9 June 1942 – three days after a victory at distant Midway which made it less likely that the Japanese would ever

overrun New Guinea – the 39th FS 'Cobras' escorted B-26 Marauders of the 22nd BG 'Red Raiders' on an all-out bombing assault on Lae. This was a serious bombing mission against a serious foe: the Japanese airfield at Lae was the closest threat to Moresby and needed to be neutralized.

But there was an arcane sidelight to the B-26 raid: flying as an observer aboard one of the Marauders was a young legislator who had taken a commission as a lieutenant commander in the Navy and was

The Airacobra as viewed from top, side and rear. Bell

on leave from his congressional seat in Washington. The crew of this B-26 would fly twenty-five missions without winning any recognition, but for just this one mission this observer from Washington would be awarded the Silver Star medal! And for decades afterwards, even when speaking to men who knew better, the observer from Washington would boast of 'many missions' in 'the war-torn hell of the South Pacific' in a 'sky full of Zeros'. He would even claim to have done 'a full combat tour', when in reality he flew a single sortie and was in battle for just eleven minutes. Lyndon B. Johnson would become president of the United States two decades later.

Over Lae

The Airacobras of the 39th engaged Zeros at 4,000ft (1,200m) near Cape Ward Hunt, fighting at an altitude where the Bell fighter was as good as the Mitsubishi, and claimed five kills. One victor in that scuffle was P-400 Airacobra pilot 1st Lt Curran 'Jack' Jones.

Gifted with the sharp eyes that distinguish a great fighter pilot from a merely good one, Jones caught the reflection of sunlight on approaching Japanese aircraft from a considerable distance. He thought at first they were bombers, and so led his Airacobra flight into a dive – and came upon eight to twelve Zero fighters. Jones nevertheless attacked and, for the first time since pre-war gunnery training back home, fired his guns. The target eluded him, and his flight of Airacobras was suddenly alone.

Or was it? On further scrutiny Jones realized there were *five* fighters in his formation of four Airacobras!

Pitched battle

The 'reinforcement' was a Zero. Jones hauled his P-400 into an abrupt, 180-degree turn. Now aware that he had been spotted, the Japanese tried to climb, hoping to force Jones into a stall situation. But he made a fatal mistake, turning so that the broad wings of his Mitsubishi fighter were temporarily broadside to the American. Jones squeezed off short bursts and drew close enough to make eye contact with the Zero pilot; he noticed that the Japanese was apparently not wearing a parachute.

The Zero was losing altitude, leaving behind a pencil-thin stream of barely visible, light grey smoke. Across a few feet of open sky, Jones and the Japanese pilot regarded each other eye-to-eye, the Japanese riding his crippled ship downwards. Almost as if flying escort, Jones followed the Zero in its lazy fall to the Solomon Sea where it vanished in a geyser of spray.

One of the Zero pilots in the fracas that day was Saburo Sakai, who would survive the war as Japan's top living ace. And as for the Zero pilot that Curran Jones followed down on that final dive to the sea: it was fifteen-victory Japanese ace Satoshi Yoshino. After claiming two Hudson bombers while flying the ageing Mitsubishi A5M Type 96 'Claude' fighter, Yoshino had claimed Airacobras among his other victories in the Zero and had been deemed one of the Imperial Japanese Navy's most promising fighter pilots. As for Jones, he eventually achieved the requisite five victories to attain acedom.

Ongoing fight

A week later, Airacobras and Zeros fought again in a more even match, at least two of the P-400 export models falling in flames.

Pilots of the 39th FS 'Cobras' were particularly proud of the way they handled a difficult aircraft under primitive conditions. Pilots of the 39th claimed at least ten aerial victories in the Airacobra, even while reviling the Bell fighter as inadequate against the Zero. These kills were achieved without a single 39th FS pilot losing his life in battle: several pilots were shot down, but survived to fight on. In other squadrons, including the 40th FS, between nine and twelve Airacobra pilots died in the battle against the Japanese.

The 39th FS finished its Airacobra era flying escort for B-25 Mitchells and A-24 Dauntlesses over New Guinea. The last Airacobra mission flown by the 39th FS came on 24 July 1942 when eight P-400s took off and patrolled without seeing any Japanese. As the 80th FS moved up to fill in for them, the 39th FS withdrew to Townsville, Australia, where it would convert to the P-38 Lightning. Lynch, who would later command the squadron and would be a top-scoring ace with twenty aerial victories, was already credited with three Zeros that had fallen to his P-400 Airacobra.

The month of June was to see more than a turning of the tide at Midway. On New Guinea, a long campaign still lay ahead – though now, with the 80th FS 'Headhunters' joining the fray. Also in June, Americans halfway round the world were taking the Airacobra into action.

Another successful Airacobra pilot was 1st Lt George S. Welch, who had shot down four Japanese aircraft at Pearl Harbor while flying a P-40; Welch would become a North American test pilot after the war. On 7 December 1942, exactly one year after he made his combat debut in Hawaii, Welch was leading a flight of four P-39s when they encountered a formation of Aichi D3A Type 99 'Val' dive-bombers that were in the process of attacking the station at Buna. As he was lining up for the attack, he spotted a Zero coming off a strafing pass and dived on it from 4,000ft (1,200m). He chased the Zero for 10 miles (16km) and finally shot it down.

Welch had the initiative. Next he climbed to 5,000ft (1,500m), latched on to one of the 'Vals' and shot it down. Then he went after another and sent it splashing to the sea. Records indicate that Welch was flying with the 36th FS at the time, but it appears more likely he was with the 80th FS that day. He eventually

P-39D Airacobra of the 31st Fighter Group during a temporary assignment to New Orleans army air base, Louisiana. This portrait was taken in the spring of 1942 before the group moved to Atcham, England, and converted to Spitfires. via Norman Taylor

finished the war as a sixteen-kill triple ace. This feat of downing three dive-bombers in one engagement may have been a record for the Airacobra.

Europe and the Mediterranean

In 1942 Americans were being overwhelmed in the Pacific, but President Roosevelt, the Army and the AAF considered Europe to be their top priority. The American perspective – and they often seemed to forget that the British had been fighting for more than two years before they began – was that they were going to use the British Isles as a stepping stone, in a war that would eventually lead to an invasion of occupied Europe and a defeat of Germany. A handful of men were busily creating what was to become history's greatest air armada: the 8th Air Force.

Harried by German submarines, merchant convoys were bringing American fighters to British ports. But on 30 March 1942, the Army General Staff formalized a plan to speed the aerial build-up in England by enabling combat aircraft to get to England on their own power. The plan to ferry bombers and fighters across the North Atlantic was given the codename Operation *Bolero*.

In April 1942, the Army identified three units that would deploy on their own power to England via the northern route, including the gruelling 1,003 mile (1,614km) leg between Goose Bay, Labrador and the airfield known as Bluie West 8 in Greenland. The 97th BG

(B-17E/F), 1st FG (P-38) and 31st FG (P-39) would make this journey, the four-engined Flying Fortresses chaperoning the smaller and shorter-legged fighters.

While Bell scrambled to complete new Airacobras and make them available for Operation *Bolero*, these complete with production-version external centreline fuel tanks holding 158 US gallons (598 litres), the Army staff mapped out the plan. Bell test-flew an Airacobra on a marathon 7hr 54min flight around the north-eastern US, covering 1,450 miles (2,333km), seemingly proving that the P-39 was up to the transatlantic challenge. The AAF even began its first tentative look at the idea of air-to-air refuelling, a concept that would not become operational until the Korean War. In connection with *Bolero*, the Army looked at possible ways to refuel aircraft in flight. At Eglin Field, Florida, several aircraft types – though not the P-39 – tested out experimental versions of a refuelling arrangement.

The 31st Fighter Group had flown P-39s in pre-war manoeuvres and was to have the distinction of being the first American fighter group to form in the United Kingdom when its troops began arriving in June 1942 at Atcham, otherwise known as Station 342, near Shrewsbury in the west of England. It appears that consider-

In its Royal Air Force battle garb, this cannonless Airacobra I makes a good appearance and could easily share any beauty contest with a Spitfire or a Hurricane. One British pilot decided, however, that with or without armament, the Airacobra I was 'a useless lump of wank', and Britain's initial dislike for the aircraft never changed. San Diego Aerospace Museum

One of the first Airacobras to reach the UK in Army Air Forces markings was this example at Bassingbourne, England, en route to North Africa for the Operation Torch landings. This is apparently a P-39F. via David Ostrowski

able effort went into preparing the 31st FG for the long jaunt in its Airacobras.

Not to be

Although other warplanes eventually followed the northern route to England, on 1 June 1942 the Army staff scotched the *Bolero* plan, reassigning the B-17s and P-38s to the west coast. The 31st FG was still scheduled to go to England, but no longer had any Flying Fortresses to escort it. Furthermore, 31st FG officers concluded that almost any other fighter would be better suited for battle with the Luftwaffe than the P-39 Airacobra. 'The P-39 just wasn't much good above a certain altitude,' one 31st FG officer remembered.

Even today, there exists a published count of the group's three squadrons (307th, 308th and 309th FS) flying combat missions in the Airacobra beginning in August 1942. One source tells how the 31st FG supported the raid by Canadian, British, American and French forces on Dieppe on 19 August 1942, and soon afterwards flew a disastrous mission in which twelve P-39s set forth from Atcham and six were shot down by Messerschmitt Bf 109s.

These accounts of the 31st FG flying Airacobras in combat are fiction. In fact, both the air and ground echelons of the 31st FG travelled to England by sea where,

instead of operating Airacobras, the group converted to the shorter-legged but more formidable Spitfire V. The haste with which this change of plans took place may be one explanation why the Spitfire, despite its yeoman service in AAF colours, never received a 'P for pursuit' military designation.

The brass in England also ordered a second P-39 group, the 52nd FG, to arrive in England minus its equipment and to take up Spitfire Vs from the start. The Airacobra would continue to fight in North Africa and the Mediterranean, and other warplanes did indeed fly the route envisaged for *Bolero*, but the Airacobra's combat career in England simply never had the chance to get started.

North Africa

P-39D-1 and P-400 Airacobras equipped the 81st FG, 350th FG, and two squadrons of the 68th Observation Group, all part of the Twelfth Air Force in the Mediterranean theatre. However, the US government spent more time ferrying Airacobras to North Africa than it gained from their operations after they arrived. In fact, as late as the end of 1942, there were fewer Airacobras in the Twelfth area of responsibility than any other fighter type.

Some encountered a different kind of problem: en route to the combat zone, a

number of Airacobras diverted to Portugal, which was then playing a delicate balancing act in its neutrality in the war. The Portuguese Air Force, or Arma de Aeronautica, confiscated eighteen of these, possibly with implicit approval from the US; and having prevented these fighters from reaching North Africa, Portugal subsequently sent officers to the Bell factories in New York to learn about the aircraft it had acquired.

The 350th FG was in action in North Africa with Airacobras by the end of 1942 but reported the usual problem: it simply could not keep up with the Luftwaffe at high altitude.

Guadalcanal

When US Marines hit the beach at Guadalcanal on 7 August 1942, they began a long battle that halted the Japanese advance towards Australia and, ultimately, turned the tide there in the Allies' favour. At first the Marines were supported only by their own Wildcats and Dauntlesses, but soon the 67th Fighter Squadron 'Fighting Cocks' sent a detachment of P-400s under Capt Dale D. Brannon. A history published by the Marine Corps describes the squadron's role:

One of the squadrons that shared Henderson Field with the Marines was the 67th Fighter

At Henderson Field on Guadalcanal in October 1942, Bell P-400 Airacobras once intended for British use (BW167 in foreground) await action against Japanese warplanes in American hands.
via Warren M. Bodie

Squadron, a somewhat orphaned group of Army Air Corps pilots who had arrived on 22 August 1942, led by Capt Dale D. Brannon, and their P-400 Airacobras, an export version of the Bell P-39. Despite its racy looks, the Airacobra found it difficult to get above 15,000ft [4,500m], where much of the aerial combat was taking place.

The 67th had a miserable time of it because of the plane's poor performance, and morale was low. The pilots were beginning to question their value to the overall effort, and their commander, desperate for any measure of success to share with his men, asked Capt Smith [John Smith, commander of Marine squadron VMF-223, 'Rainbows', equipped with Grumman F4F Wildcats] if he and his squadron could accompany the Marines on their next scramble. Smith agreed, and on 30 August 1942, the Marine and Army fighters – eight F4Fs and seven P-400s – launched for a lengthy combat air patrol.

The fighters rendezvoused north of Henderson, maintaining 15,000ft [4,500m] because of the P-400s' lack of oxygen. Coastwatcher had identified a large formation of Japanese bombers heading towards Henderson, but had lost sight of their quarry in the rapidly building wall of thunderclouds approaching the island. The defenders orbited for 40 minutes, watching for the enemy bombers and their escorts.

Suddenly, Capt Smith saw the seven Army fighters dive towards the water, in hot pursuit of Zeros that had emerged from the clouds. The highly manoeuvrable Zeros quickly turned the tables on the P-400s, however. As the Japanese fighters concentrated on the hapless Bells, the Marine Wildcats lined up behind the Zeros and quickly shot down four of the dark green Mitsubishis. The effect of the F4Fs' heavy machine guns was devastating.

Making a second run, Capt Smith found himself going head-to-head with a Zero, its pilot just as determined as his Marine opponent. Smith's guns finally blew up the Zero just before a collision was inevitable, or before one of the two fighter pilots gave way. By the end of the engagement, John Smith had shot down two more Zeros, for a total of four kills.

With nine kills altogether, Smith was the leading Marine ace at the time. Fourteen Japanese fighters – the bombers they were escorting had turned back – had been shot down by the Marine and Army pilots, although four of the P-400s were also destroyed. Two of the pilots returned to Guadalcanal; two did not.

In four days, the 67th FS lost ten of fourteen P-400s, prompting Maj Gen Alexander Vandegrift, commander of the 1st Marine Division, to issue the following statement: 'P-400s will not be employed further except in extreme emergencies; they are entirely unsuitable for Guadalcanal operations.' Soon, however, replacements arrived in the form of more P-400 Airacobras: there was nothing else to send.

At Henderson Field, P-400 pilots fought rain, mud, shellfire and harrying raids by Japanese warplanes. On 14 September 1942, following a ground assault near Henderson, Capt John A. Thompson led a series of sweeps that strafed Japanese infantry troops mercilessly. For the next month, air and ground attacks on Henderson persisted. In October, the P-400s hunted the Japanese carrying 100lb bombs, but with no real success.

Henderson, named after a Marine who lost his life at Midway, had been constructed by the Japanese who had no idea the Americans were coming to Guadalcanal, and were in no hurry to finish it: the airfield initially lacked taxiways, revetments, drainage, steel matting and proper fuel storage. At first, Marines had to defend its perimeter from ground assault, and there was a second major ground assault in September 1942 that they managed to push back; one Marine described an especially poignant moment when a P-39 shot down a Zero in front of the battle line and the Japanese pilot fell to earth in a tangle of wreckage.

For months, Henderson Field and its nearby auxiliary strip, Fighter One, fell vulnerable to air attack – although Japanese warplanes from Rabaul were stretched to the outer limit of their range to make the attacks. P-39 pilots, crew chiefs and maintainers lived a life that was in most respects similar to the men of the ground combat forces.

Typical P-39 in-flight portrait. AAF

Illness amongst pilots

It cannot be said too often that the Airacobra pilots in the South Pacific faced conditions as harsh as any encountered in any theatre of war. Every day Henderson Field and Fighter One experienced tropical thunderstorms, making things highly uncomfortable for everyone, since most were usually out of doors – but more significant, evaporation was so rapid that dust became a serious problem for safety and maintenance. When a group of Airacobras lifted off from the dusty airstrip, every pilot following behind was blinded – and was probably suffering from illness, anyway.

During the early stages at Guadalcanal, air- and groundcrews suffered a staggering illness rate, where each man was averaging 2.5 attacks of debilitating illness per year. After the Thirteenth Air Force was formed – on 14 December 1942, with Maj Gen Nathan F. Twining in command – its headquarters reported fifty-five flying days lost per 100 officers per month due to illness. The primary culprit was malaria, that pernicious disease caused by mosquito-born parasites in the blood, but Airacobra pilots and maintainers also contracted dysentery, and dengue fever. At New Guinea, which fell under Fifth Air Force (formed in February 1942 and commanded almost from the beginning by Gen George Kenney), at one point it was reported that of 800 pilots in the theatre, 10 per cent were incapacitated by normal

disease and an additional 30 per cent were out of action at any given time due to indigenous tropical maladies.

Like so many other units, the 67th FS suffered with rain, heat, dust, malaria – and the inevitable shortage of spare parts that plagued Airacobra men in the region throughout the conflict.

To Kokumbona

On 16 October 1942, the 67th FS made seven attacks on the Kokumbona area, bombing and strafing Japanese troops. However, relentless campaigning had severely compromised the firepower of the P-400 force; thus in one sortie involving four Airacobras, the first aircraft carried a bomb but had only one machine gun that worked; the second had a bomb but no working guns; and the third and fourth had machine guns in working order, but carried no bombs. With such ragged airpower, the defence of Henderson Field persisted in late October as the Japanese sought in vain to seize the airstrip.

Then in October, the first echelon of the new 339th Fighter Squadron came up to join the 67th FS at Henderson Field, and a number of its pilots flew their P-39s along with the 67th on missions. Soon, the 339th FS was operating on its own without help from the 67th. Also in October, the 347th Fighter Group was formed: headquartered in New Caledonia, it assumed responsibility for the 67th, 68th, and later the 70th Fighter Squadrons, as well as the 339th FS.

In November 1942, Major Dale Brannon brought a new force of fighters to

The significance of the ruptured duck emblem on the door eluded the author, but this close-up of a South Pacific Airacobra shows other details of the pilot's compartment. San Diego Aerospace Museum

Henderson Field for the first time: a dozen P-38 Lightnings for the 339th FS. It was the beginning of a transition process in which Lightnings would replace Airacobras throughout the combat zone. And although a Japanese battleship drew close enough to shell Henderson Field in late November, the fate of the airfield was no longer in doubt: on the ground and in the air, Americans and Australians on Guadalcanal had taken the enemy's main thrust and had begun, finally, to go on the offensive. Perhaps it is worth noting that at this point the transition was only beginning, and Airacobras were still the most numerous of AAF fighters at Guadalcanal.

The Aleutian Islands

The principal Japanese attack against US soil during the war came in the Aleutian Islands, which were part of the territory of Alaska. They first moved against the islands of Attu and Kiska, and from then on American airmen were obliged to mount a defence against a persistent enemy, in forbidding climate.

The 54th Fighter Group (42nd, 56th and 57th Fighter Squadrons), commanded by Lt Col Phineas K. Morrill and equipped with P-39D Airacobras, eventually made its way to the Aleutians on what was supposed to be a temporary assignment. The 42nd FS, headed by Major Wilber G. Miller, was the first to deploy, departing the US mainland on 8 June 1942 for Kodiak, Alaska; there it reinforced the P-40 Warhawks of the 18th FG and the F4F Wildcats of a Navy unit. The Airacobra pilots had not known their destination until the last minute, and had no special training for combat in the frozen arctic. The group's 57th FS remained at

Elmendorf Field in Anchorage until September 1942, when it shifted to the newly constructed airfield at Adak.

The terrain at Adak was mountainous, and the place seemed to be either half buried in mud or in snow. But Adak was within 250 miles (400km) of Japanese forces on Kiska, and offered the best chance of getting Airacobras – and anything else smaller than a four-engined heavy bomber – into action. In September, a film crew led by Hollywood's John Huston arrived with US troops and filmed the arrival of warplanes, including 42nd FS and 58th FS Airacobras, at the new airstrip.

On 6 October 1942, the Alaskan command began a campaign that they had hoped would last several days, their bombers pounding the Japanese on Kiska, while P-38 Lightnings and P-39 Airacobras criss-crossed enemy positions at low

Not immediately obvious in this photograph is a mechanic seated on the wing of this P-39F Airacobra (41-7341) with his back to the camera, working on the engine. This F model belongs to the 57th Fighter Squadron, 54th Fighter Group, and the location is Alaska in July 1942. via David Ostrowski

level, strafing them with cannon and machine-gun fire. It was a short-lived war for its participants, however, the Aleutian winter and the distances that had to be flown over open water simply proving too much for single-engined P-40 Warhawks and P-39 Airacobras. As it turned out, 9 October 1942 marked the last Airacobra mission of the year. By then, the P-39s had employed their heavy firepower effectively in numerous strafing missions, and had done air-to-air battle with Japanese Rufe flying-boat fighters, Nakajima A6M2-N float-equipped variants of the famous Zero. However, many pilots considered that the Airacobra's tricycle landing gear would not hold up well to the rugged conditions in the Aleutians.

Air-to-air action produced no aces on the American side. The 54th FG was credited with ten Japanese aircraft, divided among its Airacobra squadrons as follows: 42nd FS, six; 56th FS, one; 57th FS, three. All, apparently, were Rufe floatplane fighters. It appears that no Airacobra pilot in the Aleutians was credited with more than a single aerial victory. The 54th FG was to continue fighting in the Alaskan region (where it remains today), although by the end of 1942 it was trading its Airacobras for other fighters.

Pilot talk

One pilot who flew Airacobras in Alaska was Les Sponts. He provided a narrative of his experience, which begins earlier, then moves to Alaska and back:

In December 1938, I took my first flying lesson. I passed all the commercial tests in early 1941 and entered the US Army Air Corps in April 1941 as a flying cadet in San Diego, California. That was flying class 41-I. I graduated in December, and in January [1942] joined the 57th Pursuit Squadron of the 54th Pursuit Group in Everett, Washington at Paine Field. We moved within a couple of months to Baton Rouge, Louisiana, to Page Field.

The first pursuit ship that I flew was a P-39 at Paine. We read the manuals, but not very attentively, flew Stearman trainers for pay time, and looked at about six P-40s that belonged to the group but were not airworthy, a sign of how ready we were for this new war. A Capt Art Rice brought in a new P-39 Airacobra from the factory for our squadron. We had a cockpit check during which Art sat in the plane and

pointed out things to about four of us standing on the wings. After a few minutes of this we each fired it up and taxied it about one hundred yards to get the feel of the first nose-gear type airplane any of us had seen. The next day I flew it for an hour, and knew in about thirty seconds that there was where I wanted to be.

Between January and May 1942 we flew a number of P-39s and P-40s. We traded planes with the 30th Fighter Group a couple of times for reasons not known to me. Somewhere in there I flew one of the YP-39s, but I don't remember anything special about this early, service-test aircraft. The 39s were mostly P-39C, D, and F models according to my old Form 5 [flight record]. During one of our frequent trade-offs we ended up with P-39s that included D, F, and J models which we took from Page to San Diego (for about three weeks in June), then to Anchorage, Kodiak and Adak. We also flew some K and K-1 and E model P-40s while in Alaska. The P-39F was my favourite Airacobra model. Finally, in January and February of 1943 we returned stateside with the P-39s we had taken to Alaska. I was flying the same Airacobra I had taken up, with the number 31 on the side. It was full of bullet holes. Later, it was refurbished at Kelly Field. I heard later that it was pranged by a trainee in a fighter replacement training unit in Tennessee.

Airacobra assessment

Sponts' view of the P-39, based on flying in the US and Alaska, was typical, but his powers of description were unusual:

I guess the first point of importance about a P-39 was that it was a low-altitude plane – by that I mean under 10,000ft [3,000m]. We did just about anything that could be done with a plane in that performance class below 8,000ft [2,500m]. Vertical dives were common under 5,000ft [1,500m] for dive-bombing practice, and with half rolls on the way down, or whatever you wanted to do. A P-39 was a little spooky compared to a P-40. If the aileron tabs were rigged wrong so they gave too much help, a P-39 was dangerous – we always checked them before letting our trainees try one. It felt as though you could just knock the stick to one side and it would stay. Also, the later models were not built as ruggedly as the C, D, and F models were.

The guys who were killed were mostly the ones who let the airplane do what it wanted to – and sometimes it could be very nasty. High-speed stalls in a turn could result in a snap that

most newer pilots couldn't stop before completing at least one turn – and there was no warning to this snap in some of the planes, either. The only time one did that to me I was out and flying in a half turn, making it look as intentional as I could for the benefit of anyone watching! The plane could be turned very tightly, but there was a trick to it that I never found, nor any one else that I am aware of.

I really loved that little bird, and felt comfortable in it. Not too many people will say that about it. By contrast the P-40 was always solid, at any time and at any speed. And the speeds were about the same. The P-40 had a roomier cockpit and a better heater, but they used the same engines and props. The electrics in the P-40 would sometimes go into low pitch during a dive, and the whole county would know it. The Aeromatic in the P-39 would do the same thing, but in either low or high pitch as it chose. Also it would throw grease on the windshield when a seal broke somewhere, with the result that you had to land looking out the side window or maybe in formation on someone's wing.

One thing the P-39 would do was flat spin, and there was no way to get it to stop. Even the Bell test pilots could not make it stop. It would *not* tumble! [the AAF thought otherwise]. It did have a terrible oscillating snapping spin when entered inverted – I know, because I did it. I know of one lieutenant who crashed two new P-39s at the Bell plant because they believed him when he said he could make one tumble. But he couldn't, and their pilots couldn't, either.

But you would never intentionally enter a spin at the top of a loop the second time. I know pilots who have had their heads cut up where the upper door locks got to them. And I have seen pretty well bruised legs on the guys who let the stick get away from them during some wild manoeuvre.

They could be landed with the gear down and dead stick by pilots who had ten to fifteen hours' fighter time, but I am told they were a bit hot. They were great in a belly landing – I have never seen or heard of an engine coming out, or a propshaft hurting anyone. And they were not hard to jump from, as long as the doors didn't jam shut because the fuselage was twisted during uncontrolled flight (in late models). I saw one taxi in one day with the whole aft end twisted about 5 or 10 degrees from plumb, right through the radio compartments, but it flew home. The elevator came off another one in flight one day, but that one didn't get home.

Don Bryan's Recollection

Lt Col Don Bryan admits that his experience in the Airacobra 'was a long time ago, and I only flew it about forty hours before I got smart and quit it. I was a flight leader at Panels Florida, at the time – 1942 and 1943.' Nevertheless, he has some interesting recollections: 'On my last flight the propshaft bearings blew on take-off, and I had to hold the instrument panel with my feet to see the air speed. I was a flight leader and I didn't have to fly the things.'

Typical of so many of the young men rushing into Army service in the new war, Bryan was a member of Flying Class 42-G who later flew the P-40 Warhawk, then P-47 Thunderbolts and P-51 Mustangs in Europe with the 328th FS/352nd FG. His Airacobra recollections are all too familiar:

Why was I holding the instrument panel with my feet? Remember, the engine was behind the pilot. On this nice day, that long propeller shaft went crazy. It had bearings on it that blew, and it was vibrating to beat the band. Something shook loose, and I thought my aircraft was going to break apart. The instrument panel was jumping around and vibrating so bad that I took my feet off the rudder pedals and used them to hold the instrument panel in place. So I went around quickly to land.

I liked to fly the P-39 once in a while, with some of my hot pilots. At about 400mph [640km/h] the P-40 would corkscrew in a dive, but the P-39 would not.

One of my classmates put a P-39 into a flat spin, and he felt he had to get out. He was standing on the wing. He then had an idea about trying to use throttle to regain control, and thought about getting back in. So there he was, standing on the wing, thinking, 'Well, I forgot to use throttle!' And then he was thinking, 'That ground is getting too close!' So he took a step and was instantly airborne, hanging from his 'chute. The Airacobra went straight in – it hit flat, and just smacked down on the ground, and the engine went right through the fuselage. The wings were relatively undamaged.

I personally didn't like the Airacobra because it was so crowded; I'm a short guy, and it was too tight for me. I never did fire a gun out of the P-39. I have thirty-nine or forty hours. I arrived in St Petersburg, Florida, on 29 August 1942. My first flight in a P-39 (a P-39D-1) was on 3 September 1942, from Pinellas County Airport [Army Air Field].

If you idled 'em at all, they'd overheat. They had coolant ducts in the wing. So you had to get that thing airborne just as soon as you could, so you made a fast run for take-off.

1943

At the start of 1943, much of the Allied effort was focused on North Africa where troops were struggling to mount and maintain an offensive against the Axis. In January, the 81st Fighter Group received P-39s for its 91st and 92nd Fighter Squadrons, while the 68th Observation Group also began flying combat sorties in the Airacobra. The 81st FG operated briefly from Thelepte, Tunisia before moving on to a series of bases in Algeria, then returning to Thelepte. The 68th OG was stationed at Oujda, French Morocco; it made several moves in the region, and was redesignated the 68th Reconnaissance Group in the spring of the year.

Having *two* combat groups might sound impressive, but these were equipped with Airacobras, and their active role was severely compromised because of the shortage of spare parts, and because their mechanics had received no training in the Bell fighter. As late as the end of January 1943, the two groups together were able to muster no more than two dozen active Airacobras.

The flying was arduous, the results unglamorous. On 22 January 1943, ten Airacobras of the 81st FG accompanied P-40 Warhawks in strafing tanks, trucks and gun positions in Tunisia's Ousseltia Valley, where ground troops of the German Wehrmacht were pitted against friendly forces. On 30 January, half a dozen Airacobras, accompanied by P-40s and A-20 Havocs, strafed German tanks in Faid Pass and were credited with destroying eleven tanks. On a second sortie to Faid Pass, one P-39 was shot down by German groundfire.

The Airacobra was particularly vulnerable to groundfire (*see also* the section on the French air arm later in this chapter, page 98), though most of the time it got its pilot home, in often very difficult conditions. In Tunisia, the P-39 was renowned for being untemperamental, forgiving and tough – some Airacobras are reported as having returned to their bases with sand in their wingtips from brushing the soil during low-level strafing runs, and some pilots told of flying under telegraph

wires. An article in the manufacturer's house organ, *The Bellringer*, told of a P-39 landing at its North African airfield with over 100lb (45kg) of shrapnel rattling around inside the fuselage, all from German bullets. Another Airacobra returned to base with a length of telephone cable embedded in the leading edge of its wing.

As of 1 November 1943, the Twelfth Air Force in the Mediterranean theatre of operations included the 350th Fighter Group and the 154th Tactical Reconnaissance Squadron, both with P-39 Airacobras.

In the Pacific, 1943 saw further action by the 347th Fighter Group, Thirteenth Air Force, with forty-six export P-400 Airacobras, soon reinforced by P-39Ds and a handful of P-38 Lightnings. While training at Tonouta, New Caledonia, the group decided that the Airacobra lacked the manoeuvrability and high-altitude capability they wanted. But combat in the Solomons usually meant Japanese warplanes covering naval forces or attacking American positions, all of which generally happened below 10,000ft (3,000m) where the Airacobra's performance was at its best. Leaving its headquarters' flag in New Caledonia, the 347th FG soon took up residence at Guadalcanal's Henderson Field. The island was codenamed 'Cactus', but in practice many were now using the term to refer to the airfield.

As for the 347th FG (its squadrons were the 67th, 68th, 70th and 339th FS), the group had been formed by Lt Col George M. McNeese and later led by Col Leo F. Dusard, Jr.

Not much is known about this portrait of a P-39 Airacobra and maintenance men of the 53rd Fighter Group, part of the Sixth Air Force in Panama, in about 1943. Seldom recognized for their contribution to the war effort, American pilots flew the P-39 Airacobra in Central America from 1942 to 1945 when they belatedly replaced the Bell fighters with factory-fresh Lockheed P-38L Lightnings.
via Dan Hagedorn

This P-39Q-10-BE (42-20924) arrived in Panama on 8 September 1943 but did not reach the 24th Fighter Squadron until May 1944. It displays the XXVI Fighter Command's device assigned to the 24th FS at that time, the letter 'M' in a triangle. The colours are unknown. The aircraft 'battle number' 44 is repeated on the belly tank. Ole Griffith via Dan Hagedorn

Russell Islands, and although a day later the new base was attacked by four 'Val' dive-bombers, apparently no harm was inflicted.

On 9 April 1943, it was the turn of the 67th FS to take a break away from the combat zone, and twenty-three aircraft were sent to Espiritu Santo. Similarly, it was the turn of the squadron's pilots to take home leave. On 24 April the squadron moved to New Caledonia; soon afterwards it was sent to Townsville, and finally on 15 May 1943 to Port Moresby, now with a full complement of new pilots, and eighteen P-39D and P-39K models.

After several more moves and a long dry spell, on 28 August 1943 the 67th FS recorded an aerial victory when a Mitsubishi Ki-46 'Dinah' fell to the Airacobra guns of Capt Joseph Berkow. Later in the year, the 67th was to move to a liberated Munda in New Georgia – a busy place with Lightnings, Corsairs, Hellcats, Mitchells, Dauntlesses, Avengers and Venturas already on the scene – and would receive newer, P-39Q aircraft. And it was with one of these newer Bell fighters that, on 21 November 1943, 1st Lt William E. Haymes shot down a Kawasaki Ki-61 'Tony' fighter. The 'Fighting Cocks' later provided support for landings at Bougainville in December 1943.

Following heavy fighting in 1942, by February 1943 Guadalcanal seemed more secure against the risk of Japanese takeover, and so the group's 67th FS 'Fighting Cocks' was able to enjoy something of a respite in February and March, to the extent that the group commander told his troops that 'the possibility of an enemy invasion to boot us off this island is no longer looking us in the face'. As a result, life became easier at 'Cactus' and, no longer subjected to regular attacks by Japanese warplanes, the 67th FS was able to focus on escort for B-26 Marauders during strikes against the Japanese airfield on Munda. On 5 March 1943, the 67th FS sent a detachment to operate from the

At Burtonwood, England, on 16 March 1943, this export version of the Airacobra (not a P-39 but a Bell Model 14 or P-400 Airacobra I, serial BX 187) is carrying a non-standard belly tank. The aircraft was built for Britain despite its US insignia, which includes an orange 'surround' associated with Operation Torch, the invasion of North Africa. By this late date, Britons and Americans had rejected the Airacobra for combat in Europe, although it fought valiantly in North Africa, in the Aleutians, and at New Guinea and Guadalcanal.
via Norman Taylor

The P-39K, P-39L and P-39M

P-39K (Model 26A)

The P-39K designation applies to the first batch of Airacobra fighters that had been initially designated P-39G (others being the P-39L, M and N). Power was provided by the 1,325hp Allison V-1710-63(E6) engine and the 10ft 4in (3.24m) Aeroproducts propeller.

Bell manufactured 210 P-39K-1 (Model 26A) aircraft in response to an order dated 25 August 1941. Of these, six were modified to P-39K-2 standard. The P-39K-2 configuration was optimized for the ground-attack role with under-wing ordnance stations. One 'K model' was modified to become the P-39K-5 (prototype P-39N) with V-1710-85(E19) engine, 11ft 7in (3.51m) Aeroproducts propeller, carburettor air filter, new windshield and other minor changes.

210 built
P-39K serials (210): 42-4244/4453
P-39K-2 serials (6): 42-4244, 42-4273, 42-4352, 42-4387, 42-4433, 42-4437

P-39L (Model 26B)

The P-39L was also originally designated P-39G (as were P-39K, M and N). Bell manufactured 250 'L model' aircraft as the P-39L-1 (Model 26B), which were almost identical to the P-39K-1 except for the 10ft 4in (3.14m) Curtiss Electric propeller and a slight increase in gross weight.

Eleven of these were modified to become P-39L-2 photo-reconnaissance aircraft.

P-39L-1 serials (250): 42-4454/4703
P-39L-2 serials (11) 42-4457, 42-4461/4462, 42-4465/4466, 42-4470/4471, 42-4476, 42-4489, 42-4553, 42-4630

P-39M (Model 26D)

The P-39M began on engineers' drawing boards under the Army designation P-39G (as did the P-39K, L and N). Bell produced 240 P-39M-1 (Model 26D) aircraft similar to P-39L-1, but powered by the Allison V-1710-67(E8) engine rated at 1,200hp; these gave poorer low-altitude performance, but were 10mph (16km/h) faster at 15,000ft (4,572m). At this altitude, the P-39M attained 370mph (592km/h) compared with 360mph (576km/h). In part because of a recommendation by Allison, some 'M-1 models' employed the V-1710-83(E18) engine either as a retrofit or a change midway along the production line.

The P-39M-2 designation was the result when eight of these ships (of the 240) were modified to P-39M-2 standard for photo recon, in similar manner to the P-39D-3.

P-39M serials: 42-4704/4943
P-39M-2 serials (8): 42-4704/4706, 42-4710, 42-4712, 42-4751, 42-4795, 42-4824

Seen on Guadalcanal on 22 January 1943, this weathered P-400 Airacobra is very much the property of Army Air Forces, but wears a British fin flash. The name 'Lulu' has been inscribed in subdued letters beneath the battle number '18' on the nose. The number '480' on the fin does not correspond to any P-400 serial.
Jim Sullivan

Ongoing Offensives

The 347th FG finally moved its flag up to Guadalcanal at the end of 1943. It would continue to operate Airacobras for only a few more months.

At the start of June 1943, the 18th Fighter Group joined other units at Henderson Field on Guadalcanal; it was equipped with P-39N models. The group seems to have inherited the 70th FS, its other squadrons being the 12th and 44th FS.

US troops made their initial landings on Bougainville in November 1943. As at Guadalcanal, P-39 Airacobras made up much of the air cover for this amphibious operation.

In December 1943, an Airacobra of the 15th Fighter Group became the first aircraft to use the newly reconquered airstrip on Makin Island in the Gilberts: this was 'Little Rebel' (P-39Q-1-BE 42-19474), looking relatively 'clean' in its drab olive paint scheme, and with underslung wing guns. Then on 18 December 1943, Airacobras of the 15th FG's 46th and 47th Fighter Squadrons escorted Army A-24 Dauntless dive-bombers from Makin to attack the bypassed islands of Mille and Jaluit, still in Japanese hands.

Despite the oft-mentioned primitive conditions and the long supply tail, the Airacobra was doing fairly well in terms of reliability. Between December 1943 and 12 February 1944, P-39s would fly 635 sorties plus 114 aborts to interdict these two islands, which had previously received relatively little attention from American air power.

The year ended with a Bell press release issued on 31 December 1943, in which he claimed to have produced more fighters than any other US company: a total of 4,945 P-39s and twenty-eight P-63 Kingcobras. (The story of the P-63 is told in detail in Chapter 6.) However, it is unlikely that the claim was true – and if it were, then Bell would be overtaken rapidly by other manufacturers, especially North American and Grumman, in terms of overall fighter production.

Photo-Recce Squadron

Several well known American pilots flew P-39s with the 82nd Tactical Reconnaissance Squadron, which operated a mixed bag of Airacobras and Warhawks at

Groundcrew members at Segi Point, New Georgia Island in 1943 pose in front of a P-39 Airacobra based there. They are, left to right, back row: S/Sgts Stevens, Chick, and Carre; front row: S/Sgts Nichols and Donahue.
Pima Air and Space Museum

P-39N (Model 26F)

The P-39N was one of two principal production models of the Airacobra (the other being the more numerous P-39Q). In the P-39N series, a total of no fewer than 2,095 aircraft were manufactured, to say nothing of 205 more aircraft that were once assigned serials (42-19241/19445) but were not completed, these serials being later re-assigned to P-63E-1 Kingcobras.

Developmental work for the P-39N series was carried out by an aircraft that began life as a P-39K model. The first 500 'N models' had no suffix attached to the P-39N designator and were powered by the 1,200hp Allison V-1710-85(E19) engine driving a 10ft 4in (3.18m) Aeroproducts propeller. The first 166 of these had the same fuel capacity as earlier Airacobras, but thereafter Bell introduced a weight-saving measure by reducing internal fuel capacity from 120 to 86 US gallons (454 to 325.5 litres) by removing three fuel cells. The P-39M and all sub-variants were able to accommodate 75 US gal (284ltr) and 175 US gal (662ltr) belly tanks. Because the Airacobra was always somewhat short-legged, kits were produced which made it possible for internal fuel cells to be field-fitted. P-39Ns went to French squadrons in North Africa, beginning in May 1943.

The P-39N-1 (Model 26C) designation came next and identified 9,000 aircraft equipped with an enlarged 11ft 7in (3.5m) Aeroproducts propeller. This model also differed in having an altered centre of gravity.

The P-39N-2 was the photographic reconnaissance 'N model'. The Army converted 128 P-39N-1s, following a familiar pattern

that had begun with the P-39D-2.

The P-39N-3 Airacobra was another fighter modified for photo recon in the manner of the P-39D-3. There were thirty-five examples of this version.

The P-39N-5 (Model 26C-5) was like the P-39N-1, except for the installation of armour plate instead of bullet-proof glass behind the pilot's head in the cockpit. The -5 also had an improved SCR-695 radio, and it incorporated a demand-type oxygen system and other minor changes. Bell built 695 P-39N-5s.

There were other modifications to the P-39N series, some of them one-off examples.

P-39N serials (500): 42-4944/5043 42-8727/9126
P-39N-1 serials (900): 42-9127/9726; 42-18246/18545
P-39N-2 serials (128): 42-9141, 42-9145, 42-9148, 42-9150, 42-9152, 42-9211, 42-9255, 42-9416, 42-9615, 42-9677m 42-9697/9712, 42-9714/9724, 42-9726, 42-18276/18285, 42-18298/18300, 42-18302/18305, 42-18310, 42-18327, 42-18466, 42-18485/18545
P-39N-3 serials (35): 42-19479/19483
P-39N-5 serials (695): 42-18546/19240
P-39N-6 serials (84): 42-18676/18681, 42-18712/18725, 42-18768, 42-18818, 42-18829, 42-18831, 42-18841, 42-18857, 42-18870, 42-18876/18879, 42-18881/18882, 42-18884, 42-18887, 42-18889/18896, 42-18899/18907, 42-18909/18921, 42-18923/18925, 42-18927/18933, 42-18935/18941, 42-18947, 42-19043

Profile: William Fiedler, American Air Ace

On 26 January 1943 a unique achievement was recorded for the Airacobra, when 2nd Lt William F. Fiedler, flying a P-39D of the 70th FS/347th FG, shot down a Zero over Wagana Island. It was the beginning of a fighting streak that would claim a remarkable record.

In February 1943, twenty-two Japanese destroyers sped down the 'slot' near Guadalcanal with twenty-five Zeros providing cover, their instructions to evacuate exhausted Japanese troops from Guadalcanal. Led by Capt James Robinson, the 70th FS intercepted the Japanese in late afternoon, 200 miles (320km) north of Kolombangara. Fiedler shot down a Zero in the fight, his second kill.

Transferred to the 68th FS, Fiedler was in the air again on 12 June 1943 when fifty Zeros made a sweep towards the Russell Islands. The Americans managed to launch an impressive ninety fighters, claiming no fewer than thirty-one aerial victories, one of them a Zero bagged by Fiedler 10 miles (16km) from Cape Esperance – his third victory.

Four days later, an Australian coast watcher on Vella Lavella radioed at noon to say that thirty-eight Zeros, followed by another thirty of the same, could be seen escorting fifty Aichi D3A Type 99 'Val' dive-bombers, on their way from the north-west to attack US Navy transports

This looks like a crew chief but it is actually a pilot leaning against the propeller of an export P-39D (41-38514). The aircraft is nicknamed 'MARCENE' and boasts the long-barrelled 20mm cannon. Note the detail of the automobile-style door, shown with the window down. via David Ostrowski

off Guadalcanal. This was a remarkably strong Japanese bid, and the transports were virtually naked to attack. The 347th FG engaged the Japanese formations over Beaufort Bay.

Six P-39Ds of the 68th FS/347th FG were the last aircraft to take off: they had been held in reserve so they would be ready to counter any threat to the transports, a threat which had now materialized. Fiedler shot down two 'Vals', the second with his 37mm nose cannon inoperable, and using only his four small .30 cal (7.6mm) wing guns. Altogether, American fighter pilots claimed ninety-seven Japanese aircraft against a loss of five friendly aircraft – and only a barge and a merchant ship were

lost. As happened on both sides throughout the war, these claims later turned out to be exaggerated; nevertheless it was a stunning victory and one to feel good about.

William F. Fiedler went into the history books as the only American air ace to record five aerial victories in the P-39 Airacobra. Sadly, however, he can only have had a little time to enjoy the unique status he still holds today in the annals of Air Force history, because two weeks later, on 30 June 1943, he was killed when his Airacobra was hit by a P-38 Lightning while waiting to take off. No photo of Fiedler is known to have survived.

Milne Bay, New Guinea and – after 22 November 1943 – at Dobodura, New Guinea. One was 1st Lt James Deatrich, who became known in later years as a test pilot of supersonic jets, and who retired as a colonel. He describes how, in the heat and humidity of New Guinea, his squadron inherited a batch of Airacobras after they had been 'temporarily abandoned'; he also recollects that: 'I saw an order declaring them to be obsolete – but we kept flying them for about a year after that piece of paper was issued.' Furthermore, most of the P-39s in the squadron

were not equipped with cameras, and actual reconnaissance missions were few and far between.

Deatrich also remembers seeing a plan for the squadron to re-equip with a reconnaissance version of the P-63 Kingcobra at Dobodura. It never happened, however, and the Kingcobra never made it to the South Pacific. He recalls:

We felt like we were in a backwater that nobody cared much about. We had equipment that wasn't satisfactory for anything resembling a serious job of fighting the [Japanese]. There

were rumours of new equipment, and rumours of a move closer to the [Japanese], but it didn't happen.

2nd Lt William Shomo flew with the 82nd for sixteen months in New Guinea, and saw only two Japanese aircraft, a Mitsubishi L4M1 Type 0 'Topsy' transport, and an Aichi D3A Type 99 'Val' dive-bomber, both of which were demolished by alert Airacobra pilots. There was no other air-to-air action, an ironic situation for Shomo who happened to like the Airacobra and was eager to test himself

P-39 Airacobras at Cape Torokima on Bougainville in December 1943. Pima Air and Space Museum

and his aircraft against a determined foe. Shomo would later (in 1945) shoot down seven Japanese aircraft in fifteen minutes in a raging battle over the Philippines, enough to win him an award of the Medal of Honor, but he did this in an F-6D Mustang.

Shomo gave his impressions of flying the Airacobra in the South Pacific to historian Rick Mitchell:

The P-39 was good for 2hr 20min according to the tech order, but we found how to pull this out by throwing the book away: basically, we took the idiot control off – this was a co-ordinating gimmick, so that when you used your throttle, it automatically co-ordinated the mixture changes. But that was a very costly way of operating the engine [for] gas consumption, and so we had the crew chiefs yank them out and subsequently operated the mixture controls manually. On one mission [with] sixteen airplanes out of Biak [to which the squadron moved in 1944] we were up 3hr 16min according to the tech rep's report. We had a Bell aircraft tech rep in our squadron and he sent that information [as part of] his mission reports. They sent a letter and told him he'd better quit

'LITTLE REBEL' was a P-39Q-10-BE Airacobra (42-19474) of the 347th Fighter Group on Makin Island, the Gilberts, 13 December 1943. The aircraft name was derived from a popular cartoon character who was a skunk and is immortalized in silhouette on the nose of the fighter. Of interest is the spiral striping of the 0.50 cal machine guns, and the way the bar of the national insignia is carried under the gun pod. Pierced steel planking, or Marston mat, was common at Pacific bases. via David Ostrowski

drinking that jungle juice! They said one airplane wouldn't stay in the air that long, let alone sixteen flying in a combat formation!

(The quote refers to a flight with a 175 US gal (662ltr) centreline fuel tank.)

Thus the war had bypassed the 82nd squadron, with its distinctive olive-drab Airacobras with bright white trim. Deatrich remembers spotting the glint of sun against an aircraft over the green jungle canopy, peeling off to go into a chase after possible trouble, and discovering a very routine C-47 Skytrain chugging along on a routine, friendly flight. Shomo told Mitchell that, with the short-legged Airacobras, 'We were too far away to get to where the war was'. Thus every day these pilots would watch P-38 Lightnings

The name 'ONE FOR THE ROAD' adorning its nose, this P-400 (AP375) apparently belongs to the 82nd Photo Reconnaissance Squadron located at Milne Bay, New Guinea, in mid-1943. Pima Air and Space Museum

Carefully posed late in the New Guinea campaign, this image shows one maintainer leaning out of the door to signal to another that this P-400 Airacobra is working just fine. No, there is not an invisible pilot seated behind him: in real life, leaving the engine running in this manner while 'hamming' for the camera is probably not a great idea. via Dave Ostrowski

This P-39F Airacobra (41-7224) has a bulge on the rear fuselage, just behind the national insignia, for a reconnaissance camera. The P-39F was a P-39D with an Aeroproducts propeller. This one is on a training flight in the United States. via David Ostrowski

Maintenance being performed on a P-39A of the 26th Tactical Reconnaissance Squadron, stationed at Redmond army air field, Oregon, but visiting Burns Airport, Oregon during a local field training exercise in the autumn of 1943. Norman Taylor

Donald Duck is up to mischief on the nose of this mid-production Airacobra, apparently a P-39L. 1st Lt William F. McDonough, at right, was credited with two aerial victories in this aircraft over Wau, New Guinea, in 1934. USAF

Stateside Operations

At the very time when the Airacobra's star had risen and was beginning to fall, more and more Americans were learning about the Bell fighter at stateside training bases. For Howard 'Pete' Sheehan, April 1943 was the month he finished flight training at Luke Field, Arizona, and was assigned to a tactical training unit at Mills Field in San Francisco. He has clear recollections of this time:

Our aircraft were P-39s, and they came with a reputation of instability at the very least. We went through the usual training schedules, working up to navigation, aerobatics, gunnery and so on. By the time I had 100 hours or so I had convinced myself that this was a great airplane. However, it did have some peculiarities, such as the well recorded tumble effect when stalled [which now seems to have been a myth]; that stall characteristic could turn into a half-snap roll at the top of an Immelmann.

By the end of June I had become a training instructor, and saw quite a number of planes dropped into the bay due to various causes (mostly pilot error from newly commissioned pilots).

of the 475th FG take off from Dodobura to engage the Japanese, knowing that their Airacobras couldn't make the trip. In Deatrich's opinion, 'I don't think they ever gave enough serious thought to the range of the airplane. On paper, an Airacobra was supposed to be able to fly a mission out to a distance of 300 miles [480km] or so, but in the real world we were lucky to be able to get half that far.'

When 1943 came to a close, the 82nd Tactical Reconnaissance Squadron was still at Dodobura, the war was still hundreds of miles away, and the Airacobra was still listed officially (it appears) as obsolete. It was a frustrating time and place – and that was so often a vital part of the Airacobra story.

The Bell YP-39 Airacobra (40-34) bailed to NACA, the National Advisory Committee for Aeronautics and delivered to that agency on 6 February 1941. The aircraft was assigned to a 'rake survey', an apparent analysis of different flight surfaces. It is seen here on 26 June 1943, and was eventually given up by NACA on 27 July 1944.
via Robert L. Burns

The two-seat TP-39Q-5-BE Airacobra trainer (42-20024), seen here at the Bell factory in Buffalo on 16 September 1943, was never a success, although it rated praise in the company's house organ, the Bellringer. For reasons unknown, previously published examples of this photograph have been heavily airbrushed, with both the aircraft and its background altered. This is the original image, without alteration.

via Truman Partridge

In July I was assigned on temporary duty to Wright Field as a test pilot, primarily to test the alleged peculiarities of the P-39. These were labelled 'accelerated service tests', and without going into great detail they included stall and tumbling tests (and how to un-tumble), rough and muddy field take-off and landing tests, also gunnery (with both .37 and .20mm hub cannon), service ceiling, and maximum dive speeds to test compressibility.

During the two months at Wright-Patterson we tested many other planes, and I made the acquaintance of a nineteen-year old flight officer named Chuck Yeager. Even then he was an exceptional pilot. At the end of September 1943 I checked out in P-38 Lightnings, and left to join the 80th FS in New Guinea.

Evans G. Stephens made similar comments about the Airacobra:

As you probably know, the P-39 was one of the first nose-gear fighter aircraft in the US inventory; I think the P-38 was the other one. All of my classmates that went to the P-39 had no knowledge or flight instruction on a nose-gear aircraft. We soon found out that it was a snap to fly that type of aircraft without worrying about a ground loop or loss of control on take-off.

Checkout in the airplane was by another pilot telling you how to fly it – he probably had all of ten hours or less in the P-39. He would

point out the controls, tell you what speed to land at, and wish you the best of luck.

There were twenty of us that went to the same squadron. We only had one accident during the checkout phase. I found the P-39 to be a very good aircraft for that date and time – but what did I know?

The airplane was well built – I saw many accidents where the construction of the aircraft saved pilots from serious injury. The controls were very stiff during high speed, though later on there was an aileron boost added, and this helped in roll control. When we use the term 'fly by wire' today it has a different meaning: in those days we flew by wire, but it was a cable and pulley system.

On many occasions I was able to get the aircraft above 30,000ft [9,144m], though in that atmosphere the controls were very sluggish, and you were barely maintaining speed above stalling. Most of our flight experience during combat was at altitudes very seldom higher than 25,000ft [7,620m]; most of my combat experience was air ground support. Although we were not much of a match for the Japanese Zero fighters there were some exceptions: for example, a pilot from the Philippines that joined our unit by the name of Buzz Sawyer did succeed in shooting down four Zeros on different occasions.

[The pilot named Sawyer does not seem to be included on any official roster of aerial victories.]

We did have assigned to us some P-400s with the 20mm cannon in the nose; otherwise there was no difference in the aircraft. The 37mm cannon caused some pilots to have trouble firing more than one round of ammunition, but this was because they did not understand how to recharge the system. The cannon would eject a shell onto the driveshaft of the engine, and this would bounce up into the closing firing bolt and jam the cannon. There was a recharging cable that could be pulled from the cockpit, effectively causing the cannon to be usable again. I found the guns (30s to 50s and one 37mm) to be very effective on strafing of ground targets.

As a training vehicle while stationed in Northern California most of our new students came directly from T-6 Texan aircraft, so their checkout in the P-39 was not too difficult. We did encounter some students who showed a fear of flying when they were confronted with the P-39; however, their fear seemed to disappear after a few flights.

After flying the P-39 for almost 1,000 hours [this was a phenomenal amount of experience in the Bell fighter], I was assigned to P-38 Lightnings. At the same time I was engineering officer for the base. Then after six months in the 38 I had to test-fly a transit P-39. I had forgot about the vibration that was so typical to the P-39, and which was very obvious – you only had to look at the shaking control panel. I guess in those 1,000 hours I had spent beforehand in the 39, I thought it was normal for the airplane to vibrate like that. It was caused by the long driveshaft going between your legs and out to the prop.

The prosaic sameness of these accounts of a Bell fighter that was now officially a second-line flying machine is in stark contrast to the way in which pilots were experiencing the Airacobra halfway around the world. In the Soviet Union there was no piece of paper, real or imagined, declaring the Airacobra to be obsolete; there were no rumours of newer equipment; and there was no promise of a let-up in the demands of a protracted and difficult war, waged across a panorama of time- and climate zones. Here, the Airacobra was regarded with far greater enthusiasm – although records on its performance are contradictory.

Soviet Performance

As 1943 unfolded, the Airacobra continued to be an important part of the Russian air arm, the VVS. Between 1 December 1942 and 1 August 1943, the first Airacobra regiment, the 153rd IAP, fought sixty-six air battles while flying 1,176 combat sorties, and claimed sixty-three aerial victories (twenty-three Bf 109Fs, twenty-three Fw 190s, seven Fw 189s, six Ju 88s, and four Hs 126s). The regiment sustained losses of nineteen aircraft in combat.

The 30th Guards IAP became the second Airacobra I regiment and, beginning on 13 March 1943, it fought from Chernava aerodrome. The 19th Guards IAP also flew ex-Royal Air Force Airacobra I fighters in combat, after three years' experience with earlier types. Operating Airacobra Is and P-40E Kittyhawks, this unit went into action from Shonguy airfield, then began a series of moves along the central front. As early as 9 September 1942, the 19th IAP

marked the first ramming by an Airacobra: Lt Ye A. Krivosheyev, a Soviet ace, rammed a Bf 109 and destroyed it, but with the loss of the Airacobra and its pilot.

The 19th IAP also lost another pilot who might otherwise have become one of the top aces of the war: Capt I. V. Bochkov was one of the early VVS aces and made his mark in a P-400 Airacobra I (BX728). Bochkov was flying an Airacobra when he lost his life in an action on 4 April 1943.

Lend-Lease Dealings

The programme to supply Russia with warplanes from the West, begun on a modest scale, had now reached gargantuan proportions. 'Lend-Lease' was the accepted term which covered the delivery of all of the Soviet Union's Airacobras, excepting only the initial batch of ex-RAF fighters. A brief history of Lend-Lease reminds us that it began as a policy tool while most Americans were struggling to stay out of

Bell P-39D Airacobra 41-7031 suffered a nose-gear collapse near Wilmington, NC, in 1943. The band around the fuselage is thought to be insignia yellow. The 'battle number' 816 on the nose is typical of stateside markings of the era. Paul McDaniel

The P-39's Contemporaries

Almost every American fighter pilot of World War II flew the P-39 Airacobra, but for most the P-39 was merely an interim experience on the way to something else. American production of fighters included aircraft built in the following numbers:

P-39 Airacobra	9,529	P-40 Warhawk	13,143
F4F Wildcat	7,905	F4U Corsair	11,514
P-38 Lightning	10,037	P-47 Thunderbolt	15,863
P-51 Mustang	15,486	F6F Hellcat	12,275

A P-38L Lightning with an engine feathered on a flight near Burbank, California, in 1944.
via Robert F. Dorr

A P-40 Warhawk in the South Pacific in 1942.
via Robert F. Dorr

The P-39's Contemporaries

A P-47C Thunderbolt at Debden, England, in 1943. via Robert F. Dorr

A P-51D Mustang over England, in 1944. via Robert F. Dorr

The P-39's Contemporaries *continued*

An F4F Wildcat operating with the Royal Navy. via Robert F. Dorr

An F4U Corsair over the South Pacific in 1944. via Robert F. Dorr

An F6F-3 Hellcat on an early proving flight. via Robert F. Dorr

At McChord army air field, 10 miles (16km) south of Tacoma, Washington, apparently in 1943, this P-39L-1-BE Airacobra (42-4460) wears a 'plane in group' number and trim around the nose, which suggests a training role. Unfortunately the colour of the band around the nose cowling is unknown. The P-39L is badly weathered with streaks in its olive-drab paint scheme and indications that the national insignia is fading. A bar was added to the US national insignia in early 1943 but it has not been applied to this fighter. AAF via Warren M. Bodie

Close-up of the 37mm cannon on the P-39. via David Ostrowski

A well worn P-39Q-1-BE Airacobra (42-19483) at the Buffalo factory in 1943. This angle emphasizes the underslung gun armament. Although looking weathered and weary, this fighter retains a very clean separation between the topside khaki finish and the light grey underside. Bell via Truman Partridge

The big white number on the nose is a tip-off that this 1943 portrait of a P-39Q-5-RE Airacobra (42-20729) was taken at a training base in the United States. In advanced training, almost every pilot of a Lightning, Warhawk, Thunderbolt or Mustang flew the ubiquitous P-39 Airacobra before going overseas. Pima Air and Space Museum

XP-52 and XP-59 (Model 16)

Bell's engineers faced plenty of challenges solving production problems with the P-39 Airacobra and P-63 Kingcobra; yet they still found time to conjure up new fighter designs.

They were not alone. Many dozens of fighters reached the drawing-board stage during the war, and about three dozen reached the experimental flight-test stage – many of them long after the P-51 Mustang was escorting heavy bombers to Berlin. In fact American industry came up with far more designs for warplanes than were needed to win the war. Many of them advanced the cause of scientific knowledge, but many others were simply a waste of time and resources.

Bell's Model 16 designation went initially to an unorthodox, twin-boom fighter that was also given the military designation XP-52. Powered by a 1,250-hp Continental XIV-1430-5 engine rigged to drive two propellers in a pusher configuration, the XP-52 would have been a tail-dragger, an unconventional arrangement indeed for a twin-boomed aircraft. It would have had a 35ft (10.67m) wingspan, a fuselage length of 34ft 9in (10.59m), and an armament of two 20mm cannons in the nose and six .50 cal machine guns at the forward end of the booms. The AAF also intended to evaluate a second pursuit powered by the same engine, the Curtiss XP-53. In the end, the engine suffered mortal developmental problems, so the powerplant was

never built and the XP-52 and XP-53 never got beyond the paper stage.

Even after the Continental engine became available, Bell pressed ahead with work on this unorthodox fighter design. Switching to the 2,000hp Pratt & Whitney R-2800-23 driving six-bladed Hamilton Standard contra-rotating propellers, Bell redesigned the fighter with tricycle gear. It also had swept wings, another innovation that would appear on the L-39 Kingcobra. This aircraft was given the designation XP-59 – although it should not be confused with the Bell XP-59A Airacomet, which was a wholly different flying machine. Futuristic in appearance with a bullet-shaped nose enclosing the pilot's compartment, the XP-59 looked quite like the space ships that had appeared in the Buck Rogers and Flash Gordon movie serials in the 1930s. It would have had a span of 40ft (12.19m), a fuselage length of 37ft 3in (11.35m), loaded weight of 10,463lb (4,740kg) and maximum speed of 450mph (724km/h). It, too, would have been armed with two 20mm cannons in the nose and six .50 cal (12.7mm) machine guns at the forward end of the booms.

In the end, the XP-59 was cancelled before metal could be cut, and the generic P-59 designation was re-used, for security reasons, to hide details of another fighter Bell was developing. That aircraft was the XP-59A Airacomet (*see* box page 99).

---

the war, then became a means of helping Allies after the United States joined the fray.

Following his election to a third term in November 1940, US President Franklin D. Roosevelt determined to find some means of underwriting an Allied victory over Germany without huge intergovernmental loans. In mid-December he hit upon the idea of Lend-Lease, namely, the materials of war would be turned over to Allied nations immediately or when required, and would be paid for at the end of the war in goods and services. In a press conference on 17 December 1940, Roosevelt outlined in simple terms the underlying premises of the Lend-Lease programme. Two weeks later, on 29 December, in an effort to rally public opinion behind his brainchild, Roosevelt delivered one of his most famous 'fireside chats' – the 'arsenal of democracy' speech – in which he called upon the American people to assume new responsibilities as guardians of the freedom of the world.

Frank Hodgkins, a Washington DC resident who worked for the Roosevelt administration, remembers the misleadingly named programme in this way:

Lend-Lease was a device to get around Congress's isolationist prohibitions against giving aid to countries fighting in World War

II. The purpose (of the prohibitions) was to keep us neutral. Roosevelt, however, was determined to help Churchill and the British so we 'lent' them 100 (I believe) old destroyers (to escort convoys) in return or payment for a 'lease' of some British Caribbean airfields to (ostensibly) allow us to better patrol and protect our shoreline. It worked well enough, and 'Lend-Lease' became a euphemism for what is now called 'foreign aid'. I don't recall what

the Soviets 'leased' us. I don't think we got back much of what we 'lent' them either – but then we never really expected to.

Roosevelt pitched Lend-Lease to the American taxpayer in language that was innovative and memorable:

Well, let me give you an illustration: suppose my neighbour's home catches fire, and I have a length of garden hose 400 or 500ft [120 to

This well worn Bell P-39D-2-BE Airacobra (41-38416) is unique in serving with four regiments. It was flown in combat by I. I. Baback of the Russian 45th IAP (fighter aviation regiment) in March–April 1943. San Diego Aerospace Museum

A four-bladed propeller had been intended for the XP-76 variant of the Airacobra and was used on some production P-39Q models. It became easy enough, as Bell shifted to a newer fighter, to employ the four-bladed Aeroproducts propeller on Kingcobras such as this P-63A (42-68931). Bell

Airacobra I and P-39F fighters under assembly and ready for delivery at the Bell plant on 23 December 1941. The crowded look never changed throughout the war as newer models and P-63 Kingcobras joined the throng. Bell

150m] away. If he can take my garden hose and connect it up with his hydrant, I may help him to put out his fire. Now, what do I do? I don't say to him before that operation, 'Neighbour, my garden hose cost me $15; you have to pay me $15 for it.' What is the transaction that goes on? I don't want $15 – I want my garden hose back after the fire is over.

All right. If it goes through the fire all right, intact, without any damage to it, he gives it back to me and thanks me very much for the use of it. But suppose it gets smashed up – holes in it – during the fire: we don't have to have too much formality about it, but I say to him, 'I was glad to lend you that hose, but I see I can't use it any more, it's all smashed up.' He says, 'How many feet of it were there?' And I tell him, 'There were 150ft [45m] of it.' He says, 'All right, I will replace it.' Now, if I get a nice garden hose back, I am in pretty good shape.

Its rubles valueless in the West, the Soviet Union, of course, had no foreign exchange of any real value and was in no position to pay for a garden hose or an Airacobra. As far as the deal with the Soviets for the Bell fighter was concerned, Washington's Lend-Lease programme was covered in a series of agreements which had the force of treaties but were known as protocols. These followed Moscow's signature to the declaration of the United Nations on 1 January 1942 and its support for the Atlantic charter. The first American P-39s (those which followed on the heels of the ex-RAF P-400 Airacobra Is) were covered by a document called the second protocol, signed in Washington, and applicable to deliveries taking place through the end of 1943. A subsequent agreement, the third protocol, covered shipments from January to June 1943.

Even though their own industry was building and healing, the Russians could not get enough American warplanes. The third protocol, which seems to have acquiesced to unrealistic Soviet demands, promised them not 100 fighters per month (as they had received through the end of 1942), but no fewer than 500 Airacobras monthly, to say nothing of 100 Douglas A-20 Havocs and fifty North American B-25 Mitchells. By now, the southern route via Iran was the accepted way to deliver these aircraft. But as if insecure, as if needing reassurance, the Russians sent delegations to visit the Bell and Allison factories, to assure workers of the communal ties between friendly allies. There was a war on, and Hitler had to be defeated –

The Airacobra became cleaner and cleaner in appearance with each new model that came off the production line. The 188th P-39Q-10-BE is seen from an appealing frontal angle in front of the Bell factory in the late summer of 1943. Bell

but the aviation workers in Buffalo and Indianapolis knew nothing about the Gulags where Stalin was decimating his own population.

Airacobra Deliveries

It should be noted that even in the Roosevelt administration, Americans never really trusted Russia and were careful to insist that Airacobras and other war materials could not be transferred to third parties. Furthermore, when Soviet Ambassador Maxim Litvinov joined the US Secretary of State in signing the original Lend-Lease documents, the Soviet Union committed itself to make certain repayments 'as soon as the present emergency shall end'. As it turned out, the end of World War II did not bring about this result. As late as 1974, the Soviet government reneged on a commitment made in the early 1970s to repay wartime Lend-Lease debts. Today, a decade after the collapse of the Soviet Union, there is no possibility that Washington will ever ask for anything back – not even a pair of Airacobras which are rumoured to be undergoing preservation today.

The numbers needed by the Soviets were nowhere within the bounds of practical expectation. Soon after the third protocol became operative, it was quickly apparent that not even the miraculous American aircraft industry could provide the USSR with 500 Bell fighters per month (or 6,000 per year). As a stopgap, Gen Henry 'Hap' Arnold managed to find 600 P-40 Warhawks that had been slated for scrapping, and arranged for them to go to the Soviets, even though the Soviets repeatedly made it clear that they preferred the Airacobra. After some rehashing, retrenchment in Washington, and a reassessment in Moscow, the Americans committed for a total of 4,140 combat aircraft during the first half of 1943, with the number of fighters reduced from 500 to 112.5, and altered to include both P-39s and P-63 Kingcobras. Largely oblivious as to how these agreements were negotiated, ferry pilots pressed ahead with the difficult task of getting these warplanes to their destinations.

Stalin is reported to have complained that the British supplied Hurricanes, not Spitfires, and the Americans provided Warhawks, not Airacobras, a sign that the Soviets were being accorded second-class

The Soviet air arm, called the Air Force of the Red Army, or VVS (Voyenno-Vozhdushniye Sily), had thousands of pilots and maintainers who placed their trust in the P-39 Airacobra. This quintet is gathered close to the 37mm nose cannon that gave the P-39 its lethal striking power. San Diego Aerospace Museum

status. Air ace Aleksandr Ivanovich Poykryshkin is reported to have said that he would not exchange his Airacobra for any fighter provided by Mikoyan, Lavochkin or Yakovlev. While their diplomats continued to try to get more out of the Lend-Lease deal, even after it became clear that the Soviet Union was no longer in danger of imminent defeat, the Airacobra continued to be a favourite because of its performance when providing direct support to ground combat troops.

Ferry Mission

Apart from sea convoys to northern ports and aerial ferrying through Iran, there was a third route that brought Lend-Lease aircraft into Russian hands. The Alaskan-Siberian route, or ALSIB route, was launched as an alternative by the ferrying division of Air Transport Command. The division had dozens of small units of pilots who rapidly acquired cross-country experience and who were entrusted with the job of picking up aircraft and delivering them.

Lloyd P. Benjamin began by going through the 'Pursuit Transition in P-47, P-40 and P-39' airplanes with the Ferrying Division's 4th Operational Training Unit at Brownsville, Texas. After getting about twenty hours in each fighter type,

Benjamin, a flight officer who did not yet hold a commission, was entrusted with proceeding to the headquarters of a major airplane company, picking up a factory-fresh warplane, and delivering it to a user hundreds or thousands of miles away. 'I was twenty-one years old, and I had never

been given such responsibility,' Benjamin remembers.

Ferry pilots typically picked up Airacobras at the Niagara Falls factory and flew them to Gore Field at Great Falls, Montana. The AAF maintained a sub-depot of Airacobra specialists at Great Falls, who attended to the final details in preparing the aircraft for onward travel en route to the Soviet Union.

Pilots then flew the fighters from Great Falls north into Canada, with fuel stops typically at Edmonton and Whitehorse, and final delivery at Fairbanks. From Alaska, Soviet pilots took over for the journey on the ALSIB route into Siberia, with stops in Krasnoyarsk and other cities en route to Moscow. The ALSIB route eventually accommodated 1,022 Aira-cobras and 2,421 Kingcobras, with losses on delivery consisting of only twenty-three P-39s and twenty-one P-63s, or 2.25 per cent and 1.17 per cent respectively. The ferry job was an extraordinary achievement.

Benjamin ferried both Airacobras and Kingcobras. He no longer remembers which aircraft was in his hands one dark and stormy night when everything went wrong:

I was somewhere in the mid-west on the first leg of a flight that was to end in Montana,

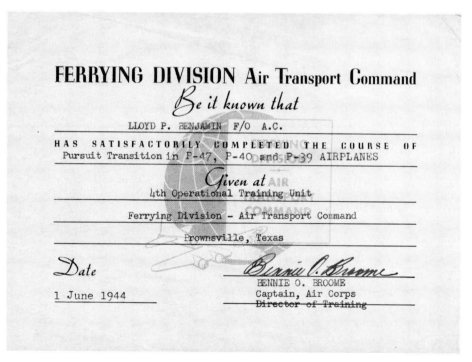

Certificate awarded to ferry pilots who completed training in the 'P-47, P-40 and P-39 Airplanes' training course. Lloyd P. Benjamin

Typical of thousands of portraits shot on a grassy plain at **Wright Field, Ohio** during the war years is this early shot of a **YP-39C Airacobra** model **(40-2974)**. AAF

where another pilot would ferry the aircraft to Alaska. Just as the weather closed in, I had a mechanical problem. I no longer remember its exact nature, but I knew I had to get down, fast. I remember the aircraft was shaking like a washing machine.

In the little light available to me, I spotted what looked like an open field with what appeared to be an aircraft runway. I learned later that this was not an airfield runway at all, but a dirt road that had been built for trucks carrying material to a construction project. Anyway, I needed both hands to keep the airplane steady as I cut power and descended, and I knew I was going to need some luck. I was happy the airplane had its wide-rack main landing gear, but I would have been even happier if it were a tail dragger without that big nose-wheel sticking out in front of me. The airplane was becoming very difficult to handle as I came near the end of my approach, and I felt I would not be able to go around.

Benjamin made a shaky landing, determined that he was still alive, and spent the rest of the night sleeping in his cockpit. The next day he walked to a source of gasoline, topped off the aviation fuel in the tanks, and continued his journey. Numerous Airacobras ferried by Benjamin later ended up in Soviet hands.

More Fighting

The long months of slaughter at Stalingrad ended with the German defeat in February, but ahead lay another critical battle along the 563-mile (900km) Kuban River in the North Caucasus, which ran beside vital Soviet oilfields. It began on

Taken near **Ladd** army air base in the territory of Alaska, this photo shows efforts to salvage a **P-39N Airacobra (42-18584)** on 13 June 1943, after the Bell fighter went into the sea on the northern ferry route to Russia. The wartime caption tells us that the watchers are 'unidentified USSR personnel who participated in aircraft Lend-Lease, 1942–45'. USAF

17 April 1943 with Junkers Ju 87 Stuka missions that were largely uncontested, but when fighting began around the village of Krymskaya, VVS fighter units began tearing into the Luftwaffe with a vengeance.

In the Battle of Kuban River, most of the fighters on the Soviet side were foreign-built, including the Supermarine Spitfire Mk VB, which the Russians found disappointing and often confused with the Bf 109. Airacobra action was spearheaded by Russian pilots who would later become legends. Aleksandr Ivanovich Poykrysh-kin, later to be recognized as the third-ranking Allied ace, had begun his career in the MiG-3 but was flying Airacobras throughout the Kuban battle, sometimes with Airacobra pilot Grigori Rechkalov, who would emerge as the second-ranking ace, on his wing. Unlike American pilots in England or the South Pacific, these men did not finish their missions and then have leave to go home: they would be in the war until its end.

Rechkalov, who later flew a P-39Q model (44-2547), seems to have been a little too much of a fighter pilot and has long been accused of being more interested in his personal tally of aerial victories than in his role as an officer and leader. As we shall see, he fell out with Poykryshkin; but no amount of animosity between the two can change the fact that they shared the honours as the USSR's top Airacobra aces.

Newer Airacobras

Having begun with ex-RAF Airacobra I models, the Russian air arm subsequently received model P-39D-2 Airacobra fighters; these came exclusively via the southern route, through Iran. This route became almost essential after the shattering losses inflicted on convoys taking the northern route, especially convoy PQ-17, and because of the general increase in losses in Arctic convoys, to 11–12 per cent of transport vessels. The shipment of needed war materials via northern sea convoys continued unabated – bar P-39D-2 models – and at least three Soviet regiments equipped with ex-RAF Airacobra I models, the 17th IAP and 78th IAP, drew the hapless job of covering convoy arrivals at Archangelsk and Murmansk. As noted earlier, Airacobra Is were also delivered to fighter squadrons of the Soviet Navy.

Bell P-39N-1-BE Airacobra (42-9302). A major production version with over 2,000 articles manufactured in the early part of 1943, the P-39N introduced powerplant changes, an Aeroproducts propeller, and a reduction in internal fuel capacity to save weight. via David Ostrowski

The Navy, too, provided air cover for arriving Allied convoys, flying over waters so cold that any downed pilot would freeze to death in minutes. One Airacobra pilot who drew this duty, Maj V. F. Sirotin of the 17th IAP, flew an Airacobra bearing twenty-one kill marks and a personal nose emblem which showed a powerful eagle chasing a German aircraft away from a ship.

By the time of the Kuban River campaign, the ex-RAF P-400 Airacobra Is were being joined in action by P-39D-2 Airacobras from the USA. The first of these to be lost in combat was 42-135031, of the 45th IAP, shot down in the Kuban fighting on 10 March 1943. Another P-39D-2, 41-38444 of the 104th Guards IAP, was shot down on 19 March 1943 with the loss of a promising pilot, G. I. Belayakov.

The Allies shipped aircraft by sea and offloaded them at Abadan. Assembled by Soviet specialists and given a test-hop by Soviet pilots, they were then ferried by air to the Kvali Margi airfield in Teheran, where they underwent formal acceptance by Soviet officials. Then, pilots ferried the American-built Airacobras to Aji-Kabul, Azerbaijan, or to a ferry airfield in the vicinity of the city of Kirovabad. The

acceptance process was unquestionably hindered by a xenophobia prevalent in Russia at the time – Stalin himself distrusted foreigners intensely – which meant that only a small number of American and British experts were on scene to be part of this process, and no more than the odd one was present on the delivery route beyond Tehran.

A newly formed 25th ZAP at Aji-Kabul, analogous to the 22nd ZAP which accepted foreign aircraft on the northern route, was in operation to accept fighters arriving from Teheran and to move them on to combat units. These units trained Airacobra and P-40 Kittyhawk pilots, and also had a role training fliers on the MiG-3 and LaGG-3. Models of the Airacobra pouring into Russia now included the P-39D-1, P-39D-2, P-39K, P-39L, P-39M, P-39N, and – eventually – the P-39Q.

In February 1943, the 19th Guards IAP began to receive Lend-Lease P-39N and P-39Q Airacobras to supplement its waning fleet of Airacobra Is. It is not clear how long some Soviet units kept the older Airacobras after newer ones were available, but many pilots remained faithful to the more reliable 20mm cannon – as occurred elsewhere.

Kuban River

In the Kuban River fighting, a young Luftwaffe Bf 109 pilot named Erich Hartmann was among the members of three crack German squadrons that engaged the newly arrived P-39D-2s in March 1943. On the 23rd, eight Russian Airacobra pilots took on thirty Messerschmitts and shot down thirteen of them – but at high cost. Two Airacobra flyers in burning aircraft, seeking to alter the balance of the fight as it unfolded, rammed their foes and died. In that same engagement, another Soviet Airacobra pilot who would become well known – Boris Glinka of the brothers Glinka, Boris and Dmitry – was wounded in the fighting while at the controls of a P-39D-2. Though he would eventually gain thirty-one aerial victories (thirty personal and one group), this was a serious setback for Boris Glinka, who never had the opportunity to catch up with Dmitry, whose final score was fifty (all personal).

April 1943 was a month of horrendous fighting along and above the Kuban. One Airacobra pilot claimed fourteen Luftwaffe aircraft destroyed, and both Glinka brothers added to their scores; but Hartmann bagged an Airacobra, his own seventh aerial victory (and his first Airacobra) of a tally that would eventually rise to 352, to make him the top-scoring air ace of all time.

It appears that Hartmann did not hold the Airacobra in any higher regard than many American pilots who dismissed their own aircraft. In a 1980 interview, he referred to the Bell fighter as 'meat on the table'. That was hardly the case, however, if Russian claims – usually exaggerated – are to be believed: according to these, during the Kuban fighting the 45th IAP shot down 118 Luftwaffe warplanes with the loss of just seven Airacobras and one P-40E. Soon afterward, the regiment began exchanging its P-39D-2s for fresh, newer P-39L and N models. Numerous Airacobra veterans of the Kuban River campaign were awarded Hero of the Soviet Union status, including the two Glinkas.

Heavy Fighting

A remarkable Ukrainian history of Airacobra operations, reprinted in the *Journal of the American Aviation Historical*

During the war era, Bell mastered the technique of photographing its fighters while they fired guns on the ground at night, then altering the photos to make it look as if the planes were in flight. These nearly identical shots of a P-39 Airacobra and a P-63 Kingcobra were created using this method. The tracer gunfire is certainly authentic, but in real life neither the P-39 nor the P-63 was especially useful at night. Bell

This excellent Bell publicity shot shows the wing-mounted armament to advantage. via Robert F. Dorr

French Cobras

On 13 May 1943, l'Armée de l'Air squadrons in North Africa received their first P-39N Airacobras, starting with Groupe de Chasse (Fighter Group) III/6 Roussillon in Ain Sefra, Algeria. French pilots also began flying Airacobras with Groupe de Chasse I/4 Navarre and I/5 Champagne. These were weathered, war-weary Airacobras apparently greeted with something less than total enthusiasm by their French charges, and they were employed initially for the prosaic job of patrolling the Mediterranean and guarding North African ports.

Eventually added to the roster of P-39 Airacobra units were Groupes de Chasse I/3 Corse, I/9 Limousin, II/6 Travail, and II/9 Auvergne. Following delivery of used AAF Airacobras, a batch of P-39Qs apparently came to the French directly from the factory; but by then, l'Armée de l'Air was

Society, contains statistics for the 19th IAP, which retired its last ex-RAF Airacobra Is (AH658, 628) at the end of 1943 and was now flying some twenty-five P-39N and Q models in addition to Soviet-built Yak-3 and LaGG-3 fighters:

By 31 December 1943, the 19th Guards IAP had made 7,451 sorties with a flight time of 5,410hr 19min. It had shot down fifty-six Bf 109Es, forty-three Bf 109Fs, fifteen Bf 109Gs, one He 113, 30 Bf 110s, seven Ju 88s, nine Ju 87s, one He 111, two Do 215, five Hs 126s, one Fi 156 and one Fw 189. During that time it experienced the following losses: forty-six pilots (including thirty-six in air combat) and eighty-six aircraft (including fifty-nine shot down in air combat, of which twenty were Airacobras). Non-combat losses were three in collisions (one being an Airacobra). Of 128 aircraft received, 56 were Airacobras.

All claims for aerial victories in combat are exaggerated, and the figures given above must be read with some scepticism, particularly since we know today that the Germans never had an aircraft called the He 113 (it was a fictional creation based on the He 100D, which was manufactured in small numbers and never reached the combat zone). It is also grounds for scepticism that the Ukrainian document is so precise about which model Messerschmitt was being claimed (aircraft recognition being a far more difficult challenge than this precise document would suggest). Nevertheless, the figures put to rest the myth that the Airacobra was solely an air-to-ground weapon in Soviet hands.

They all had a picture like this, all those young men who flew the Airacobra in the ZI (the 'zone of the interior', meaning the United States) – but they found themselves piloting some other fighter once they got abroad. These members of the 380th FS/363rd FG are clustered around an Airacobra named **FOOLS PARADISE II** at Oakland, California. Municipal Airport on 17 November 1943. Their squadron is an obscure one: the 380th appears in no history, but officials confirm that it existed briefly before being re-designated 160th FS and then (more familiarly) 16th FS. Both squadron and group soon became tactical reconnaissance units, flying F-5 Lightnings and F-6 Mustangs at Staplehurst, England, as part of the Ninth Air Force. Earl Otto

The P-39N was used by the Free French Forces in Sicily. This example from Spa-165 was photographed at Catama in October 1943. Howard Levy

beginning to fly the much-preferred P-47 Thunderbolts. The Airacobras were useful in southern France and northern Italy in air-to-ground work and, as noted below (*see* Chapter 6), were joined in 1945 by P-63 Kingcobras.

In French hands, as elsewhere, the Airacobra seems to have demonstrated some weaknesses and vulnerabilities, but to have acquitted itself well as a ground-attack weapon. Early P-39s had lacked adequate pilot protection, but the later-model Airacobras used by the French came along after Bell added armour protection around the cockpit and elsewhere. There was still no protection for the oil and glycol cooling radiators located in the wing centre section, which was particularly vulnerable to groundfire – the same problem which made the P-51 Mustang less than ideal for air-to-ground work – and even late-model French aircraft apparently did not have enough armour on the bottom. Very few details have emerged regarding French use of the aircraft, but it does appear to have done well.

P-59A Airacomet (Model 27)

In 1941–42, Bell began building prototype fighters that were so secret that no serial numbers were assigned to them until after they had flown. The AAF gave the new aircraft the designation XP-59A, re-using a number that had been assigned to a different Bell aircraft (the XP-59). The secrecy was aimed at concealing the fact that the aircraft had an entirely new kind of powerplant, devised by Britain's Wg Cdr Frank Whittle and built under license by General Electric. With a pair of British-built, General Electric-assembled I-A turbojets rated at 1,300lb (590kg) thrust, the XP-59A Airacomet prototype was to become the United States' first jet fighter at a time when jet power was unknown to the press and public.

Because Great Britain was so far ahead of the US in gas turbine development, the UK supplied the General Electric Company with specifications of what became the 2,000lb (907kg) thrust I-16 powerplant, later re-designated J31-GE-5 (replacing the British-built 1-A model employed in the interim). On 5 September 1941, Bell was tasked to build three XP-59As (42-108784/108786), and the first of these was trucked in secrecy to Muroc Dry Lake, California, draped in tarpaulin with a fake propeller affixed to conceal its revolutionary power source. First flight of the XP-59A

The Bell XP-59A Airacomet was America's first jet fighter – though it was never fully operational, and would have had difficulty fighting anybody; it was developed and flown while the production of the P-39 Airacobra and P-63 Kingcobra was continuing. via Robert F. Dorr

was achieved on 1 October 1942 with Bell's chief test pilot Robert M. Stanley at the controls. The first military flight was by Brig Gen Laurence C. Craigie on 2 October 1942.

P-59A Airacomet (Model 27) *continued*

P-59A Airacomet (Model 27)

The twin-jet, mid-wing, tricycle-gear XP-59A offered only modest improvement in performance over the best propeller-driven fighters of the early 1940s, but AAF planners recognized that jet power was the wave of the future. Following the three test craft which had been powered by the 1-A, thirteen service-test YP-59As (42-108771/108783) flew with the I-16. Production orders followed for twenty P-59A aircraft (44-22609/22628).

The P-59B was originally to have been a single-engine variant, but the thirty P-59Bs completed (44-22629/22658) of eighty originally ordered retained the twin-jet layout, albeit with minor changes. A sole YP-59A (42-108773), in 'trade' for a Gloster Meteor flown by the AAF, was shipped to the RAF's test facility at Farnborough, given the RAF serial RJ362/G, and evaluated only briefly. The US Navy designation XF2L-1 is sometimes quoted for Airacomets tested at NATC Patuxent River, Maryland, and the three XP-59As in Navy markings (44-22651, 44-22657/22658) did acquire Navy bureau numbers (64100, 64108/64109); however, the XP-59A nomenclature was retained.

The XP-59A Airacomet was credited with a maximum speed of 409mph (658km/h). The Airacomet cruised at 375mph (604km/h), and had a service ceiling of 46,200ft (14,080m) and range of 400 miles (644km). It was significantly larger than an Airacobra, witness this comparison:

	XP-59A	P-39D
wingspan	45ft 6in (13.87m)	34ft (10.36m)
length	38ft 1½in (11.62m)	30ft 2in (9.21m)
wing area	386sq ft (35.84sq m)	213sq ft (19.80sq m)
empty weight	8,165lb (3,704kg)	6,300lb (2,853kg)
loaded weight	13,700lb (6,214kg)	7,650lb (3,465kg)

Armament was one 37mm M4 cannon and three .50 cal (12.7mm) machine guns mounted in the nose, although most P-59s flew with no guns installed.

The Airacomet was not, as many believe, the second or third jet aircraft to fly: it was, in fact, the fifth, being preceded into the air by (in chronological order) the Heinkel He 178 (24 August 1939), the Caproni-Campini N.1 (27 August 1940), the Heinkel He 280V-1 (5 April 1941), the Gloster E.28/39 (15 May 1941) and the Messerschmitt Me 262V-2 (18 July 1942).

All production had been completed by the end of the war, and many Airacomets were assigned to the AAF's 412th Fighter Group for use as drones or controllers, some aircraft having a second open cockpit in the nose for an observer. In fact, it was in this unique open cockpit that Lawrence Bell made his first ride in a jet aircraft. No P-59, however, reached fully operational status or saw combat.

Though none is flyable, several P-59 Airacomet airframes remain in existence today. A lesser known example is a P-59B (44-22656), preserved indoors at the Harold Warp Pioneer Village Museum in Minden, Nebraska.

CHAPTER FOUR

1944

For most purposes, 1944 was the final year of the war for the Bell Airacobra: in the Pacific, North Africa and Italy, P-39 fighters flew their last combat sorties in American hands; briefly, they equipped the famous Tuskegee airmen, who went on to greater achievements flying newer fighters; and not so briefly, Airacobras finally brought to a close their prolonged campaign on Guadalcanal. In the Soviet Union, however, 1944 was merely another year, and the Russians continued to use the Bell fighter with greater imagination and enthusiasm than anyone else – indeed, by the time 1944 came to an end they were flying as many of them as ever.

This was also the year when the last of these fighters came off the production line, superseded by the P-63 Kingcobra, a model which by the year's end was flowing smoothly out of the factory doors in Niagara Falls. Exactly how these P-63s sent to the Soviet Union were deployed and used is, however, not quite so clear: as we shall see, there are conflicting claims about their combat use in Russian hands.

Kwajalein Landing

As a preliminary before the better known battle for Saipan, in late January and early February 1944, the US Army 7th Infantry Division assaulted Kwajalein Island, and the other small islands in the southern half of Kwajalein Atoll. Simultaneously, the US Marine Corps in its northern half assaulted Roi Island and Namur Island, and then the remaining smaller islands of that area. This part of the Pacific island-hopping campaign has never received much attention – perhaps because American losses were just 142 and 845 wounded – however, the seizure of Kwajalein Atoll and its neighbouring islands gave US forces staging points for air and naval forces moving onwards in later months to attack the vast Japanese naval base at Truk, and other lesser Japanese installations en route to the Mariana Islands.

When US forces landed on Kwajalein Island on 29 January 1944, the 318th Fighter Group's 46th and 72nd Fighter Squadrons covered part of the landings by flying continuous daylight combat air patrols over Japanese-held Mille Island. The record doesn't say how much action the Airacobras saw, but these patrols continued for several days. Airacobras were at their best in this kind of air-to-ground environment, and the sorties were credited with forcing the enemy into a low profile.

P-39Q-15-BE Airacobra (44-2506) in the snow at Buffalo. Bell via Truman Partridge

Bell P-39Q-5-RE Airacobra 42-19993 at **New Guinea in April 1944**. Mike Moffitt

In January 1944, the 347th Fighter Group moved from Guadalcanal to Stirling Island, to support ground forces on Bougainville in the Solomons, to assist in neutralizing the Japanese bastion at Rabaul, and to fly patrol and search missions in the northern Solomons. The fight on Bougainville, in particular, was taking far longer than Americans expected (it dragged well into March) and the Airacobra was an essential part of the slow, grinding struggle.

To 'backfill' for the departed 347th FG at Henderson Field, the 12th FS, or 'Dirty Dozen' (also dubbed the 'Foxy Few'), part of the 18th FG, remained on Guadalcanal with Airacobras. The 12th FS motto was *In Omnia Paratus*, or 'Prepared for All Things', but by the time the men reached Guadalcanal they learned that the war had moved on; and soon afterwards the squadron converted to P-38 Lightnings.

On 8 March 1944, 347th FG P-39s dropped 500lb bombs on Japanese troops closing with American GIs on Bougainville. With the completion of an airstrip on Nissan, the relatively short-range Airacobra was finally able to reach Rabaul: on their first mission, also on 8 March 1944, they encountered no fighters

Bell P-39Q Airacobras of the 82nd Reconnaissance Squadron at New Guinea on 28 May 1944. The P-39Q-6-BE bears the nickname 'LITTLE SIR ECHO' at the far right, it also has the word 'TEXAS' painted beneath the rear canopy, and it boasts shark's teeth on its belly tank. Under a microscope, the nicknames of other aircraft in this line-up are evident, including 'SHREVEPORT SACK RAT', 'RUTHIE II', 'EILEEN', 'JULIE 2ND' and 'REBA'. The trim on the tail, the wing leading edge, and a band around the nose is understood to be yellow. via Warren M. Bodie

Apparently belonging to the 89th Reconnaissance Squadron, 'BRINKLEY'S BUM' is a P-39Q-5-BE Airacobra (42-10993), high over New Guinea in April 1944. via Norman Taylor

but plenty of anti-aircraft fire. The availability of Airacobras to join in the massive aerial siege of Rabaul was welcomed by officers who wanted to free B-24 Liberators to devote their attention to the Japanese base on Truk.

By now, however, the condition of the 347th Group's P-400 and P-39D Airacobras was described by one pilot as 'wretched'. As a case in point, on one occasion a handful of mechanics was to be seen standing about watching hydraulic fluid leak from the heavy back-side of an Airacobra; but instead of stemming the haemorrhage, they were taking bets on how long it would last! A technical sergeant won $80 in bets, though fortu-

nately he was happy to fix up the whole mess afterwards. That was no exaggeration. The Airacobras had, in fact, been in wretched condition for more than a year.

The handwriting was on the wall. In April 1944, a report on the 82nd and 110th Tactical Reconnaissance Squadrons in the South Pacific said that the squadrons' P-39 Airacobras had reached 400 flying hours and were worn out. The report praised their contribution to close-support work but suggested that their days were numbered. Gen Ennis Whitehead, who commanded the advanced element of Fifth Air Force under Gen George Kenney (and was known as 'Ennis the Menace' to troops), wanted P-51 Mustangs as replace-

ments but was told that because of demands in the European theatre of operations he would have to wait. A member of his staff believes Whitehead saw the Airacobra as one of life's necessities: '. . . not a spectacular airplane, but his men had to make do with what they had'. The 82nd and 110th were bolstering their strength with P-40 Warhawks cast off by the 7th and 8th Fighter Squadrons (both of which were being newly equipped with the P-38 Lightning) and were being told to be patient. As it turned out, the Mustangs would come later.

1st Lt James Deatrich led a detachment of the 82nd Tactical Reconnaissance Squadron which operated from Finschhafen, New Guinea, from December 1943 into April 1944. He has one particularly cogent memory:

I was cruising along over the jungle at 1,000ft [300m] when I looked out at my left wing and saw it starting to peel off. It looked as if the skin of the aircraft had been installed from front to back in tiny little segments, because portions of the wing were coming open like the top of a tin can. My Airacobra became unstable, and its responses to my touch on the controls became sluggish – but the controls were still working, and the thing was still flying. I did a 180 [degree turn] and an RTB [return to base]. The airplane started shaking and shuddering, but continued to work as I approached the airfield, lowered the gear without difficulty, and let down.

Apart from the biggest bounce since my early cadet days, it was an eventless landing – but when we looked at the plane after I stepped out,

we couldn't figure out what had happened. There simply was no logical explanation for the skin of the wing coming apart in narrow slabs. The next time I saw a Bell tech rep, he told me this was impossible. We could find no way to repair this unusual skin damage so we simply pushed the Airacobra into a pile of scrap near the end of the runway and left it there. I can only think of one explanation for this odd and disturbing incident and that is some kind of metal fatigue. Our planes were very, very tired.

On 28 June 1944, the 82nd with its P-39 Airacobras moved up to Owi in New Guinea along with the first P-61 Black Widows of the 421st Night Fighter Squadron. It was a relatively large and comfortable airfield with good taxiways and support facilities. Within weeks, the 82nd was finally told it would convert to the F-6D, photo-reconnaissance version of

the P-51D Mustang. The beleaguered 110th squadron was also allowed to convert to Mustangs, albeit belatedly.

In June 1944, the last P-39Q Airacobras to be delivered to Twelfth Air Force in the Mediterranean were signed for. At one point, fighter strength of the Twelfth was listed as including fifty-two P-40 War-hawks and twenty-three P-39 Airacobras, relegated to 'rhubarb' strafing missions (and the Airacobras, as we shall see, eventually assigned to the 322nd FG). The Airacobra's war in American hands was approaching a close. In August 1944, the 347th FG moved to New Guinea and completed its 22-month process of re-equipping with the P-38 Lightning. This was the last American fighter group in the combat zone to give up the Airacobra.

On 14 February 1944, the Buffalo snow stranded a pair of P-39Q-20-BE Airacobras (44-3785, foreground, and 44-3719) replete with long-range belly tanks. Bell via Truman Partridge

Tuskegee Airmen

The 332nd Fighter Group consisted of black Americans who had trained in Tuskegee, Alabama; in American society they were segregated from whites. They joined the Fifteenth Air Force in Italy in February 1944; the group was equipped with P-39Q-20-BE Airacobras. The commander of these 'Tuskegee airmen', Col Benjamin O. Davis, complained long and hard about the Bell fighter in private – and put his best face on the Bell fighter in public. Called Negroes in the parlance of the time, and African-Americans today, Davis and his men wanted to prove that skin colour was no barrier to performance in combat; in this, however, they fought prejudice all the way from boot camp to flight school to the combat zone. Davis never said so, but according to Lee Archer who later became one of the group's best-

known pilots, he considered that the P-39 Airacobra stood as a symbol of the men's frustration.

Davis, a big man, regarded the P-39 Airacobra as follows:

> [It was] a beautiful, small-looking fighter-bomber with a tight, crowded cockpit – especially tight when it was flown by a six-footer. My head rubbed against the canopy and I had to keep my back bowed. Although the Russians had used the P-39 successfully on the Eastern Front and it was doing well in the war in the Pacific, it could not fly as high as the Fw 190s and Bf 109s we were likely to encounter in Europe. I liked the four .50 cal machine guns mounted in the wing toe to concentrate fire, and the 37mm cannon that extended through the hollow propeller hub in its nose. The pilot could use all the guns or any combination of them by flipping a selector switch in the cockpit. I actually would have preferred another

airplane, but because the P-39 had already been chosen for the unit, I declared it to be the best airplane we could possibly have, and belittled all criticism of it.

In the US, Davis practised using the P-39 for the 'skip-bombing manoeuvers I supposed would be our bread and butter in Europe'.

Davis's 332nd FG included the 100th FS commanded by Capt Robert Tresville, Jr, the 302nd FS commanded by Lt Red Jackson (both flying from Capodichino), and the 301st FS commanded by Capt Charles DeBow (at Montecorvino).

Davis had made it through the US Military Academy at West Point, N.Y. (class of 1936), even though he was shunned by other cadets for four years because of the colour of his skin – and now he had brought a combat group to the battle zone only to be handed the P-39, a

P-39M (42-4770) being scrutinized at a training base in the United States. Based upon the P-39L version, the P-39M entered production in 1942 and offered improvements to the powerplant and to internal systems. The 37mm cannon installation on the Airacobra received plenty of press attention, but Bell made no effort to point out that the gun frequently jammed. San Diego Aerospace Museum

P-39Q

The ultimate Airacobra on the production line was the P-39Q, which was more a family than a single variant. The 'Q model' represented the final attempt to mould the Airacobra into a world-class fighting machine. The first P-39Q was produced in March 1943, and it was the standard on the manufacturing line until the final Airacobra was produced thirteen months later. Bell manufactured 4,905 before production ended in April 1944. Like the P-39D and P-39N models, the P-39Q had a wingspan of 34ft (10.36m) and length of 30ft 2in (9.21m). Like the P-39N, it was 8in (20cm) taller than the P-39D model, with a height of 12ft 5in (3.79m).

The P-39Q-1, first of the sub-types in this series, retained the reduced 87 US gal (329ltr) internal fuel capacity of the P-39N, but restored armour plate weighing just over 231lb (105kg). Later aircraft in the P-39Q series restored the 120 US gal (454ltr) internal fuel capacity of Airacobras built before the P-39N.

Significantly, the 'Q-1' dispensed with four .30 cal (7.62mm) wing machine guns, replacing these with one .50 cal (12.7mm) machine gun added to each wing in an under-wing pylon, with 300 rounds of ammunition per gun. This armament change was applauded by American pilots who felt the smaller calibre weapon to be inadequate; but ironically, virtually all 'Q' models were flown by Russians, who were just as happy to dispense

with the under-wing machine guns. The Soviets credited the 'Q model' Airacobra with a maximum 376mph (605km/h) as compared with 279mph (449km/h) for the LaGG-5 and 370mph (595km/h).

The 150 P-39Q-1 fighters were otherwise similar to the P-39N-1; they were powered by the now familiar V-1710-85(E19) engine.

Five P-39Q-2 aircraft were created by modifying 'Q-1s': these were to carry cameras for the photo-reconnaissance mission in the manner of the P-39D-3.

The P-39Q-5 (Model 26Q-5) sub-variant was similar to the P-39Q-1 and used the same V-1710-85(E19) powerplant, but had minor internal changes. Bell manufactured 950 of these with lighter armour and increased wing fuel capacity.

The P-39Q-6 model (148 built) was brought about by modifying P-39Q-5s for photo reconnaissance, again following the tradition of the P-39D-3.

The P-39Q-10 (Model 26Q-10) designation applies to 705 Airacobras that were similar to the P-39Q-5 but with revised armour plate, additional winterization of the oil system, rubber engine mounts, and various other minor changes. This model had an internal fuel capacity raised to 120 US gallons (454ltr) and armour weighing 227lb (103kg). Bell turned out 705 'Q-10' models, but did not build 995 more that were assigned serials

Wearing the national insignia adopted in September 1943 and used through the remainder of the war, the 474th P-39Q-20-RE model (44-3474) chugs its way through an acceptance flight near the factory. Bell via Truman Partridge

P-39Q continued

(42-21251/22245): these later appeared on the books as P-63E-1 Kingcobra fighters.

Eight P-39Q-11s were modified from among the P-39Q-10 population for photo reconnaissance, in yet another follow-up to the P-39D-3.

The P-39Q-15 (Model 26Q-15) became a major subvariant. Bell turned out exactly 1,000, similar to P-39Q-10, but with the oxygen system changed to two bottles instead of four, besides other minor alterations.

The P-39Q-20 (Model 26Q-20) was similar to P-39Q-15 with numerous equipment changes. The US Army acquired an unknown number of these with wing-gun pylons installed, but the majority went to Russia without the under-wing gun pods. Free French forces also operated 'Q-20s'. Bell built 891.

109 P-39Q-21s (Model 26Q-21) were built: these were similar to the P-39Q-20, with a four-blade Aeroproducts propeller; wing guns were normally deleted on Russian aircraft.

The RP-39Q-22 (Model 39) identifier was a two-place fighter trainer converted from P-39Q-20. The AAF modified twelve aircraft to this configuration. Engineers removed armament, added an interphone, and created an additional fin area on the top and bottom of the rear fuselage. Changes included a ventral fin for stability which was somewhat different in shape from the ventral fin on the first TP-39 built by Bell (see TP-39Q-5 entry). At least two of these two-place Airacobras reached the Soviet Union. A Soviet source identifies these as TP-39Qs.

Bell made 700 P-39Q-25 (Model 26Q-25) fighters which were similar to the P-39Q-20, but with a reinforced after-fuselage and horizontal stabilizer structure, and a four-blade Aeroproducts propeller. The manufacturer deleted wing guns from these aircraft that were exported to the Soviet Union.

The P-39Q-30 (Model 27Q-30) was the final Airacobra, and it reverted to the proven three-bladed propeller. Bell built 400. The 'Q-30' was otherwise similar to the P-39Q-25 with minor changes; for instance wing guns were deleted from those bound for Russia.

The first P-39Q-5-BE, or Model 26 (42-19596) on the flight-line at the factory, with under-wing guns protruding smartly.
Bell via Truman Partridge

P-39Q-1 serials (150): 42-19446/19595
P-39Q-2 serials (5): 42-19479/19483
P-39Q-6 serials (148): 42-19608, 42-19610, 42-19612, 42-19614, 42-19616, 42-19624, 42-19626, 42-19628, 42-19636, 42-19638, 42-19640, 42-19642, 42-19644/19646, all even numbers 42-16948/19694, all odd numbers 42-19697/19719, 42-19723, 42-19725, odd numbers 42-19927/19975, 42-19977/19979, 42-19981, 42-19983, 42-19985, 42-19987, all odd numbers 42-19989/20011, 42-20013/20015, 42-20017/20019, odd numbers 42-20021/20065, 42-20067/20069, odd numbers 42-20071/20093, 42-20095/20097, 42-20099, 42-20101, 42-20103, 42-20105.
P-39Q-10 serials (705): 42-20546/21250
P-39Q-15 serials (1,000): 44-2001/3000
P-39Q-20 serials (891): 44-3001/3940 (minus 49 aircraft, including 22 Q-22s)
RP-39Q-22 serials (22): 44-3879, 44-3885/3887, 44-3889, 44-3895, 44-3897, 44-3905/3906, 44-3908, 44-3917/3918
P-39Q-25 serials (700): 44-32167/32666; 44-70905/71104
P-39Q-30 serials (400) 44-71105/71504

fighter that another officer told him was 'on its way out'. Davis and his men wanted to shoot down Messerschmitts and Focke-Wulfs – they wanted to have an impact on the war – and the big bosses were telling them to use P-39s to attack convoys, protect harbours, and fly armed reconnaissance missions.

Italian Fighting

The Allied landing at Anzio took place while 332nd FG pilots were boring holes in the sky in their Airacobras. During the early morning hours of 22 January 1944, troops of the Fifth Army swarmed ashore on a 15-mile (24km) stretch of Italian beach near the pre-war resort towns of Anzio and Nettuno. The landings were

carried out so flawlessly and German resistance was so light that British and American units gained their first day's objectives by noon, moving 3 to 4 miles (5 to 7km) inland by nightfall. The ease of the landing and the swift advance were noted by one paratrooper of the 504th Parachute Infantry Regiment, 82nd Airborne Division, who recalled that D-day at Anzio was sunny and warm, making it very hard to believe that a war was going on and that he was in the middle of it.

Unfortunately, timidity on the part of commanders, and a series of tactical blunders on the ground, neutralized the Allies' advantage and cost them a chance to seize Rome quickly and so divide the German forces. The men in the 332nd FG watched all this and felt it spoke volumes of their situation. Like the troops ashore at Anzio, they had come to fight, not to waste time.

For three months in early 1944, the fired-up pilots of the 332nd FG lived a largely eventless life on the fringe of the war. There were only three encounters with Luftwaffe aircraft, in each case a solitary Junkers Ju 88 on a reconnaissance mission, and in two instances Airacobra pilots inflicted damage on the Ju 88s. On 18 February 1944, 1st Lt Lawrence Wilkins of the 302nd FS spotted a Ju 88 near Ponza Island, in the Tyrrhenian Sea. Wilkins, possibly overestimating his available fuel, followed the Junkers as far as the Anzio beachhead and poured bursts of gunfire into it. Now Wilkins saw that his

fuel was low and broke away, but not before he saw the Ju 88 beginning to disintegrate; it then vanished into a shoreline mist. The evidence was not good enough for a confirmed aerial victory, but Wilkins was certain the Ju 88 never returned to its base.

Soon afterwards, 2nd Lts Roy Spencer and William Melton combined forces to attack another Ju 88, riddling it with gunfire until Spencer's guns jammed. Melton emptied all of his Airacobra's ammunition into the Luftwaffe warplane. The two Tuskegee airmen dogged the Ju 88 and followed it for 60 miles (90km), but they were unable to inflict a *coup de grace*. Leaving wisps of smoke behind it, the Junkers escaped, 'damaged', but not 'a kill'.

Davis and his pilots were frustrated. Was the Airacobra a sign that black Americans would only be allowed to fight when given second-rate equipment? Quietly, Davis argued for a greater role in the war in Italy. In March, he was summoned by Mediterranean Allied Air Force commander Lt Gen Ira Eaker, and told

that he would get what he wanted: the 332nd FG would acquire a fourth squadron, the 99th (which had entered the war with P-40 Warhawks), and would move to Ramitelli. Instead of routine patrol missions, the group would escort bombers attacking the Third Reich. However, Davis had to ask, 'What about the Airacobras?'

The answer, to his infinite relief, was: 'They're out.'

In an important, symbolic way, it was the end of the line for the Bell P-39 Airacobra. The subsequent achievements of the 332nd FG, of Col Davis, and of the Tuskegee airmen are well known and reflect great dedication and heroism. Popular belief has it that the Tuskegee airmen never lost a bomber they were escorting. One of their members, Lee Archer, was ultimately credited with 4.5 aerial victories – the closest an African-American came to becoming an ace. Another, Roy Brown, shot down two Me 262 jet fighters. But all of these achievements came after the Eaker-Davis

With a neatly painted, wavy division between the khaki topside and the grey underneath, this P-39K Airacobra was captured on film in 1944. As can be seen here, the window on the car-style door opened in exactly the same manner as those on automobiles. Peter M. Bowers

conversation, and after the 332nd FG converted to the P-47 Thunderbolt and, subsequently, to the P-51 Mustang. It would appear that the 332nd FG's Airacobras may be among the airframes discarded by the AAF which eventually reached the Italian air arm.

Stateside

The end of the line came at the factory, too. In August 1944, Army Air Forces took delivery of the last P-39 Airacobra, manufactured the previous month. The Airacobra was the first of the principal American fighters of the war to reach the end of its manufacturing run. The final tally was 9,529 Airacobras of all models, as compared with eventual totals of 10,037 P-38 Lightnings, 13,143 P-40 Warhawks, 15,863 P-47 Thunderbolts, and 15,486 P-51 Mustangs. Larry Bell's company was still very busy – indeed, it was secretly pioneering jet aviation while continuing to manufacture the P-63 Kingcobra. But the Airacobra was now out of the factory door – and as far as Army Air Forces were concerned, it was also out of combat.

Already, many were looking back at the Airacobra and reflecting on its accom-plishments and tribulations. To some, the P-39 was an aircraft that would have been perfect with turbochargers and would have acquitted itself well against the best fight-ers of the war. To others, the flaws of the Airacobra ran deeper. It was a fighter that had limited range and offered limited potential for growth. Either way, many were already talking about it in the past tense.

Despite the proliferation of P-39 vari-ants, all Airacobras were very similar. In one central Pacific squadron, US Army mechanics created an extra Airacobra, nicknamed SPARE PARTS, from hulks and scrap. Painted black with a question mark on the fin in place of a serial number, this fighter flew night intercept missions. It never really had a serial number or an identity.

Some things about the Airacobra were different from all other fighters: for instance, many P-39s had 'door art' in place of nose art.

Features in common to all models of the P-39 (not including test ships such as the XP-39, XP-39B, and XP-39E) included a wingspan of 34ft (10.36m) and length of 30ft 2in (9.19m). All, with propeller blade vertical, were 11ft 10in (3.63m) in height, until the P-39Q at 12ft 5in (3.79m). All models had the same ailerons, although

several minor changes were made in the design of flaps on different Airacobra vari-ants. All models had the same rudder area and movement, but there were minor changes in other tail features. Minor changes were found in export aircraft, including those for France, Italy and Australia.

Usually described as a small fighter, the Airacobra had a lesser wingspan and length than a P-40N Warhawk, a P-47D Thunderbolt, or a P-51D Mustang. It was, however, larger than a Yakovlev Yak-3. No major fighter of World War II had a wider main landing-gear track than the 11ft 4in (3.45m) track of the Airacobra. Its internal fuel capacity, however, dropped markedly, from 200 US gallons (757ltr) to 120 US gallons (454ltr) from the first experimental models to the first produc-tion machine, the P-39D; this assured a career-long reputation for short legs, even with the standard 175 US gal (662ltr) external centreline tank affixed. P-39NS and some P-39Qs had internal fuel capac-ity further reduced to 87 US gal (329ltr).

Bell produced 9,529 Airacobras, out of 9,588 once planned, between 1939 and 1944, or 9.6 per cent of the 100,090 fight-ers manufactured by American industry during the war years. The US Army Air Forces reached a peak inventory of P-39 Airacobras in February 1944 with 2,105 aircraft, a figure which is also reported in one source as 2,150. 4,924 P-39s were sent to the Soviet Union under lend-lease, of which 4,758 reached their destinations. During the production run, the cost per aircraft rose from $50,666 to $72,000. Production ended with the assembly on 25 July 1944 of the final aircraft, 44-71504. This final ship was an olive-drab P-39Q-30-BE model which differed from earlier Qs in having no wing guns, and a three-bladed propellor that was slightly reduced in diameter.

As for Great Britain, having dispensed with the Airacobra with undue haste in 1941, it was still flying the Airacobra in 1944. The Royal Air Force fitted one P-400/Airacobra I (AH571) with a reduced-area rudder for aerodynamic studies. Another aircraft (AH574) was equipped with an arrester hook and was tested aboard HMS *Indefatigable* during 1944, although no photo of this remark-able naval test appears to have survived. AH574 was still soldiering on as a dog ship (test aircraft), not only in 1944, but when the war ended.

By 1944, the offspring of the Airacobra, the cleaner P-63 Kingcobra, was becoming the dominant sight at the Bell factory. The P-63 was exported to Russia in vast numbers but never really found a home in the US Army. This P-63E has been preserved. Pima Air and Space Museum

Nearing the end of the line: the last Airacobras on the production line at Bell. Visible is aircraft 44-71422, one of the last 100 P-39Q models built. The end of the line was approaching in the spring of 1944. Bell

The Airacobra as Training Fighter

For the remainder of the war, most of the Americans who flew Airacobras would do so in the United States, at training bases. One of them was 1st Lt George Gunn, who logged seventy-five hours in the P-39 between March and September 1944 at Victorville Army Air Force Base in California. Gunn remembers:

We were called simply the Provisional P-39 Training Squadron, our students new pilots just graduated from Luke and Williams [bases in Arizona]. We got our aircraft from training bases all over the US. I was with a group of seven or eight who picked up aircraft in South Carolina and flew them back to Victorville. Also, I brought one in from Tacoma, Washington. I don't know the total number, but we had around seventy-five Airacobras at one time.

We had two shifts in operation. Because of the heat and the problem of engine overheating in the summer of 1944, one shift would fly from 11am to 3pm one day and 6am to 10am

the next morning, then be off until the following afternoon. On Saturday the instructors would fly practice formations, and occasionally take part in a little dogfighting. The Marines were stationed at Mojave flying Corsairs, and we would occasionally mix it up with them. One flight went over the Marine base and we had three Corsairs attacking us in less than fifteen minutes.

The flight that I was in, saw the dogfight and joined in, right over Victorville airfield. The tower was transmitting for us to break it off and land. I turned my radio off and we had a ball until the Marines left. After we had all landed and gathered in our flight room we wondered what the brass would do. Nothing was ever said to us. Later one of our instructors met a Marine and they thought we were flying P-63s. Below 10,000ft [3,000m] the P-39 was a good fighter.

We had a very high accident rate, in most cases due to mechanical failure, but of course [also due to] pilot error. In the first twenty-one days of June 1944 we had twenty accidents, two of them fatal, as far as I recall. Most deaths were caused by spinning at low altitude. I saw one spin on the turn to final. Another was found after being missing for ten days just west of the

field where he had spun in. The word got back to Luke and Williams and we had pilots who refused to fly the P-39. I had one student who lost it on a go-around and the torque caused his bird to start a roll. My student survived, but spent about three months in the hospital.

As instructors, we tried to talk pilots out of quitting. We flew demonstration flights, too, to show them we thought the aircraft were safe. Those who quit were sent on as co-pilots in bombers.

Because of its build-up in producing pilots, the AAF had run out of places to send them after graduation. That's why they opened the Provisional P-39 Training Squadron at Victorville. They were given ten hours flying the P-39. Most stayed at Victorville and flew BT-13s for flight pay until there was room to move them on to replacement training units. By late summer 1944, there was room for the new pilots in the system.

On 6 June 1944 at about 3pm we got word of the D-Day landings. We sat around talking about how the war was nearly over and we had missed it. I think all of us wanted combat and a chance to be an ace. We had one instructor who was so bitter and hard to get along with

---

TP-39Q-5 (Model 39)

Although no fewer than six photos of this aircraft appeared in a Bell publication in November 1943 (and an image has been widely published with the tail number and background touched out), the identity of the first TP-39 two-place trainer modified by Bell was not clear until recently. The first Bell-modified two-seater is now known to be a TP-39Q-5, aircraft 42-20024. This aircraft is referred to, simply, as 'the TP-39' in manufacturer's literature, and was apparently rolled out on 16 September 1943.

Fourth Air Force, the AAF command responsible for tactical training, asked Arthur L. Fornoff of Bell's service division if a two-seater could be built 'to handle just like the 'Cobra and, at the same time, carry an instructor to lend the student a guiding hand'. Chief project engineer F. M. Salisbury headed the design team for the TP-39 and added a dorsal fin plus a small auxiliary ventral fin, both aimed at alleviating centre-of-gravity changes. The work was done at Bell's Modification Center at Niagara Falls. Test pilot Jay Demming and Norman Bethune of the service division were apparently the first to fly the two-seater, identified

in Bell literature solely as the 'TP-39' and depicted without a visible serial number. Demming and Bethune made a tour of the US west coast in 1943 in this aircraft, described as follows:

> The space for the instructor in front of the standard cockpit was provided by removing the guns and cannon and the gun cowling, extending the cabin, and adding a second set of controls and a simplified instrument panel. An inter-phone set allows conversation between the two pilots. The rear controls and instrument panel are identical with those of the production P-39 so that the student gets actual experience in the operation of the Airacobra.

The notion of having an instructor *in front of* his pupil might seem odd today, but Bell's Salisbury apparently saw no other way to do it. Several company employees, including president Larry Bell (who hated to fly) were apparently given 'rides' in the TP-39.

---

that they shipped him out. He went to the Pacific in P-38s. We got the word back that on his first mission he saw Jap planes and broke formation and went after them. Before the rest of the flight could help, he was shot down. He was just too eager.

Also at Victorville was Dino Cerutti of Flying Class 44-C, whose reaction to the P-39 Airacobra was similar to others:

I flew the 39 at Victorville after graduating from flight school, and then went on to fly the P-38 and P-51.

I flew at Victorville from 6 June 1944 to 12 June 1944. We went to Gila Bend, Arizona for gunnery and bombing training and I found the Airacobra to be extremely accurate as a strafing platform. My log book also shows I flew the P-39N and P-39Q. Both models had 1,150hp. The group of new graduates was sent there for 'transition training'. Here is what my official records say, and don't ask me what the abbreviations stand for: Station: Victorville, Calif; Organization Attached: (Unassigned (WFTC 37th, Group: 3035th B.U. Section L. My order assigning me to Victorville read: 'Transferred to Victorville AAF, Victorville,

Calif. Transfer Date: 23 May, 1944.' I hope this helps.

I remember being struck by the short wingspan, the closeness of the pilot to the propeller, and how the pilot straddled the engine. The plane was not very fast and did not do well over 10,000ft [3,000m] because it had no supercharger. And its stall characteristics were horrible. We lost – meaning they were killed – many pilots in our first week of transition because they stalled out on final approach and snapped and crashed to the ground a few hundred feet below. We used a 360-degree overhead landing pattern it order to reduce speed rapidly to enable us to lower gear and flaps. But the pilots were concentrating on lining up with the runway as they hauled back on the stick so they were not watching the airspeed indicator. Personally I liked the plane, but not as much as the P-38 and P-51, which were supercharged and much faster.

Combat Abroad

In 1944, the Airacobra was still very much a combatant elsewhere in the world.

In Russia

Russian pilots often had opportunities to engage the Messerschmitt Bf 109 at low altitude, where the American-built fighter performed best. The 'Cobrastochka' ('dear little Cobra') clearly performed better in Russian hands than American. Lt Col Alexandr I. Pokryshkin became the Allies' second-ranking ace of the war with fifty-nine aerial victories, forty-eight of them

Beautiful study of a P-39K Airacobra at a stateside base circa 1944.
Robert F. Dorr

When examined under a magnifying glass, this photo shows the term 'RP-39Q-5-BE' in black stencilling on the side of the forward fuselage. One of the few two-seat Airacobras to have been extensively photographed, this aircraft (42-20024) is sometimes identified as an RP-39Q-22-BE; it was one of 12 two-seat trainers created by modifying P-39Qs, removing armament, and installing an extra seat and an interphone. Warren M. Bodie

accomplished in his Airacobra. Eight other Soviet P-39 pilots are reported to have claimed twenty or more aerial victories. Pokrushkin assessed the Bell fighter much like many others:

It was a shapely aircraft. One thing I particularly liked about the Airacobra was the armament. That was really something to shoot the enemy down with – a hard-hitting 37mm cannon, two fast-firing heavy machine guns, and four normal caliber machine guns. I wasn't put off when other pilots warned me that the Cobra was dangerously prone to spinning because of a C of G located well aft.

Yvgeney Zolotov, who flew Airacobras with the 57th IAP, told British author Bill Gunston years later that 'all along my sector of the front, regiments equipped with Spitfires or Hurricanes were converting to the Airacobra as fast as they could'.

The various terms of endearment heaped upon the Bell fighter were obviously sincere, and occasionally they were ribald. Gunston remembers another Soviet pilot, Feodor Rumyantsyev, who quipped, 'In the Soviet Union we have a proverb about the Airacobra. We never let any pilot over thirty-five fly one.' Asked why, Rumyantstyev responded: 'Too dangerous. Get balls caught in propshaft.'

Among Russians praised in Bell documents were the brothers Glinka, Dmitri and Boris. Dmitri was reported to have flown 240 sorties and to have downed thirty-nine German aircraft; Boris' score was listed as twenty-six.

It is not clear how many Airacobras remained in Soviet Service once more as better Soviet-built fighters became available. But there are grounds to believe that the Soviets never lost their high regard for the Bell fighter. American ambassador

Airacobra Aces

On 1 May 1944, tensions between the two top Soviet Airacobra aces came to a head. As commander of the 16th Guards IAP, Rechkalov apparently was accused of abandoning wingmen in the midst of a battle and of providing inadequate leadership. Aleksandr Pokryshkin filed a complaint, then relieved the pilot who had once flown on his wing. Rechkalov lost his post as commander, and was replaced in it by Boris Glinka.

Nevertheless, the availability of the P-39Q model and the seemingly endless nature of the war, provided Rechkalov with opportunities for further aerial victories. He was made a Hero of the Soviet Union twice and ended up neck-and-neck with Pokryshkin for the distinction of being the second-ranking Soviet ace (*see* next chapter).

Reflections in a thaw: P-39Q-25-BE Airacobra fighters (44-32338 in foreground) at the factory on 14 March 1944, wearing red stars and awaiting delivery to the Soviet Union. Bell via Truman Partridge

W. Averell Harriman was quoted by Soviet foreign minister Vladimir Molotov on the significance of the P-39:

There is one type of aircraft, specifically the Airacobra, which is used very well by the Soviet Air Force. Harriman says the Russians use this airplane even better than the Americans. Therefore it would be of benefit for Vandenberg [Maj Gen Hoyt S. Vandenberg, Twelfth Air Force commander and a future US Air Force chief of staff] to become acquainted with the experience of Soviet pilots ... Vandenberg would like to be informed about this and visit Soviet squadrons composed of Airacobra aircraft.

Molotov blessed the proposed meeting as 'useful'.

Bell Aircraft expressed a similar request. Gen Vandenberg and company representatives visited the 6th ZAB (Zapasnaya Aviabrigada, or Reserve Air Brigade) in Ivanovo and two other units. The Soviet pilots had some requests – for example, they wanted an improvement in the ballistics and rate of fire of the 37mm cannon. The Russians asserted that late-model P-39Qs were much less stable than earlier Airacobras, and that the armoured headrest introduced on this model impaired

Side view of P-39 in flight in 1944. Bell

rearward visibility. Bell representatives said they would take these complaints into account, although it is not clear what they might have done about them.

The visit of the American delegation to the 6th ZAB was marred by the crash of a P-39Q-5 when the pilot became disoriented after recovering from a spin and had to bail out. Sure enough, the spin had been induced by too-far-aft centre of gravity.

If anything, the Russians became more obsessed with the downside of the Airacobra's flying characteristics than the Americans. A number of evaluation programmes were undertaken including these: spinning and aerobatics tests of a P-39Q-10-BE (43-2467), which showed that the Q Model spun more powerfully and irregularly than earlier P-39 variants; tests of the same airframe, to determine the Q model's maximum safe dive angles with

Two P-39Q-25-BE Airacobras for the Soviet Union (44-32648 in the foreground), paid for with donations from East Aurora, N.Y. public schools, at the Buffalo factory in 1944. Bell via Truman Partridge

Bell P-39Q-25-BE Airacobra (44-71053) heads a line-up of Soviet Air Force fighters fitted with ferry tanks at the Buffalo, N.Y. factory in 1944. These warplanes appear to have fabric or tarpaulin protective covers draping the exhaust stacks on the fuselage under the cockpit. via Norman Taylor

220lb (100kg) FAB-100 and 551lb (250kg) FAB-250 general-purpose bombs (with a finding thereafter that the Airacobra would have no problems carrying out fighter-bomber missions); tests of a P-39Q-30-BE (44-71117) with the elevator trim tab locked into the neutral position; and spinning and aerobatics tests of a P-39Q-15-BE (44-29115) with altered centre of gravity and reinforced tail unit and rear fuselage. The tests apparently raised no problem, which justified this much effort and expense; however, there are indications that some Russians continued to have problems with the C. G. situation.

On the Eastern Front, the Airacobra continued to be a regular sight until the end of the war. The Bell fighter was operated by twenty-five air regiments in eight fighter divisions.

In France and Italy

As noted in the previous chapter, French pilots received the first of 247 P-39 Airacobras at Maison Blanche in North Africa in May 1943, and a few days later claimed their first kill, a Dornier Do 217. L'Armée de l'Air's Airacobra units were part of North African Coastal Command based in Algeria and included the G. C. 1/4

'Navarre' Squadron. The French painted out all American insignia and serial numbers and applied the French insignia roundel with a yellow surround in all six positions. Aircraft carried a single-digit 'plane in group' number for identification.

Italy, once it changed sides, took delivery of seventy-four P-39Ns and seventy-five P-39Qs late in the war. By late 1944, both French and Italian pilots were scoring aerial victories and striking ground targets.

The Italian role in the Airacobra story had followed Italy's capitulation to the Allies on 8 September 1943. At that time, the Regia Aeronautica had been whittled

They all had a picture like this. Every time Army pilots visited the Bell factory to pick up new fighters, they posed on the wing, or beside the nose, and the company photographer clicked away. These men in 'Class A' uniform are picking up P-63 Kingcobras, those big brothers to the P-39 Airacobra, and will ferry them to a receiving unit. Bell

down from 8,448 first-line aircraft to just 1,265, of which 447 were operational. Following Marshal Badoglio's call to surrender, Italian air units based in the vicinity of Rome flew south to form the nucleus of the Italian Co-Belligerent Air Force. The Co-Belligerent Italian regime had declared war on Germany on 13 October 1943; 246 warplanes went with the defecting airmen, but the Allies made certain that they soon received more, including Supermarine Spitfires, Martin Baltimores and P-39s.

The 9th, 19th and 12th Gruppos of the Italian Air Force had begun training in newly acquired P-39s on 20 June 1944; they refrained from combat while practising through September, and seemed for a time unable to master the aircraft, which gave them relentless engine problems. The first operational mission for the Italians took place on 8 September 1944 when P-39s escorted by Macchi fighters went after German ground troops. Still not really adequately trained for their new aircraft, and handicapped by an inadequate maintenance infrastructure, the Italians suffered high losses due to engine problems. Two months later, in November, they lost ten aircraft in a thirty-day period.

In December 1944, Free French P-39s were being operated by GC11/6 in southern France.

CHAPTER FIVE

1945 Onward

The Soviet Union's air arm, the VVS, continued to operate the Bell P-39 Airacobra throughout 1945 – the most destructive year in human history – and was constantly making innovative changes to the Bell fighter. For instance, it appears that the Soviets received a couple of two-seat TP-39Q Airacobras made in the US, and then created more two-seaters of their own design.

In the US, the Q model was one of several examples which were converted into trainers. A second cockpit was installed forward of the first, with a conventional sideways-opening canopy. It was located in the gun bay forward of the original cockpit. A shallow ventral fin and sometimes a dorsal fillet were added to make up for the increased side area forward of the centre of gravity. Since

these were field-modified aircraft, the TP-39Qs had many detail differences. At least two US-modified TP-39Qs were delivered to the VVS. Regrettably, accurate identification is impossible because the aircraft wore neither original AAF serials nor Soviet tactical codes. One aircraft had a dorsal fillet and the other did not, and the shape of the ventral fin and the forward canopy frame was also different.

Neither of these TP-39Q models compared in appearance with aircraft that were field-modified into two-seaters within the Soviet Union. Referred to as the 'Whales', a handful of Airacobras were modified in a most bizarre fashion, ending up with a bloated and ungainly appearance. The records on these aircraft have not survived, but it is unlikely that their flying performance could have been satis-

factory. A two-seat Airacobra, in any event, had almost no war-fighting potential, and probably would have been even shorter-legged than the single-seat aircraft. Nor is it clear how any useful training could have been either given or received in an aircraft with such an unorthodox appearance and such apparently poor handling qualities.

Nevertheless, work continued throughout the war to refine and improve the Airacobra, and Soviet pilots continued to fly them in combat – once again, often in preference to the well-known Lavochkin and Yakovlev fighters made at home. The P-39 saw active service on the Eastern Front until the end of the war. Eight fighter divisions and twenty-five regiments operated the type.

As of 9 May 1945, the Soviet Air Force inventory included 1,178 Airacobras, including 536 aircraft serving with the PVO (the defensive air arm), 478 in the naval air arm, and 164 in tactical fighter units.

In the closing stage of the war, the Airacobras of A. I. Pokryshkin's unit operating from tactical airfields in Germany used the excellent German highways (Autobahns) as landing fields. Airacobras also routinely took off from thoroughfares such as the Berlin-Breslau highway.

Longevity Plus

The Soviet Union appears to have phased out the P-39 Airacobra with some haste, mostly in 1945 once more and better warplanes of other types were available. Years later, there would be reports of P-39 Airacobras and P-63 Kingcobras being operated by the North Korean air force in 1950, but these reports were almost certainly in error (although as late as 1955, when the North Atlantic Treaty Organization created reporting names for Soviet aircraft, it invented 'Fred' for the P-63).

The Airacobra was only one of many fighter types that contributed to the even-

American P-39 Airacobra pilots of the 28th Fighter Squadron, Chame, Panama, June 1945. 1st Lt Joe Dehlert is at left. 1st Lt Jimmy Burns (centre) died shortly after this photo was taken when his P-39 caught fire and he inexplicably ignored a call from a wingman to bail out. 1st Lt Winton W. 'Bones' Marshall (right) trained in the Airacobra to fight the Japanese, but did not see combat until six years later in Korea, where he recorded 9.5 aerial victories. Winton W. 'Bones' Marshall

Two late-model P-39Qs were converted by Bell into radio-controlled target aircraft for the US Navy's Bureau of Aeronautics. This is a P-39Q-10-BE (42-20807) assigned bureau no. 91102 and apparently painted in standard olive-drab with the number '1' in white on the fin. These aircraft were initially designated XTDL-1 and were later re-designated XF2L-1K; they were operated in postwar years. This ship was badly damaged in a wheels-up landing after an engine failure on 8 April 1946. via Kevin Grantham

tual Soviet victory. It also marked the end of an incredible fight. According to official Russian sources, the Luftwaffe lost 60,000 aircraft during the fighting on the Soviet-German front, and the VVS ended up with an average of 2,000 sorties per day.

During the final campaign as Russian tanks advanced on Berlin, the VVS flew 91,000 sorties and destroyed 1,172 German aircraft in 1,317 engagements, and the total number of operational sorties flown during April 1945 was a remarkable 216,000. Figures on Russian air aces are constantly being modified as new information becomes available, but at least twenty-five Russian flyers claimed to have destroyed between thirty and forty enemy aircraft each, and there were 137 pilots credited with between twenty and thirty aerial victories. The most successful Russian fighter pilots all had at least some kills in the Airacobra.

Among them were Ivan Nikolaevich Kozhedub (sixty-two personal aerial victories), Aleksandr Ivanovich Poykryshkin (fifty-nine), Grigori Rechkalov (fifty-six), Nikolai Dmitrievich Khulayev (fifty-seven), Kirill Aleksandrovich Yevstigneev (fifty-two), Dmitry Glinka (fifty), and N. Skoromokhov, A. Koldunov and A. Vorozheikin, each with forty kills. Poykryshkin is widely accepted as the top Airacobra ace with around fifty aerial victories in the Bell fighter. At the end of the war, the Russian air forces boasted 17,500 aircraft – so perhaps it is understandable that the Airacobra did not linger long in inventory.

A final footnote: the above numbers must be viewed as approximate, since there are no fewer than seven supposedly authoritative lists of Soviet air aces, each of which lists a different total of personal aerial victories plus a much smaller number of group aerial victories credited

to each pilot. Kozhedub's place on the roster seems more secure than that of Poykryshkin and Rechkalov, who appear in reverse order in second and third place on some of the lists.

The P-39 stayed in Soviet service until the early 1950s. When the original US armament became unserviceable it was replaced by Soviet 20mm B-20 cannon and .50 cal Berezin UBS machine guns. In general, the Airacobra was a reliable aircraft which matched the requirements of Soviet warfare and was remembered with affection by Soviet pilots. Indeed, it was the best loved of the lend-lease aircraft.

Italian Cobras

In April 1945, the Italian air force – no longer a foe to the Allies as they stood on the brink of victory in Europe – began to

The source of this photo calls it a '1945 view of Soviet Airacobras'; the location and circumstances can only be speculated upon. An American B-17 is visible in the background, and the Marston mat on this parking apron has a distinctly Western appearance. But Soviet Yakovlev Yak-9 fighters are also visible in the background. So where is this, and what is going on? No explanation seems to have survived. via Norman Taylor

Bell XP-77

The link between the well known P-39 Airacobra and the rather obscure Bell XP-77 pursuit ship is far closer than the mere coincidence that both fighters come from the same manufacturer. The XP-77 (or Bell Model 32), in a much larger sense, is the aircraft that the Airacobra might have been if the builder had forged ahead with its initial response to Army specification X-609, which in the event led to the Airacobra instead.

It will be recalled that Bell submitted two designs to meet the mid-1930s specification, the Model 3 (never built) and the Model 4 (which became the Airacobra). Long after the Model 3 was dropped from Army consideration, Bell engineers used the basic concept to develop the XP-77. Today it has been all but forgotten, but in its time the XP-77 was a remarkable machine.

It was an all-wood lightweight fighter made from Sitka spruce, patterned after racers of the 1930s and intended to operate from grass runways. It was also an astonishingly attractive machine. Yet when the first of two XP-77s (43-34915/34916) flew on 1 April 1944 at the Bell facility at Niagara Falls, NY, with Jack Woolams at the controls, it was not unfitting that the date was April Fools' Day.

Because of early concerns about a possible shortage of strategic materials (which did not materialize), initially the idea of a small, cheap, all-wood fighter built with readily accessible materials held high appeal. Using their earlier engineering documents on the defunct Model 3, in early 1941 Larry Bell's upstate New York fighter team began work on a plane at first called the 'Tri-4' – shorthand for an informal Army Air Forces

requirement for '4– hp, 4,000lb, 400mph'. On 16 May 1942, the Army ordered twenty-five 'Tri-4' aircraft.

Delays, technical problems with subcontracting on plywood construction, and disappointing wind-tunnel tests caused the manufacturer to suggest by early 1943 that the number of pursuit ships on order be reduced to six. In May 1943 the AAF pared this number to two: by now thinking had changed, there appeared less need for a fighter which would be so short-legged as to be useful for point-defence only, and the Army saw the XP-77 as having no operational utility, but as useful in lightweight fighter research.

The XP-77 was a single-seat aircraft with a tricycle undercarriage and a single in-line Ranger SGV-770C-1B engine developing up to 450hp. The original design had called for an XV-770-9 engine, then under development for the US Navy, with a two-stage supercharger.

Gross weight was 3,583lb (1,625kg). With a fuel capacity of 56 US gallons (212ltr), the XP-77 had a range of 550 miles (885km) when cruising at 270mph (441km/h). Service ceiling is listed in documents as 30,000ft (9,144km) although one wonders, in retrospect, whether it could ever have got that high.

If the predicted shortage of critical aluminium alloy materials for aircraft had materialized, the XP-77 might have served a purpose ('such as defending Chicago', quipped one Bell company sceptic). Plans existed to arm the sleek XP-77 with two synchronized .50 cal (12.7mm) machine guns, firing through the propeller shaft mounted on the engine, or – an

BELL XP-77

The United States Army's largest and smallest combat aircraft in 1945. The Boeing B-29 Superfortress was caught up in the final campaign against Japan when this stately example posed beside the second Bell XP-77 (43-34916). An immediate relative of the P-39 Airacobra, the latter aircraft was lost in a crash during the test programme. AAF

idea that always seemed present at Bell – a cannon firing through the propeller hub.

When the wings for the first airplane were delivered they were found to be structurally deficient due to problems in the plywood veneer bonding process during manufacture. In order to expedite test-flying it was decided to use the defective wings and restrict the high-stress flight manoeuvres of that airframe.

The anticipated low cost also turned out to be a delusion. The contracted cost for six aircraft was $698,761.88. The final figure (for two aircraft and one static test airframe) was $2,686.750.

Following the 25min maiden flight on 1 April 1944, on 2 May the first aircraft was ferried from Niagara Falls to Wright Field where flight tests there were limited due to the structural restrictions. The no. 2 aircraft (43-34916) flew for the first time on 2 May 1944 and remained in Bell's hands for exhaustive tests until mid-July.

On 21 July 1944, the Army ordered both aircraft to Eglin Army Air Field, Florida, for operational suitability tests. But the no. 1 aircraft had been damaged at Wright Field when the nose-wheel

collapsed, so only the no. 2 XP-77 was used in the Eglin tests. By 2 October the suitability tests had been successfully completed, and the aircraft was being checked out prior to a planned ferry flight to Wright Field. The pilot attempted an Immelman turn and fell into an inverted spin from which he recovered, only to go into a flat spin from which he could not. The pilot parachuted to safety, but the aircraft was a total loss.

But although the pilot survived, the programme did not. Plagued by noise and vibration, an unexpectedly long take-off run, and general performance inferior to existing Army fighters (according to a test-pilot report), the XP-77 was killed by an administrative decision on 2 December 1944.

The exact route of the first aircraft is not certain, but it appears the prototype 43-34915 went to Wright Field, then Eglin, then back to Wright. It was seen at postwar displays wearing spurious markings including bright bands of an unknown colour around the fuselage. At one point, pilot and aviation writer Cole H. Morrow attempted to purchase the XP-77 as war surplus, but 'they just wouldn't sell it'. It ended up on outdoor display at

Bell XP-77 *continued*

Purdue University and was eventually scrapped.

   Those who saw the XP-77 might have admired its racy lines, never realizing that when it achieved its peak speed of 330mph (531km/h), the disappointing XP-77 fell almost 70mph (108km/h) *short* of the speed its designers had been charged with attaining.

   This was a harsh reality, not like a wartime press release, aimed at making the Bell pursuit ship sound 'hot' by describing it, in cowboy terms, as 'an engine with a saddle on it . . .'.

An unpublished postwar photo of the first XP-77 aircraft (43-34915) shortly before it was scrapped. The all-Sitka spruce Bell pursuit ship spent its final years on display at Purdue University; here it is being examined by cadets of the Reserve Officer Training Corps (ROtc). Robert F. Dorr

A Soviet P-39 pilot. The myth persisted that the 37mm cannon on the Airacobra could routinely rip open the armoured hull of a tank and transform it to twisting, smouldering wreckage. In fact the gun was nowhere near that powerful, but the Soviets did use the Airacobra and its armament with extraordinary success. San Diego Aerospace Museum

A P-39D-2-BE Airacobra of the Soviet air arm; the latter is called the Air Force of the Red Army, or VVS
(Voyenno-Vozhdushniye Sily). San Diego Aerospace Museum

show results with a handful of P-39 Airacobras it had acquired. Assigned to the 4th Stormo, the P-39s proved effective in strafing German ground positions.

The Italian Co-Belligerent Air Force ended the war with a motley collection of military flying machines that would have been a joy to visiting enthusiasts, had any existed at the time: there were Macchi C.202 and 205 fighters, Spitfire IXs, and P-39Q Airacobras. There were Savoia-Marchetti S.M.79 and Martin Baltimore bombers, and Douglas C-47 and Savoia-Marchetti S.M.81 transports, to say nothing of Cant Z.506B float seaplanes.

The Italians never really met the challenges presented to them by the Airacobra's complex power arrangement or its cantankerous electrical system, and they always had a significant number of P-39s that were not airworthy. On VE Day, the strength of the Italian air arm included eighty-three P-39s, of which sixty were

serviceable. Italy replaced its Airacobras with P-38 Lightnings soon afterwards, but a few remained on duty in training roles until 1951.

War's End

On 7 May 1945, peace came to Europe at 2.41am in a small red schoolhouse in Rheims where General Eisenhower, the Allied Supreme Commander, had his headquarters. After General Alfred Jodl, Army Chief of Staff, the German emissary, had signed the instrument of unconditional surrender, he said: 'With this signature, the German people and armed forces are, for better or worse, delivered into the victors' hands.' General Bedell Smith, Eisenhower's Chief of Staff, signed for the Western Allies, and General Ivan Suslapatov was witness for Russia.

The Airacobra might not have been in frontline service in American units at that time, but there were still plenty around. However, it may well have been Britain who operated the last P-400/Airacobra I: the aircraft (AH574), which was tested on a carrier in 1944, continued to wear RAF roundels until it was withdrawn from use on 18 March 1948. When he was searching out the designations of US military aircraft in the 1950s, the noted researcher James C. Fahey found evidence that at least one P-39 Airacobra remained in inventory – although not actively flying – as late as 1949. If that is correct, the Airacobra would have survived the creation of the United States Air Force as an independent service branch on 18 September 1947 and the re-designation of pursuit ships as fighters (the 'P' being replaced by 'F' on 5 June 1948), so that technically, the airframe in question would have been not a P-39, but an F-39.

Natural-metal P-39Q-5-BE, or Model 26 (42-19517), fitted with belly ferrying tank and lined up at the Buffalo factory.
In later years, this AAF veteran became the Confederate Air Force's sole flying Airacobra 'warbird'.
Bell via Truman Partridge

A late-war factory portrait of a P-39Q-15-BE Airacobra (44-2506). This final version of the Airacobra was built in greater quantity than all other versions combined.
In production from 1943 on, the Q Model looked like other Airacobras except for substitution of a pod-mounted .50 cal machine gun under each wing, replacing
.30 cal guns. via Warren M. Bodie

A cutaway photo of a P-39D fighter (42-6878) being run up by mechanics, apparently in Hawaii. With
propeller hub, armament access and engine panels removed, this Airacobra will not be flying anywhere in
a hurry. Just in case, the aircraft is tied down and is being carefully watched over by an attendant with a
fire bottle. San Diego Aerospace Museum

Japan capitulated on 15 August 1945, of course, and a surrender document was signed aboard the battleship USS *Missouri* in Tokyo Bay on 2 September 1945. The event was accompanied by the largest flyover of aircraft in formation ever to occur on this planet – about 2,000 warplanes, nearly all of them belonging to the Navy and Marine Corps: but there was not an Airacobra amongst them. One individual who happened to be aboard the *Missouri* to witness the end of humankind's worst conflict was an AAF sergeant named James Patton who had maintained P-39s and P-400s on Guadalcanal.

The ink was scarcely dry on the surrender document marking the end of World War II when Bell test pilots Jack Woolams, Tex Johnston and Chalmers 'Slick' Goodlin purchased two relatively pristine P-39Q Airacobras that had been in the hands of the manufacturer. The pilots set forth to install 1,500hp Allison V-1710-135 engines, replacing the V-1710-85s installed on the Q model. Cobra I, painted a brilliant red, and Cobra II, wearing brilliant yellow with black trim, were expected to be stars in the coming 1946 Thompson Trophy Race. But just days before the start of the races, Woolams was killed while testing Cobra I when the

aircraft dived into Lake Ontario on a high-speed run; it is thought that the bullet-proof windshield fractured, and blew in and killed him.

When the National Air Races resumed in 1946, P-63 Kingcobras soon outnumbered P-39 Airacobras among the participants seeking the newly revived Thompson Trophy in Cleveland, Ohio. The P-63 was more powerful and heavier than the P-39, and had a larger wing with a greater wing area – although this was not an advantage, indeed it was not really needed, for pylon air racing. Nevertheless, twelve P-63s participated in the postwar races, as opposed to only three P-39s.

Bell XP-83

On 24 March 1944, with the war in Europe signalling the need for a long-range escort fighter to accompany bombers to their targets, the AAF tasked the builder of the first American jet aircraft to develop a larger, longer-legged jet fighter. One factor in the selection of the builder was that Bell was deemed to have sufficient capacity to handle the job; production of the P-39 Airacobra was nearing an end at its Niagara Falls, NY, facility and while production of the P-63 Kingcobra would continue, there were expertise and resources for this additional job.

Bell assigned engineer Charles Rhodes to 'bring along' the new fighter, the bulky XP-83. The XP-83 was to be a mid-wing single-seater powered by two General Electric I-40 turbojet engines (later designated J33-GE-9) expected to produce 4,000lb (1,845kg) of thrust each. Armament was to be a hefty battery of six .50 cal (12.7mm) Browning M3 nose machine guns.

The ill-fated first of two Bell XP-83 fighters (44-84990). The AAF's order to develop and build the XP-83 came while Bell was finishing its production run of P-39 Airacobras and turning out P-63 Kingcobras. Under better circumstances, the XP-83 might have proved to be a suitable replacement for the Airacobra, but other jet fighters showed better performance and greater promise. Bell

Bell XP-83

First flown on 25 February 1945, apparently with company test pilot Jack Woolams doing the honours, the first XP-83 (44-84990) soon proved to be under-powered and unstable. The actual thrust developed by its I-40 engines was 600lb (283kg) less than projected, and the close proximity of the two underslung powerplants caused hot exhaust gases to buckle the tailplane unless, during run-ups, fire trucks were used to play streams of water over the rear fuselage!

The second XP-83 (44-84991) was completed with a slightly different bubble canopy and an extended nose to accommodate six .60 cal guns, the .10in increase in machine-gun barrel diameter being based on anticipated firepower needs for the planned amphibious invasion of Japan. No photographs of the second XP-83 appear to have survived, and while it is known that the aircraft was used in gunnery tests at Wright Field, its final disposition is not recorded.

Notwithstanding its early difficulties, the Bell fighter showed promise. The XP-83 could reach 322mph (515km/h) at 15,000ft (4,570m) and had a service ceiling of 45,200ft (13,776m). The extreme forward position of the pressurized cockpit gave such good visibility that the pilot could visually check his own main gear when down. Modified tailpipes, angled outwards, resolved the heat/buckling problem. Wind-tunnel tests showed that an 18in (0.45m) extension of the vertical tail would enhance stability, though it is not clear whether this modification was actually made.

Specification data include a wingspan of 53ft (16.15m), a length of 45ft (13.71m), a height of 14ft (4.26m), and a wing area of 431sq ft (40sq m). Empty weight was 14,105lb (6,397kg) and maximum take-off weight was 27,500lb (12,473kg), making the XP-83 as heavy as some wartime bombers.

Except with respect to range, the performance of the Bell fighter – however creditable – offered no improvement over the Lockheed P-80 Shooting Star which was then entering production. For the escort role, the AAF turned to the equally long-legged P-82 Twin Mustang. Both fighters would later fight in Korea, leaving the Bell XP-83 with no prospect except to fall between the cracks of history as a 'might have been'.

Once it became clear that the XP-83 would not be produced, 44-84990 was assigned to a ram-jet engine test programme. A hatch was cut into the belly to provide entry into the aft fuselage, and an engineer's station – 'blind' except for a small port-side window – was created behind the pilot. Experimental athoyd ram jets were slung under the wings. The intent was for the XP-83 to serve as a test-bed – once aloft, flying on ram-jet power alone. In the late forties, similar tests were conducted with P-51s, P-80s and other types (an Airacobra with a ram jet-looking device under its fuselage was actually testing an experimental supercharger). Much was learned even though no practical application was ever found.

On 4 September 1946, just as this test programme had begun, a ram jet caught fire and the flames soon spread to the wing. Pilot Chalmers 'Slick' Goodlin and engineer Charles Fay, without the benefit of ejection seats, bailed out, and neither man knew whether the other had got out safely until they met on the ground. The Bell XP-83 bored into the ground. The other XP-83 was scrapped soon afterwards, and the programme was ended. There is no record that a Bell model number was ever assigned to the XP-83.

This P-39Q-20-BE Airacobra (44-3919) was apparently employed for miscellaneous duties at Wright Field, Ohio, late in the war. By the time the tide of war had turned and victory was in the air, P-39s were being employed as 'hacks' at numerous bases around the country. Thousands of AAF pilots acquired a secondary qualification in the P-39 while carrying out their principal duties in some better-loved aircraft type. James C. Fahey

With the Allies on the brink of victory, it became less and less likely that a squadron-sized gaggle of P-39 Airacobras would be found anywhere. These late-war P-39Q Models are lined up at an airfield in Hawaii, but it is not clear whether they are going anywhere. By 1945, no Airacobras remained in any American combat units. San Diego Aerospace Museum

Racing Cobras

Cobra I

For the first postwar Thomson Trophy Race, Bell test pilots Chalmers 'Slick' Goodlin, Alvin M. 'Tex' Johnston and Jack Woolams prepared and entered two P-39 Airacobras. Jack Woolams was the driving force behind the scheme and flew Cobra I, a P-39Q-10 (42-20733). Tex Johnston flew Cobra II, a P-39Q-10 (42-20869). The two Airacobras were the aircraft that surrendered their three-bladed, 400lb (181kg) propellers for use by the two swept-wing L-39 Kingcobras, which were balanced too finely to use the four-bladed, 460lb (209kg) Kingcobra propeller. This left two Airacobra aircraft – which Bell had purchased for less than it would have been charged, had it purchased only Airacobra propellers – plus two Kingcobra propellers at Bell's Niagara Falls factory; and thus the two Cobras were created.

The two Cobras swapped their V-1710-85(E19) engines for the V-1710-135(G4) powerplant also used on the RP-63G Kingcobra. The carburettor air scoop area was increased.

Cobra I never managed to see the finish line because,

tragically, Woolams was killed in a flight from Bell's Niagara Falls factory in Cobra I, and it was left to others to attempt to score in the National Air Races.

Cobra II

Flying Cobra II, or P-39Q-10 (42-20869/N92848), Johnston redeemed Woolams' loss by taking the 1946 Thompson Trophy Race at an average speed of 373.908mph (601.745km/h). Jay Demming, one of Bell's first helicopter pilots, persuaded an entrepreneur to purchase Cobra II, and flew it to a third-place finish in the 1947 Thompson event at an average speed of 389.837mph (627.380km/h). With many modifications, including a change to the V-1710-143/145(G6) engine developed for the North American P-82 Twin Mustang, Allison test pilot Charles 'Chuck' Brown flew Cobra KF-1, as Cobra II was re-named, in the 1948 Thomspon. Brown established a closed-course qualification record in this craft at 418mph (673km/h), but was forced to drop out without finishing. Cobra KF-1 was abandoned for many years

Cobra II was P-39Q-10-BE Airacobra 42-20869, registered as N92848. Test pilot Tex Johnston flew it to take the 1946 Thompson Trophy race at an average speed of 373.908mph (601.745km/h). It was a kind of last fling for the P-39, and it was the first and last time a Bell test pilot achieved fame for a civilian racing event. via Clyde Gerdes

Racing Cobras *continued*

before being brought to Ed Maloney's museum in Clairemont, California. The plane was purchased in 1969 by Mike Carroll, who intended to re-name it Cobra III. However, this Airacobra was lost soon afterwards: Carroll bailed out, was struck by the airframe, and lost his life.

Other Cobra Racers

A P-39Q-15 Airacobra (44-2433/NX 57521) was flown in the 1946 National Air Races by Earl Ortman. This aircraft now belongs to the National Air & Space Museum at Silver Hill, Maryland, and is displayed with the nickname 'Galloping Gertie'.

A P-39Q flown by C. W. Bing, and another P-39 flown by James Harp in the postwar races, were not sufficiently modified to be competitive.

A P-63C Kingcobra (N62995, race no. 28), flown by Charles Tucker, entered the 1946 Thompson race. He purchased two P-63s for $1,000 each just after the war at Kingman, Arizona, hoping to excel in air racing. He cropped off the wing of N62995, reducing its span from 38ft 3in (11.67m) to 25ft 9in (7.86m) and its wing area from 248sq ft (23sq m) to 187sq ft (17.4sq m). He also removed the ventral fin. He entered the 1946 races with an unmodified V-1710-117(E21) engine in N62995. Tucker sold this aircraft to Russ Hosler at the end of the 1948 races.

Tucker's second P-63C Kingcobra (44-4126/NX63231, race no. 30) was intended for the 1946 Bendix cross-country race, operated between Van Nuys, California and Cleveland over a distance of 2,048 miles (3,296km). This aircraft initially retained its wing size and was fitted with two wing-tip drop-tanks. In 1947, Tucker removed the tip-tanks, cropped the wingspan to about 28ft 6in (8.68m), and flew the Tinnerman event which was for Kingcobras only. For the 1949 races, Tucker modified this ship further and painted it a brilliant purple. In 1949, he took third place in the Sohio Trophy Race and fifth place in the Thompson: the crash of Bill Odom's P-51 Mustang, 'Beguine', in the latter event marked the end of air racing in the US for a decade and a half, and Tucker remains on record as having got more speed out of a Kingcobra than any other race pilot before or since. His qualifying speed in the 1949 Thompson was an enviable 393.328mph (632.998km/h).

A P-63C-5 Kingcobra (NX63941, race no. 72), Lucky Jack, entered in the 1947 races by 'Lucky' Jack Singleton and flown by Raymond E. Eiche, was lost in a pre-race mishap; Eiche managed to parachute to safety.

A P-63C-5 (44-4393/NX62822, race no. 92) owned by Joseph M. Kinkella, never finished the 1947 Bendix race, also Van Nuys-Cleveland. Kinkella was forced out at Pueblo, Colorado with engine troubles.

A P-63C-5 (44-4178/NX67115, race no. 47) piloted by Spiro 'Sammy' Diles, dropped out of the 1946 Bendix event.

A P-63E-1 (NX69702, race no. 65) operated by Wilson V. 'Bill' Newhall appeared at the 1946 races, but because it was unmodified – probably too heavy and with too much wing area – it was never a serious pylon-turning contender. Newhall returned in 1948.

A P-63A-7 (42-69063/NX69901, race no. 64 in 1946, 55 after 1947) modified with V-1710-133(E30) engine and revised intake

duct, with an 11ft 1in (3.36m) Aeroproducts' three-bladed propeller, was flown in several postwar events. Bill Bour flew this aircraft in the 1947 Tinnerman, but was unable to retract his landing gear and ended up in last place in a reduced field of five competitors. Bour also reached sixth place in this aircraft in the 1947 Thompson.

NX69901 returned in 1948 with a four-bladed propeller and the nickname Spirit of Tick, honouring pilot-owner Howard 'Tick' Lilly who was also a test pilot and was killed flying the Douglas D-558-I Skystreak at Muroc. Bob Eucker flew it to second place in the 1948 Tinnerman, and to first place that year in the Sohio. With the Aeroproducts three-bladed propeller restored, Eucker flew it again in the 1949 Thompson.

A P-63C-5 (NX62797) was flown by Steve Wittman in the 1946 and 1947 races, including the latter year's Tinnerman. This was essentially a stock aircraft without modifications.

A P-63C-5 (44-4181/NX73744, race no. 53) in natural metal finish was brought to the 1948 air races by Frank Singer. A year later, Singer returned with a P-63C-5 painted dark grey and trimmed in red. Decades later, it is not clear whether Singer had one Kingcobra or two. Re-registered (B9009/ race no. 90), this ship was extensively modified and distinguished by a tiny bubble canopy when flown in the 1971 San Diego air races piloted by Larry Havens. This aircraft had a shortened wing, concave wing tips, V-1710-135(G4) engine. Plans existed to convert the craft to a Merlin engine, but before they could materialize, it was lost on a trials flight on 7 September 1972 when Havens bailed out. The aircraft was salvaged and is being used by the Yankee Air Corps, Chino, California, to provide parts in the restoration of another ship (43-11117).

A P-63A-10 (42-70455/NX4699N, race no. 51), once slated for Free French Forces, was the 1947 mount for Ken Knight, and victor in that year's Tinnerman.

A P-63A-7 (42-69097/N52113, race no. 87) was flown by Alfred T. 'Al' Whiteside in the 1947 national races (with the nickname 'Kismet') and again in 1949 (without the nickname). The aircraft had a reduced wingspan and rounded wing-tips. As G-BTWR, this ship resumed standard P-63 configuration, and is listed today at the Fighter Collection at Duxford, England.

The sole surviving P-63F of the two built (43-11719/NX1719, race no. 21) emerged in the postwar era as H. L. Pemberton's mount in the 1946 Cleveland Air Races, appearing again in 1949. No modifications were ever made to the 'F model', and it was not a serious contender in the speed competition. This ship reappeared in the 1970s in bogus Soviet markings. It is active today (as N6763) with the Confederate Air Force, Midland, Texas.

A P-63C (44-4393/N62822, race no. 28) was flown in several post-1964 Reno air races by John Sandberg and Lefty Gardner. It was later part of the Fighter Collection at Duxford. This aircraft remained active until it was lost in a 4 June 1990 crash in France that killed pilot John Larcombe.

44-2333 is a P-39Q located at a training base in the US. via Norman Taylor

A final look at a P-39 Airacobra against a sunset. By 1945, the war had passed the Airacobra by, and the Army air forces no longer had a single P-39 combat squadron in any front-line combat zone. The Airacobra always remained one of the best looking of fighters, even if it was not the best performing, and even its strongest detractors had to admire the way it posed in silhouette. Bell

Arriving on the scene in the wake of the Woolams tragedy, Tex Johnston won the 1946 Thompson in Cobra II at a spectacular average speed of 373.9mph (601.73km/h). It was a surprise to those who still clung to the Airacobra's reputation as an inferior fighter. But Bell wanted Johnston to stop flying in the races, so Cobra II was sold to Rollin Stewart of Indianapolis, Indiana. Jay Demming, another company test pilot, resigned from his position with Bell in order to fly this aircraft in the 1947 Thompson, and came in at second place.

The P-63 Kingcobra gave a good account of itself in the 1946 and 1947 Thompson Trophy races in Cleveland, Ohio and in the 1947 Tinnerman Trophy Race, a seven-lap event created especially for P-63 Kingcobras in the unfulfilled hope of producing a close race. The Kingcobra did less well in the 1946 and 1947 Bendix cross-country events which began in California and terminated at Cleveland. 1947 was apparently the last year a Bell fighter flew in a cross-country event, though P-39s and P-63s appeared in pylon racing when it was restored in 1964.

CHAPTER SIX

P-63 Kingcobra

Jerry C. Scutts

On 27 June 1941, roughly coinciding with its decision to cancel the P-76, the US Army placed an order for two Bell XP-63 Kingcobra prototypes (41-19511/19512) to be powered by the 1,325-hp Allison V-1710-47 liquid-cooled engine in the same rear-mounted location as the Airacobra's. The P-63 was in fact a new aeroplane, capitalizing on the P-39 layout and the positive experience with the XP-39E's laminar-flow wing. However, most of its design features had been 'set in concrete' before Pearl Harbor, when the design looked (then) as good as anything likely to fly in the near future.

Then, there came delays. For a time, it must have seemed that the P-63 Kingcobra programme was never going to get off the ground. The first aircraft flew on 7 December 1942 but was lost in an

accident just weeks later. The second prototype flew on 5 February 1943 but crashed the following May.

Fortunately, a third prototype, the XP-63A, had been ordered in June 1942 and flew on 26 April 1943. This XP-63A (42-78015) had been conceived as a Merlin engine test-bed under the designation XP-63B but was never flown in that capacity, as the few available Merlin engines were needed elsewhere for the North American Mustang. Powered instead by a 1,500-hp Allison V-1710-93, the XP-63A became an effective third prototype and test ship for the continuing development programme.

The XP-63A was the fastest Kingcobra built. It attained 426mph (686km/h) on military power at 20,000ft (6,000m). But air combat was not to be the Kingcobra's

strong suit: the P-63 was intended for the ground-attack role. Its nose armament of one 37mm M-10 cannon (an improved T-9) and two .50-caliber guns with a total of 900 rounds for all three guns, bolstered by additional wing guns in most models, was well suited for air-to-ground action. The Kingcobra also boasted 88lb (40kg) of armour, 100 US gallons (387ltr) of internal fuel, and provision for a 500lb bomb or 75 US gallon (284ltr) drop tank beneath the fuselage. Later aeroplanes were equipped to carry three 522lb bombs. All of this boded well for the harsh needs of the Soviet Union on the Eastern Front.

The basic P-63A version is representative of the Kingcobra series. The aircraft weighed 6,375lb (2,892kg) when empty, a figure which rose to a maximum take-off

As late as late 1943, the trio of XP-39Es, including 41-19502 seen here, were flying as test ships for the P-63 Kingcobra, which Bell developed while the P-39 was in production. This aircraft was belatedly painted olive-drab and given the red-bordered national insignia introduced in June 1943. via Warren M. Bodie

weight of 10,500lb (4,763kg). This made it a lightweight by the standard of most wartime fighters, although the Kingcobra was a sturdy machine and could absorb considerable battle damage.

P-63 Production

On 29 September 1942, the US Army ordered production of the Kingcobra, which began in October 1943. The production P-63A, 1,725 of which were built in eight sub-variants with minor changes in armament, armour, and ordnance, was followed in 1943 by the P-63C with an 1,800hp Allison V-1710-117 engine with water injection. Two P-63As (42-68937 and 42-69423 were tested by the RAF as the Kingcobra Mk I (FR408 and FZ440) but no production for the British service materialized.

The first P-63C (42-70886) introduced a distinctive small ventral fin to improve lateral stability. 1,227 P-63Cs were manufactured, with an internal fuel capacity of 107 US gallons (405ltr) and 201lb (91kg) of armour. A Russian fighter pilot is reported to have called this aircraft a 'tank of the skies', and the P-63 Kingcobra was both highly survivable and very capable against all sorts of ground targets, including main battle tanks.

The sole P-63D (43-11718) introduced a wingspan increased to 39ft 2in (12.11m) and a distinctive, one-piece bubble canopy for enhanced visibility. The first P-63E (43-11720) introduced the improved wing but retained the standard canopy. Just thirteen E models (43-11720/11721; 43-11725/11735) came off the factory line before contracts for 2,930 more were cancelled at war's end. A sole P-63F (43-11719) introduced the V-1710-135 pow-

erplant, a taller vertical fin, and survived the war to become H. L. Pemberton's mount in the 1947 Cleveland Air Races, though a second F model was cancelled.

This trio of improved Kingcobras – the P-63D, P-63E, and P-63F – which warranted a new manufacturer's designation as the Bell Model 41 – came much closer to measuring up to the war's later and better-remembered fighter types, including the P-47 Thunderbolt and P-51 Mustang.

Plans to equip the AAF's Ninth Air Force with Kingcobras did not materialize, nor did plans to equip a Pacific reconnaissance squadron with P-63s. The relatively few Kingcobras retained by the US Army were used primarily for training. None reached the war zone or served in combat.

Total Kingcobra production reached 3,303 airframes. 2,421 Kingcobras were

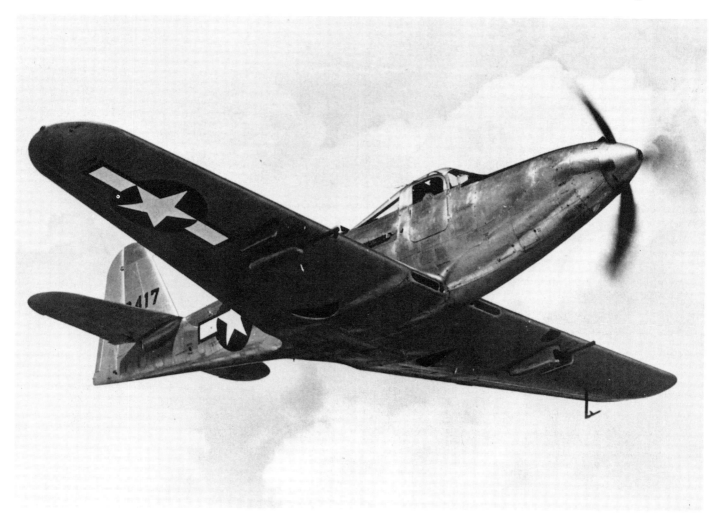

In-flight view of a production P-63A-9 (42-69417) showing half the standard machine-gun armament. Two 0.50in guns were located in the forward fuselage with two in the underwing pods. Bell

Soviet orders for the P-63 followed on from the P-39, one of the most popular combat aircraft used by the VVS in World War Two. Here, scores of P-63A-10s destined for delivery to Russia wait on the ramp at Niagara Falls Airport near the Bell plant in autumn 1944. The P-63A-10 introduced the M-10 37mm nose cannon. Bell

Specification – P-63A Kingcobra	
Powerplant:	1,325hp Allison V-1710-93 liquid-cooled 12-cylinder Vee piston engine driving a four-blade propeller.
Performance:	maximum speed 410mph (660km/h) at 25,000ft (7,620m); cruising speed 378mph (608km/h); service ceiling 43,000ft (13,106m); range 450 miles (724km).
Weights:	empty 6,375lb (2,892kg); maximum take-off 10,550lb (4,763kg).
Dimensions:	span 38ft 4in (11.68m); length 32ft 8in (9.96m); height 12ft 7in (3.84m); wing area 248sq ft (23.04sq m).
Armament:	one 37mm cannon and four (two wing-mounted and two nose-mounted) fixed forward-firing 0.50-calibre machine guns, plus up to three 522lb bombs.

delivered to Russia and just over 100 P-63Cs went to France's Armée de l'Air.

Kings in Combat

With the end of World War in August 1945, the first years of peace cast a number of late-war fighters such as the Bell P-63, North American P-51H and Grumman F8F into a form of limbo. Too late for wartime service and no longer needed in quantity, they nevertheless weathered a mass cutback in orders. All three were built in numbers high enough to fulfill second-line requirements at home or to equip air arms overseas. In the case of the P-63 it served the USAAF only in a training role and the interesting frangible

Bell P-63 Kingcobra Serial Numbers		
XP-63	41-19511/19512	(2)
XP-63A	42-78015	(1)
P-63A	42-68861/70685	(1,825) (100 delivered as RP-63A)
XP-63B	(cancelled)	
P-63C	42-70686/70860	(175)
	43-10893/10932	(40)
	43-11133/11717	(585)
	44-4001/4427	(427)
RP-63C	43-10933/11132	(200)
P-63D	43-11718	(1)
P-63E	43-11720/11721	(2)
	43-11725/11735	(11)
P-63F	43-11719	(1)
RP-63G	43-11723/11724	(2)
	45-57283/57312	(30)
XP-63H (one converted)		
Total: 3,303		

bullet programme known as Operation *Pinball*.

Pinball was the result of extensive research into improving methods of training bomber gunners. The AAF soon realized that its teachings were not working through to great success in combat – gunners were not affording bombers the protection they required from enemy fighter attacks, even with the dozen or so guns mounted in each B-17 or B-24. The primary problem was that practice shoots at friendly interceptor fighters had to be safe yet reliable – the gunner had to be convinced that his dummy rounds would have destroyed the attacking fighter, had the situation been real.

The ultimate answer lay in safe rounds not only being fired but actually hitting the fighter; if the latter could be well armoured and the bullets made to break up on coming into contact with the airframe, then the major problems inherent in judging closure speed, range and the correct 'lead' to destroy the incoming 'enemy' aircraft would be all but solved. The frangible bullet, made of a plastic and lead compound and designed to shatter on impact, was the answer.

In selecting a suitable fighter for the *Pinball* programme the choice soon fell more or less naturally on the P-63. It was in plentiful supply, it was not required for combat and it had already been integrated into the AAF training programme. Bell enthusiastically worked out the engineering involved in reskinning most of the P-63's airframe with armour plate, adding the thickest sections in the front fuselage (which would absorb the most rounds) and tapering these off in thickness towards the rear. A similar protective plating was applied to the wings, and the cockpit of each *Pinball* was armoured to protect the pilot.

The name *Pinball* was derived from the system of placing sensors under the skin to record hits, via an electrical charge, as a blinking light. The RP-63 also carried a blinking light in its propeller spinner. The name was a 'natural' and it struck. The programme involved 100 P-63A models, 200 P-63Cs and 32 RP-63Gs, the first conversion flying in August 1944.

The RP-63G was the culmination of a lengthy series of aeronautical design studies undertaken by Bell with the P-63.

A striking portrait of the best-looking Kingcobra, the one-off P-63D fighter (43-11718) with its almost unique bubble canopy, an A model being fitted with one in England. This Kingcobra variant appears to offer the pilot spectacular vision. The big-wing, tall-tail P-63D or Bell Model 41 came too late in the war for a major production order, but proved valuable in flight-test work. Bell

In 1945, the Airacobra's cousin, the P-63 Kingcobra, was chosen by the US Navy to test the swept-back wing configuration then being considered for jet fighters. The result was the US Navy's first – and for many years, its only – swept-wing aircraft, a single P-63 Kingcobra test-flown under the non-standard designation L-39. Some sources refer to the aircraft as the XF2L-1K, but this is incorrect. via Jim Sullivan

Briefly, the experimental Kingcobras included two XP-63s, the sole XP-63A, a single P-63D fitted with a bubble canopy replacing the 'car door' cockpit entry and two P-63Fs, both of which had extended vertical tail surfaces. Research into alternative tail configurations led to a Bell-developed butterfly tail modification on the first P-63A-1 (42-68861) followed by an independent, post-war, air force-derived 'V' tail design fitted to RP-63G 45-57300 for flight trials.

For more than 35 years, an RP-63G (45-57295) has been on outdoor display at Lackland AFB, Texas, where enlisted airmen undergo basic training.

Kingcobras in England

Considerable international interest in the laminar-flow principal in wing design led to two examples of the P-63 being sent to England. These Kingcobras, a P-63A-6 and a P-63A-9 with British serials FR408 (AAF s/n 42-68937) and FZ440 (42-69423), respectively, were used by the

Royal Aircraft Establishment at Farnborough. It appears that FR408 first flew in the UK on 18 May 1944 and was the aircraft subsequently fitted with a British-designed bubble canopy which differed in detail to the similar canopy fitted to the single P-63D. Damaged in a landing accident in August, this aircraft was still able to participate in the laminar flow study before being finally struck off charge on 18 October 1945.

The accident to FR408 appears to have resulted in FZ440 undertaking most of the test-flying of a system designed to make wing airflow visible. The Kingcobra, which had a NACA series 6 laminar flow aerofoil, had sets of static pitot head 'combs' fitted to each trailing edge and instrumentation in a blanked-off canopy rear section. Each inner wing section was coated with paste to create a slipstream of visible mist when a Miles Master 'chase' aircraft sprayed a trail of chlorine through which the P-63 was flown. Darkening of the wing surface indicated transition from laminar to turbulent flow. The programme involved thirty flights during March and

April 1945. FZ440 was on public display at Farnbough that September. It was finally scrapped in September 1948.

Swept Wing

One of the most radical modifications made to the P-63A was the Navy-sponsored L-39 programme to investigate the low-speed handling characteristics of swept wings. Two P-63A airframes, initially identified unofficially by Bell as XP-39Ns, were refitted with wings swept back 35 degrees and spanning 33ft 7in (10.25m). Both the L-39-1 (BuAer 90061) and L-39-2 (90062) had lengthened fuselages compared to the P-63, greater ventral fin area and wing slats. After the first flight of the L-39-1 on 23 April 1946, the fuselage was further lengthened by 4ft (1.2m). With the wing slats deployed, the extensively instrumented L-39 showed some interesting stall characteristics including a tendency to snap roll with little warning. Different span slats produced a fund of basic data for further development of wing slats, which became standard fittings on carrier aircraft.

The L-39 was tested by Bell until 26 August when the first aircraft was turned over to Langley for wind-tunnel evaluation. The company retained the second L-39 for further tests, these focusing on a further modified wing associated with the Bell X-2 research aircraft.

Honduran Kings

America's 'embarrassment of riches' in terms of surplus combat aircraft in 1945 was not duplicated in many other countries and some, particularly those in South and Central America, urgently needed more modern aircraft. Only one nation in that part of the world was to receive the P-63, this being Honduras.

Bell built thirteen examples of the final Kingcobra production model, the P-63E-1. This was powered by a 1,100hp Allison V-1710-109 engine, which was capable of an output of 1,750hp at sea level with War Emergency Power (WEP). Five of these (43-11727–11731) were ordered by Honduras, the first two of which arrived in October 1948 with a third in December and the final two in July 1949. Given the Fuerza Aerea Hondurena (FAH) serial numbers 400 to 404, the Kingcobras were to become the mainstay of the country's air defence for a half-decade, along with six P-38L Lightnings.

Having one P-63E (401) badly damaged in a landing accident on 15 October 1948 proved fortuitous, in that the aircraft thus became a source of spares that were otherwise in short supply. The Hondurans also had some problems with the armament of their Kingcobras, the 20mm nose cannon proving temperamental and rarely working. The aircraft were, however, equipped with bomb racks and wing guns, and at least one later acquired a 37mm cannon which was the 'design standard' centreline weapon of all Kingcobra subtypes after the P-63A-10.

Armed and bombed up, the FAH P-63s were placed on alert status on 22 April 1954 to defend the country against a threatened insurrection. This did not eventually directly involve Honduras in armed conflict, but the air force was placed on alert for a second time on 21 June, remaining so for the rest of the summer. Days of flying airfield defence sorties, prac-

tice bombing attacks and standing patrols, despite being good training for pilots and groundcrews, did serve to highlight the inadequacy and the age of the P-63s and P-38s by the 1950s.

Kingcobras 402 and 403 were also damaged in landing accidents during their FAH service, which lasted until 30 June 1955. A single example (403) was preserved and mounted on a plinth outside the FAH Officers' Club at Tegucigalpa-Tocontin airbase, firstly in its original finish of light grey but subsequently in a 'creative' four-tone camouflage.

The FAH Kingcobras were replaced by F4U Corsairs in March 1956, whereupon the four survivors were sold to American buyers eager to have a now-rare WWII combat aircraft in their growing warbird inventories. One of the ex-Honduran Air Force machines, 43-11728, currently resides in the USAF Museum at Dayton, Ohio.

Russian Kings

P-63s were ferried to Russia in seemingly endless numbers (beginning with the P-63C variant), using the ALSIB route (*see page 94*) and pausing at way stations in Alaska and Iran. The conventional wisdom goes like this: in Soviet hands, the P-63 Kingcobra was short-changed again in terms of its reputation: though the Kingcobra, as noted, proved to be a potent ground attacker and tank-buster, it never received the 'press' of the Ilyushin Il-2 Shturmovik.

Military action was taking place elsewhere in the Far East even as the world war ended. Having invaded Manchuria in August 1945, Stalin set about grabbing Sakahlin Island and parts of the Kuriles chain from the exhausted Japanese, an action which would foster bad relations between the two countries for decades.

Japanese Army fighter *Sentais* struck back at the invaders and among the sixty-two Soviet aircraft lost to all causes, at least one was a P-63 Kingcobra, further details of which are presently unknown. The Soviets had, of course, been the leading customer for the Kingcobra in World War II, their air arm taking delivery of the greater part of total Bell production, at 2,421 aircraft, or 24.3 per cent. All examples were supplied under Lend-Lease and delivered over the ALSIB

(Alaska-Siberia) route. The number of Kingcobras despatched to Russia made it the third most numerous US fighter supplied after the P-40 (2,430) and the P-39 (4,924), a massive 49.4 per cent of the aircraft produced.

Racers and Warbirds

With the end of the war and jet re-equipment looming for the new USAF, thousands of piston-engined fighters were scrapped, among them the P-63. The role that led to the long-term survival of a number of Kingcobras in the US was as racing and cross-country record machines.

Clearly taken with the unusual configuration of the Kingcobra, Charles Tucker went to Kingman, Arizona, where acres of unwanted military aircraft awaited the scrapper's torch, parted with $2,000 – and came away the proud owner of two P-63s.

Tucker was only one of several civilian owners of Kingcobras, but he was one of the most successful. He flew one P-63 in the 1946 Thompson Trophy Race as N62995, having clipped its wings and removed the ventral fin. He also entered the Bendix cross-country race, the P-63 (NX63231) competing in the Tinnerman event which was restricted to Kingcobras. In 1949 Tucker came fifth in the Bendix and gained a third place in the Sohio Trophy Race, his qualifying speed of 393.328mph (632.865km/h) in the Thompson standing for some fifteen years when air racing was banned throughout the US after a fatal crash in the Sohio event.

When racing was revived, the P-63 was represented in the competitors' pit line-up for several of the Reno races in the mid-1960s. As late as 1971 Larry Havens entered an extensively modified P-63 with a tiny bubble canopy in the San Diego races. This machine was unfortunately destroyed when Havens was forced to bail out on a pre-race trials flight.

Fortunately for what came later, not all the P-63 racers were modified out of all recognition – for their next manifestation was as warbirds, invariably painted up in wartime military markings. A mid-1990s listing put the world Kingcobra inventory as a least a dozen examples either in flying trim or enjoying 'under restoration' status, this total not including aircraft on permanent display in museums.

French Kings

Shortly before the end of WWII, on 14 April 1945, the USAAF began transferring P-63s to France for use by the Armée de l'Air (AdeA). All examples supplied were the penultimate series production model, the P-63C-5 fitted with an Allison V-1710-117 engine rated at 1,325hp and 1,800hp with WEP at 24,000ft (7,300m).

Having equipped seven wartime Groupes de Chasse with the P-39, the French had originally placed orders for 300 P-63s, a number later reduced by about one third. An initial contract for forty P-63C-5s was signed on 3 May with a second, for seventy-two aircraft, following on 4 June, making a grand total of 112 aircraft to which two more were apparently added. Kingcobras were despatched to France without delay during the spring of 1945 and had all arrived by July.

The Kingcobra had originally been intended to replace the few ageing P-39Q and -L Airacobras remaining in French front-line service, but early post-war rationalization resulted in some P-63s going straight into storage. Others were used to equip several AdeA units in the early post-war years. They included part of the old 'Airacobra Escadre' which had comprised GC I/9 and II/9, the latter being the first to fly the P-63 in July 1945. Based at Meknes, Morocco from September 1944 until disbandment in April 1946, GC 9 became the first fighter Escadre to fully equip with the P-63.

Of the seven wartime Groupes de Chasse equipped with the P-39, only two, GC II/6 and II/9, still operated Airacobras on 8 May 1945. All the others had been re-equipped by the war's end, GC 9 ultimately being the last French unit with P-39s.

By late 1945 France was rebuilding its air force with numerous foreign military aircraft from Allied and Axis sources. Post-war commitments in the former colony of Indo-China, recently liberated from Japanese wartime occupancy, required forces to police increasing unrest from the Viet Minh nationalist movement. Having contributed to the defeat of Japan, these patriots felt they had won a right to govern themselves, but the colonial powers aimed instead to return to the 1939 status quo. Armed conflict was the almost inevitable result.

Combating the Viet Minh

When the French returned to Indo-China in 1945 they had to contend with armed guerillas who gradually set about taking over the country by force of arms. At first French troops contained the small-scale outbreaks of violence but guerillas with pro-communist leanings were a worrying development to some Western powers who feared a 'domino effect' if any part of South-East Asia came under their control.

The US was particulary aggrieved at the turn of events in China; having shored up a Nationalist regime during the war, it was faced with the reality that the 'long march' of Mao Tse Tung's communists had carried them to the Indo-Chinese border at Tonkin. To forestall any takeover of the country the US agreed in April 1949, to lift an embargo on the export of combat aircraft to France. Officially this aid did not take place – but covertly the Truman

Twin 75gal wing drop tanks helped boost the relatively short range of the P-63C-5, this example from GC II/9 exhibiting typical Indo-China combat configuration and markings. All known French P-63s were uncamouflaged. J.Mutin/Aero Journal

government provided considerable material support to the French in their expanding war against the Viet Minh.

At that time AdeA fighter units based in metropolitan France were equipped with an assortment of piston-engined types including the P-47 and Spitfire IX, which were the most numerous. Thunderbolts had been supplied to France under wartime Lend-Lease contracts and direct transfers from Army Air Force stocks.

When the need arose to re-equip units in Indo-China, there was some possibility of the P-47 fulfilling this role. However, with home-based units having first call on this still-capable fighter and considering the state of some Indo-Chinese airfields, which were 'paved' with pierced steel planking (PSP), the Armée de l'Air decided against using the heavy (14,500lb/6,600kg gross) P-47D in Indo-China. When it was fully laden, the Thunderbolt would also have required every yard of available runway on the well-worn airstrips in the Far East, with a forseeable and unacceptable risk of accidents. France opted instead to deploy the lighter (10,813lb/4,900kg gross) P-63C to meet its immediate needs. This decision was partly influenced by an apparent reluctance on the part of the US to agree to the P-47 being deployed in combat, despite its age, and the upshot was that some eighty-five P-63s were shipped to Indo-China between July 1949 and October 1950 for

use by five Groupes de Chasse on a rotational basis.

Early in 1949 the 5th Escadre de Chasse at Sidi Ahmed (Bizerte) in Tunisia was selected as the first unit to deploy with 'Kings' to the Far East. The pilots, many of whom had considerable experience of the Kingcobra, as the unit had been flying it since August 1945, greeted the news of the posting with some excitement. The P-63C-5s that GC-5 would fly in Indo-China were not their standard machines, some of which were getting a little long in the tooth, but brand new aircraft that had been stored soon after delivery to France. Apart from occasional engine runs, they had hardly been flown.

Ferried from storage at El Aouina to Sidi Ahmed where they were stripped, inspected and reassembled, the P-63s were then flown to Marseilles-Marignane to be crated. Loaded aboard the Aeronavale carrier *Dixmunde*, the first twenty were then shipped to Saigon to arrive on 23 July. Aircraft were moved to GC 5's main operating base at Tan Son Nhut and on 10 August 1949 the P-63 made its first flight over Indo-China, in the hands of Commandant Prayer, the Groupe CO. Pilots of GC I/5 *Vende*, led by Commandant Boudier and II/5 *Ile de France* (Capitaine De Pinson) drew up flight rosters, each adopting a basic system of two- and four-ship sections for routine combat sorties.

All the P-63C-5s used in Indo-China

were armed with the standard centreline M-10 37mm cannon with fifty-eight rounds firing through the airscrew spinner, plus four .50 cal machine-guns, two in the nose and a pair in underwing gondolas. A 175gal contoured belly tank was usually carried, this extra fuel load being supplemented on extended-range missions by two 75gal drop tanks on hardpoints outboard of the gondolas. Napalm could be carried in place of the fuel tanks, as could a pair of 500lb bombs, one under each wing. The centreline rack was also wired for bomb release, and although numerous early AdeA P-63 combat flights were undertaken without underwing ordnance, paired wing launchers for up to four HVAR were also used in combat.

The French pilots found that to effectively counter guerilla activity their sorties had ideally to be closely integrated with offensive operations on the ground, the requirement being for the Army to 'flush out' the elusive guerillas. The aim was to neutralize as many Viet Minh personnel as possible to prevent the organization growing large enough to constitute a major threat to French rule. Such support missions occupied the P-63 pilots for the first few months in their new combat zone. On 30 August ground attack sorties were flown by five Kingcobras, the pilots aiming to dovetail their strafing runs with pursuit of the Viet Minh by Moroccan troops – but the so-called 'Great Viet Hunt' yielded few tangible results on that occasion.

On 4 September II/5 moved to Gia Lam, near Hanoi, for operations in the Tonkin area. Some success attended two-ship strafing missions against guerilla hideouts and storage dumps, the P-63 using cannon and machine-gun fire to deadly effect. Targets were located in many places including Thai Nguyen, Than Hoa and Hao Binh. Armed patrols also intercepted junks and small boats plying the waterways of the Red River delta in support of the guerillas.

The 1,100hp Allison engine of the P-63C-5 stood up well enough to the rigours of the tropical climate although there were inevitably accidents within a normal attrition rate for a front-line unit. In November GC II/5 sent a detachment to Lang Son where ground support sorties were flown in response to local briefings on a day-to-day basis.

Further shipments of P-63s had meanwhile been made to Saigon and an official

Groupe de Chasse II/5 was one of three Groupes that retained a full unit code prefix on their P-63C-5s in Indo-China. In this line-up view 44-4118 has an individual code duplicating the last letter of its civil registration (F-UGOR), as per standard Armée de l'Air practice. The aircraft later served with GC I/9 with the identity F-UGWM. J.Mutin/Aero Journal

The nearest aircraft of this flight of P-63s belonging to GC II/5 is 44-4021, registered F-UGOL, which lasted until 14 August 1950 when it was wrecked at Gia Lam. The aircraft has not had its individual code 'L' applied in this view, unlike the other 'Kings' in the flight. J.Mutin/Aero Journal

AdeA statement of 15 December 1949 confirmed the following distribution of the aircraft then in-theatre: Staff flight of GC 5, four aircraft; GC I/5, fourteen; GC II/5, fifteen; and GC II/6, seventeen. In addition, the maintenance unit Parc 482 then held ten P-63s.

Operational use of napalm began less than spectacularly for the P-63 on 10 January 1950 although this weapon continued to be used.

With the Chinese supplying the Viet Minh with anti-aircraft guns and mortars, the 'guerrilla phase' of the war ended and on 19 January a P-63C of GC II/5 became the first example of the type to be shot down by anti-aircraft fire.

As the Viet Minh gained strength French military posts were increasingly attacked and occasionally overrun. Such actions were difficult to stop by air attack; flying a number of sorties to support the garrison at Pho Luc, GC 5's pilots failed to prevent the post being captured on 13 February.

On 3 August 1950, having flown 3,703 hours of combat sorties in its P-63Cs, GC I/5 prepared to return home. It left Haiphong on the 6th bidding farewell to II/5 which stayed behind, to be joined by the third P-63 Escadre in the area, GC III/6 *Roussillon*. Stationed initially at Gia Lam under Commandante Motte from 5 August, III/6 maintained the pressure on the guerillas in much the same type of fighter-bomber operation as the French forces had conducted previously, but without appreciably decreasing the Viet Minh's hold on the country. The Armée de l'Air shouldered an increasingly frustrating and difficult task against an elusive enemy who rarely indulged in pitched battles against superior French firepower. Lacking any air support, the guerillas invariably sought to avoid damaging exposure to air attack.

Armed reconnaissance sorties for III/6 had begun on 9 August and by the end of the month the unit had completed 131 flying hours. The following month recorded the first P-63 losses, on the 8th and the 17th, when Adjutant Begaud was shot down at Dong Khe. The Viet Minh, now well equipped with anti-aircraft artillery (AAA), became a tougher opponent as GC III/6 found to its cost on 4 October when a second King was damaged by enemy fire in the same area.

To provide air cover for Route Coloniale RC 4, one of the main French supply routes, III/6 sent six P-63Cs on temporary detachment to Lang Son on 6 October. This move led indirectly to an operation that ended somewhat unusually. Hit by small-arms fire on 17 October, Lt Perrotte made an emergency landing at Lang Son when his aircraft began leaking glycol. Almost immediately the French airmen were forced to abandon the base as the Viet Minh were about to overrun the town. This they did and the following day GC III/6 sent one of its Kingcobras to strafe Lt Perrotte's machine, primarily to prevent its weapons falling into guerilla hands.

Edging close to the camera ship, P-63C-5 44-4028/E of GC III/6 was registered F-UGYE. The aircraft appears to have rocket launch rails fitted. J.Mutin/Aero Journal

On 3 November 1950 GC III/6 moved its base to Cat Bi, near the port of Haiphong, where it remained apart from a temporary detachment to Bach Mai.

There followed a steadily increasing sortie rate as the French airmen fought a tough enemy who, despite their efforts, gradually gained control of the countryside, if not the towns which remained nominally under French control. By 12 February 1951 III/6 had flown its 1,000th sortie and on the 23rd the unit had a new commander, Capitaine Sales.

The P-63's operational record in Indo-China was boosted by a fourth unit, GC II/6 *Normandie-Niemen*. Possibly the most famous French air force unit, the *Normandie* or *Neu Neu* had arrived at Saigon on 29 October 1949 and flown its first P-63 sortie on 11 November. With an establishment of twenty-seven P-63Cs, the unit was led until 19 December by Capitaine Billoin.

GC II/6 carried out ground-support sorties in many areas of the country and in March 1950 the *Normandie*'s Kingcobras used napalm while participating in a large-scale attack on Viet Minh infantry at Tra Vinh. Detachments were based at Phnom Penh, Hanoi and Tourane during the course of operations.

Among the unit's combat losses were those of Adj Leon Perrier, who was hit by AAA fire at Ap An Thai on 5 May, and Capitaine De Royer Dupre, who was downed during a strike on 14 September. This latter sortie was a minor saga for

Undernose view of GC II/6's Kingcobra flight line at Tan Son Nhut in 1950. To the left is the standard 175gal contoured belly fuel tank almost universally carried by French P-63s, while in the background is 44-4077/A (F-UGXA) of the Normandie-Niemen, complete with 'barred' national insignia. J.Mutin/Aero Journal

Armée de l'Air P-63C Kingcobra units		
Unit	Date re-equipped	Date P-63s phased out
GC II/9 *Auvergne*	July 1945	March 1946**
(GM) GC I/9 *Limousin*	c. September 1945	May 1951*
GC II/5 *Ile de France* (previously EC IV/2)	c. July 1946	Jan 1951*
GC II/6 *Normandie-Niemen*	c. July 1946	Dec 1950*
GC I/5 *Vendée*	c. April 1947	Aug 1950*
GC III/6 *Roussillon*	c. May 1950	April 1951*

*denotes combat service in Indo-China
** unit disbanded & later reformed on F8Fs

Dupre, who was flying 44-4149/H armed with two 500lb underwing bombs as well as the contoured belly tank. Experiencing a loss of engine coolant either en route to or in contact with enemy gun positions at Tay Ninh, the aircraft went down to crash in a plantation at Cau Khoi from whence it was subsequently recovered, Dupre himself being wounded.

This particular Kingcobra had been delivered to GC II/6 on 16 November 1949; a *Normandie* pilot named Pichoff flew it during the month and had experienced a flat spin from which he recovered – but there was a slight indication that 44-4149's problems did not stem entirely from the stresses of combat.

Sgt-chef Turpin was lost on 22 October,

by which time II/6 was anticipating the arrival of a P-63 replacement, the F8F Bearcat. Enough of these had arrived by December, and P-63 sorties tailed off.

Fifth and last P-63 unit to see combat in Indo-China was Groupe de Marche I/9 *Limousin* which arrived at Saigon on 28 December 1950 to take over the P-63s left behind when GC I/5 departed. Led by Commandant Cavoroz, GM I/9 was based at Haiphong and flew its first mission on 1 January 1951, when eight aircraft attacked ground targets at Cho Phong. During its first period of combat the unit was redesignated as a Groupe de Chasse.

On 19 January two 'Kings' flew an armed reconnaisance mission along RC 3 south of Thai Nguyen. Enemy guns opened fire and hit the aircraft flown by Sous-Lt Grob, who went down. On the 20th I/9 lost another P-63 while strafing in the Dong La/Bich Thuy area. Two machines failed to return on 28 January when they flew a rocket strike south of Thai Nguyen.

Having completed seventy-six missions by January 1951, GC I/9 was to suffer proportionately more pilot losses (eight killed

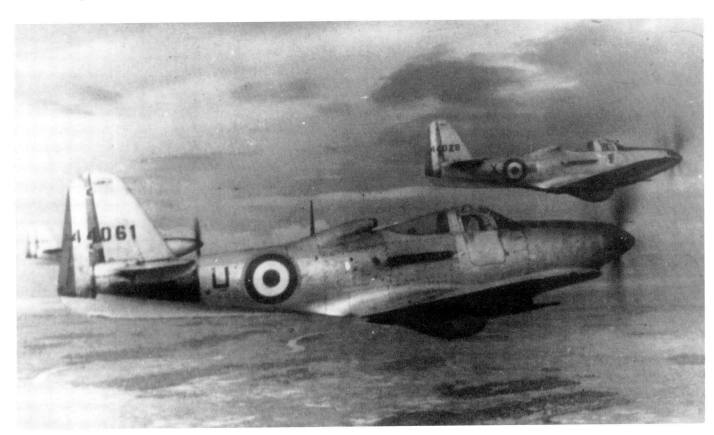

P-63C 44-4061/U, delivered to France in September 1951, was serving in GC III/6, its third operational unit, when it was wrecked at Cat Bi on 14 February 1951. J.Mutin/Aero Journal

After a seemingly gentle wheels-up landing at Tan Son Nhut on 28 January 1950 this P-63 (43-11614/F-UGQE) flown by Capitaine Jacques Guillemin de Monplanet, CO of GC II/6, was deemed a write-off. J.Mutin/Aero Journal

with nine aircraft lost) than other *Escadres* during its time in the Far East on both the P-63 and the Bearcat.

Now committing regular troops in considerable strength under the able leadership of Gen Vo Nguyen Giap, the Viet Minh demonstrated that they could absorb heavy casualties and still fight hard. Tenaciously holding territory in the face of air attacks, paradrops and the extreme efforts of crack French regiments to dislodge them, the enemy systematically overran garrisons and forced evacuations. Giap, launching an 'open battle' phase with several divisions of Viet Minh regulars, embarked on securing a series of objectives designed to so wear down the French that they would abandon Indo-China entirely. He knew that time was on his side. Confident that their weaponry would ultimately prevail, the French fought on.

In the meantime the AdeA P-63s continued to take the war to the enemy, strafing, bombing and rocketing troops and strongholds wherever these could be found. Change was, however, looming. As effective, if not more so than the P-63, were the F6F Hellcats and F8F Bearcats already in action and it was decided to re-equip all Armée de l'Air Groupes de Chasse with these and phase out the P-63. Lighter, smaller, highly manoeuvrable and able to carry a substantial weapon load, the Bearcat in particular proved its superiority over the Kingcobra in the harsh conditions of Indo-China.

The final mission for the P-63 in Indo-China took place on 30 April 1951 when GC I/9 and GC III/6 fielded twelve aircraft each to bomb Quynh Lu. According to intelligence reports twenty-one of the twenty-four bombs dropped hit the target.

At the end of their service in Indo-China twenty-five P-63s had been lost on operations or in accidents, twenty had been struck off charge as 'war weary' or damaged beyond repair, and forty which were still in good condition were earmarked for shipping back to North Africa, though apparently only a very small proportion of these were actually despatched.

It was common for French P-63s to serve with more than one unit and among those that also saw front-line combat duty was 43-11567. Initially taken on charge by GC I/5 where it took the code '5T-J', it passed to GC II/6 in September 1949, having meanwhile being allocated the registration F-UGOH, and to GC II/5 in 1950. It then returned to GC I/5 (coded 5T-I) before service with GC I/9 (becoming F-UGWH) from 1 January 1951. Damaged at Don Lai on 4 April, it passed to Parc 482, the maintenance unit at Bach Mai, on 13 April after which it was presumably scrapped.

Several P-63s survived the scrapping process and soldiered on in various French test establishments until the early 1960s, but after service in Indo-China the P-63 otherwise faded quickly from the French aviation scene. Although its contribution in that conflict, which later ended so disastrously for France, was in no way decisive, the 'second generation' of the radical Bell fighter design had been available for duty when required – a fitting enough epitaph for any combat aircraft.

CHAPTER SEVEN

Airacobra Survivors

As with many aircraft that did not have long post-war careers, the number of surviving Airacobras is relatively low when compared to types such as the P-51 Mustang.

A few museums do have a P-39 in their inventory, though few of these are wartime veterans. The United States Air Force Museum at Wright Patterson AFB has a P-39Q 44-3887 that has been converted back from a TP-39 two-seater. This was owned by the Hardwick Aircraft Company until 1966, by which time it was derelict. It was acquired by the USAFM and restored as a single-seat P-39Q, before being flown by Jack Hardwick to Wright Patterson in July 1966, where it remains on display.

The National Air and Space Museum have a former air racer, P-39Q 44-2433:

this was raced by Charles W. Bing in 1946 and Betty Hass until 1950 when it was retired to the NASM. It has since been restored as a United States Army Air Service example named 'Galloping Gertie', and is now on display in the Niagara Museum.

Another ex-racer is P-39Q 44-3908, acquired from the War Assets Administration from Altus AFB Oklahoma by W. H. Osterberg. This was owned and raced by a number of people, including former Czech refugee Mira Slovak of Van Nuys, California; he raced the aircraft at Reno in the early 1970s. It was subsequently bought by the Confederate Air Force, who passed it on to the Kalamazoo Aviation History Museum where it was restored to fly in the colours of a USAAC P-400.

Another airworthy example is that

operated by the Confederate Air Force based in Midland, Texas, a P-39Q that was abandoned in Hobbs, New Mexico in July 1945 after a forced landing. It was recovered and remained in storage until restoration started in 1968. This was finished by 1974 – although sadly the Airacobra belly-landed on its first flight; however, it was soon repaired and it now flies in a Soviet Air Force colour scheme.

Airframes for the Future

The number of airworthy Airacobras is set to rise, with several being rebuilt. Many of these are from a large number recovered in the mid-1970s by Charles Darby and Monty Armstrong of New Zealand, who scoured Papua New Guinea looking for

One of the earliest civilian Airacobras was P-39Q, NX92848, which was raced in the 1949 Thompson Trophy.

145

NX92848 taking off with Bell Aircraft Chief Test Pilot Alvin 'Tex' Johnson at the controls. He would win the 1946 Thompson in this aircraft.

warbirds, finding over a dozen Airacobras in varying states of preservation. A number of these have been passed on to warbird dealer David Tallichet of Los Angeles: some remain in storage in the United States, but others are under active restoration. One example has been identified as 42-19995, a P-39Q that was recovered in 1974 and is now with the MAPS Air Museum in Akron-Canton, Ohio. Another ex-Tallichet example is P-39N 42-8740, restored to fly by the Yankee Air Corps at Chino in California.

Kermit Weeks has a P-39K under restoration at his Florida museum, an ex-Papua New Guinea aircraft recovered by the South Australia Aviation Museum during the 1980s. It was restored to static condition in Australia before passing through The Fighter Collection at Duxford and on to the Weeks Air Museum. It was heavily damaged when Hurricane Andrew ripped through the museum in August 1992, but is being rebuilt.

Another former Papua New Guinea example that was statically restored in Australia found its way to the Museum of Flying in Santa Monica, California; it has since passed to The Fighter Collection at Duxford for restoration to flying condition: this work is being undertaken at Chino.

Not all examples found in the Far East were returned to the United States: a small number has remained in Australia, and some are now on display in Papua New Guinea itself. In Australia, Sid Beck has P-39D 41-6951 which he is statically restoring, and the National Musuem and Art Gallery in Port Moresby has P-39D 41-38351. Two P-400s are also on display in the Solomon Islands, with BW157 at the High School War Museum at Beti Kama, and another example at the Vilhu Cultural Village and War Museum. Wrecks have also been recovered from Alaska, and at least one of these may be rebuilt to fly.

Since many P-39s were operated in northern Russia, many would have strayed over the border with Finland: it is therefore no surprise that examples have been found in Finnish forests and lakes. One of these is now under active restoration by the Aviation Museum of Central Finland, a P-39Q that force-landed in June 1944 near Aunus. It was recovered by the Finnish Air Force and was stored until 1981 when they transferred it to the museum.

The United States Air Force Museum P-39Q 44-3887 on display at Dayton, Ohio. Eric Dumigan

'Galloping Gertie', the NASM P-39Q, pictured while on loan to the museum at Niagara Falls in 1998. Eric Dumigan

Mira Slovak's P-39Q at the Reno Air Races in 1972. Although prevented from racing after a late arrival, Slovak did fly the aeroplane, named 'Mr Mennen', around the course. This aeroplane in now airworthy with the Kalamazoo Aviation History Museum.

The cockpit of the Kalamazoo Aviation History Museum P-39.
Eric Dumigan

This unidentified fuselage was photographed in the late 1980s at Genesco in New York. Eric Dumigan

In February 1999/2000 the Kalamazoo P-39 was badly damaged when a truck smashed through the hangar wall, damaging its tail. Eric Dumigan

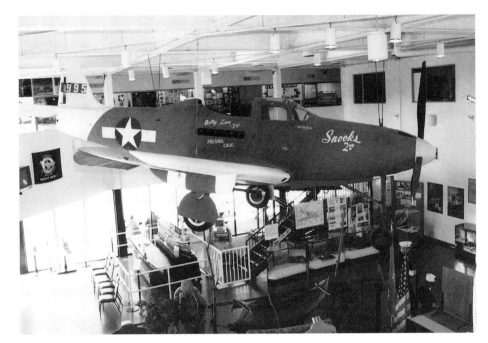

The Buffalo Naval and Servicemans Park had a P-39 painted in the colours of 42-19995 'Snooks 2nd', which was flown by Medal of Honor Winner Lt William A. Shomo whilst with the 36th fighter squadron of the 8th Fighter Group based in New Guinea. There is some confusion since the MAP Museum in Canton, Ohio, also claim to have this aeroplane, which is being restored to fly.

Eric Dumigan

The MAP museum at Canton has two P-39s on inventory, and both are dismantled.

The most interesting recent development in aircraft preservation has been the opening up of the former Soviet Union. Rumours of Western aircraft had been circulating for years, though few people had seen any of these. One story was of a museum close to Moscow that had examples of the Hurricane, the P-39, Spitfire and P-51. Some of these stories have proved to be unfounded, or

the aircraft have been scrapped; however, P-39s can be found in Russian museums. The Central Museum of the Armed Forces at Monino in Moscow has a P-39, as does the museum at Safonavo Air Force base at Severomorsk on the Kola peninsula, about 15 miles (24km) north of Murmansk. Another example is said to be held at the Pouryskin Museum in Novobirsk.

Rumours also abound of a compound full of World War II, Allied aircraft – although the principal source of rebuildable aircraft is from crash sites in the inaccessible areas of Northern Russia. With no free enterprise to trigger a profitable scrap-metal industry, many former wartime wreck sites were left as they were, because they were too far from major roads to be worth recovering. With the value of the

N9009 is an airframe with a confused history. Originally P-63C 44-4181, it was raced in the late 1940s and reportedly crashed in June 1968. Passing through the hands of former piston-engined world air speed record holder Darryl Greenamyer, it was rebuilt in 1971/72, using parts from several airframes, into a highly modified racer as seen here. It crashed into the sea near Long Beach, California, during a test flight with the pilot baling out. The wreck was salvaged in 1984 and parts were used in the restoration of 43-11117, which acquired the identity. It is now registered as N91448 with **Kermit Weeks** at **Polk City** in Florida. Howard Levy

P-63 420-68941 pictured at a Confederate airshow in 1971 whilst owned by Olin Crabtree and operated by the Confederate Air Force.

The sole P-63F, 43-11719, was raced in 1946 and passed through several owners before being bought by Jack Flaherty of Monterey, California. He also raced the aeroplane for several years before passing it on to the Wittington brothers of Fort Lauderdale who, in turn, passed it on to the Confederate Air Force.

Ex-racer 'Tipsy Miss' pictured at the 1989 airshow at North Weald in Essex. Its career was to be short-lived, as just one year later it crashed while departing from La Ferte Alais in France.

Melvyn Hiscock

Seen here in 1949 with clipped wings, P-63A 42-69097 was entered into the Thompson Trophy as number 87 'Kismet' but failed to qualify. This aircraft now flies as 269097 'Trust Me' with Stephen Grey's Fighter Collection at Duxford.

aircraft now being known to the Russians and the desire for the dollar being an acceptable part of life, these are now being actively sought, and more airframes are bound to emerge in the future.

Fewer P-63s have survived, although Russian sources suggest that some may still emerge from the USSR, and an example is on display at the museum in Monino. Examples are held by the National Air and Space Museum, and by the United States Air Force Museum, whose aircraft is one of four ex-Honduras Air Force examples that have survived. Two of these remain on display in Honduras, and the fourth is at the Pima County Air Museum in Tucson, Arizona.

Several examples are still airworthy, with several more under restoration; of the airworthy examples, two are operated by the Confederate Air Force. The first, P-63A 42-68941, was acquired in 1966, and P-63F 43-11719 was raced for several years before arriving at the Confederate Air Force in 1981.

Another ex-racer was P-63C 44-4393, which operated from 1946 until 1951 when it fell into disuse. It was bought by racing pilot John Sandberg in 1969 and restored as racer no. 28, 'Tipsy Miss'. It became a well known sight with several owners, and by 1981 was flying in an all-red scheme as 'Cobra'. It was acquired by The Fighter Collection at Duxford in 1988, and was repainted in a Soviet scheme. Sadly this aircraft was destroyed when departing the La Ferte Alais airshow south of Paris in June 1990, killing pilot John Larcombe.

The Fighter Collection soon replaced it with another former racer: P-63A 42-69097, that had been entered for the 1949 Thompson Trophy but had failed to qualify. It passed through several owners until finally it was acquired by Biggin Hill-based collector Doug Arnold. He passed it on to The Fighter Collection and it was restored, flying again in August 1994; it remains as the only Cobra in airworthy condition in Europe.

In the United States several more are airworthy, and of these perhaps the most impressive is P-63A 42-69021, now owned by former astronaut Frank Borman. This aircraft was purchased from the military, and is said to have had the central cannon removed. The new owner then flew it to California where he landed at Van Nuys airport. The change in the centre of gravity from removing the cannon must have made flying the aeroplane very hazardous, and it remained at Van Nuys, its owner having apparently lost interest in it; the airport authorities eventually sold it to cover its mounting parking fee. It was partially restored in California before being sold to Doug Arnold in England – but he did not take delivery. Instead the aircraft was bought by Frank Borman who entrusted its rebuild to Square One Aviation at Chino, in California. Square One had recently completed a P-51 Mustang rebuild for Borman that had won prizes as best warbird at the Oskosh Fly-In and at Lakeland, two of the most important events in the vintage aeroplane calendar.

Borman wanted his P-63 to win the prizes the following year too, and so all stops were pulled out to complete an immaculate rebuild in a short time. Under the leadership of Simon Brown, the missing parts were found and refurbished, and by September 1997 the airframe was ready for final fittings. These included all weaponry and a complete set of inert ammunition and original cockpit equipment. The attention to detail was stunning, with careful research revealing the details of paint shades and stencil details which were all applied, even if not visible on the final aeroplane. The end result was a masterpiece and, fittingly, walked away with all the prizes Borman had hoped for, and a few more besides.

As with the P-39, the prospect of finding rebuildable wrecks in the former Soviet Union is bound to increase the numbers of flyable and static Kingcobras: and a new generation of pilots will be able to see the Bell fighter in all its glory.

Bibliography

Bergerud, Eric M., *Fire in the Sky: The Air War in the South Pacific* (Boulder, Colorado: Westview, 2000)

Berliner, Don, 'Bell XP-77', *Model Airplane News* (July 1982)

Davis, Benjamin O. Jr, *American: An Autobiography* (Washington: Smithsonian Institution Press, 1990)

Dean, Francis H., *America's Hundred-Thousand: U.S. Production Fighters of World War Two* (Atglen, Pennsylvania: Schiffer Military/Aviation History, 1997)

Dorr, Robert F., *US Fighters of World War II* (New York: Sterling Press, 1991)

—— 'The Bell XP-83 Fighter of 1945–46' *Aviation News* (10 October 1984)

Drucker, Ronald, 'Limited Editions: The Bell XP-77 Fighter of World War 2' *Aviation News* (14 April, 1985)

Green, William and John, Fricker, *The Air Forces of the World: Their History, Development and Present Strength* (New York: Hanover House, 1958)

Gunston, Bill, *An Illustrated Guide to Allied Fighters of World War II* (London: Salamander Books, 1981)

—— *Plane Speaking* (Northampton: Patrick Stephens Limited, 1991)

Hagedorn, D.P., *Central American and Caribbean Air Forces* (Air-Britain, 1993)

Hammel, Eric, *Aces Against Japan: The American Aces Speak* (New York: Pocket Books, 1992)

Johnsen, Frederick, *Bell P-39 Airacobra* (Osceola: Specialty Press, 1991)

Matthews, Birch, *Cobra: Bell Aircraft Corporation, 1934–1946* (Atglen, Pennsylvania: Schiffer Military/Aviation History, 1996)

McDowell, Ernie, *P-39 Airacobra in Action* (Carrollton, Texas: Squadron/Signal Publications, 1980)

Mersky, Peter B., *Time of the Aces: Marine Pilots in the Solomons, 1942–1944* (Washington: History and Museums Division, Office of Marine Corps History, 1993)

Mitchell, Rock, *Airacobra Advantage: The Flying Cannon* (Missoula, Montana: Pictorial Histories Publishing Company, 1992)

Morrow, Cole, 'Guess What?' *Air Line Pilot* (April 1990)

Pelletier, Alain J., *Bell Aircraft Since 1935* (London: Putnam Aeronautical Books, 1992)

—— 'French Kings', *Air Enthusiast* 72

—— 'From Guadalcanal to Luzon: 67th Fighter Squadron' *Air Fan International* (December 1995)

Roman, V. *Aerokobry vstupayut v boy* [*The Airacobras Enter into Battle*] (Kiev: Kiyec-skaya fabrika drukovanoy reklamy, 1993.

Index

Aichi D3A 'Val' 67, 76, 79
Air Fighting Development Unit (AFDU) 25, 34
Aircraft & Armament Experimental Establishment (A&AEE) 25, 34
air racing 125, 129–130, 132, 138
Allison V-1710 13, 17, 19, 20, 25, 48, 51, 107, 133, 135
ALSIB route 94–95, 138
Aleutian Islands, defence of 72–73
American Volunteer Group 38, 39, 63
Archer, Lee 109
Armstrong, 1st Lt Patrick 63
Armstrong, Monty 145
Army Air Corps (AAC) 9
Army Air Forces (AAF) 9
Arnold, Doug 155
Arnold, Maj Gen Henry 'Hap' 9, 12, 16, 27, 93
Augusta Herald 27

Bachelor, Col Jerome 40
Badoglio, Marshal 117
Beck, Sid 146
Bedell Smith, Gen Walter 123
Begaud, Adjutant 141
Belayakov, G.I. 96
Bell aircraft
    Model 3 12, 13
    P-39C (Model 13) 25
    P-39D (Model 15) 27
    P-39F 51
    P-39G 51
    P-39J 39
    P-39K 77
    P-39L 77
    P-39M 77
    P-39N (Model 26F) 78
    P-39Q 107
    P-400 (Model 14), 34
    P-63 Kingcobra 50, 135
    TP-39Q-5 (Model 39) 112
    XFL-1 Airabonita (Model 5) 16, 19–20, 51
    XFM-1 Airacuda 13
    XP-39 (Model 4) 16, 17
    XP-39B 20-22
    XP-39E (Model 23) 48–49
    XP-52 (Model 16) 91
    XP-59 (Model 16) 91

XP-59A Airacomet (Model 27) 91, 99–101
XP-77 16, 120–122
XP-83 126–127
YP-39 (Model 12) 18
Bell, Larry 7, 9, 11, 19, 20, 48, 112, 120
The Bellringer 11, 34, 75
Benjamin, Lloyd P. 94-95
Berkow, Capt Joseph 76
Bethune, Norman 112
Billoin, Capitaine 142
Bing, Charles W. 130, 145
Bochkov, Capt I.V. 85
Boeing B-17 Flying Fortress 12, 27, 68, 69
Boeing F4B 19
Boeing P-26 11
Bolero, Operation 68, 69
Borman, Frank 155
Boudier, Commandant 140
Bour, Bill 130
Brannon, Capt Dale D. 69, 71
British Overseas Airways Corporation (BOAC) 29
British Purchasing Commission 29
Brown, Charles 'Chuck' 129
Brown, Roy 109
Bryan, Don 74

Cant Z.506B 123
Caproni-Campini N.1 101
Carroll, Mike 130
Cavoroz, Commandant 143
Cerutti, Dino 112
Chance Vought F4U Corsair 76, 86
Chennault, Col Claire 18, 38, 63
Christian, Frank 27
Churchill, Winston 11, 34, 36
Clarkson, Christopher 29
Consolidated B-24 Liberator 104
Consolidated Aircraft Corporation 11
Continental XIV-1430-5 91
Craigie, Brig Gen Laurence C. 99
Curphy, Dr M.P. 18
Curtiss A-12 12
Curtiss C-46 Commando 53
Curtiss P-36 Mohawk 12
Curtiss P-40 Warhawk/Kittyhawk 7, 15, 24, 38, 42, 58, 60, 62, 64, 67, 72, 73, 74, 75, 78, 85, 86, 95, 96, 104, 105, 109, 110

Daimler-Benz DB 601N 57
Darby, Charles 145
Davis, Col Benjamin O. 106, 108, 109
De Pinson, Capitaine 140
Dean, 1st Lt Fred 27
Deatrich, 1st Lt James 79, 81, 104
DeBow, Capt Charles 106
Demming, Jay 112, 129, 132
Diles, Spiro 'Sammy' 130
Dixmunde 140
Dornier Do 217 58, 116
Douglas A-20 Havoc 75, 93
Douglas C-47 27, 81, 123
Douglas D-558-1 Skystreak 150
Douglas O-36 12
Douglas SBD/A-24 Dauntless 69, 76, 77
Dupre, Capitaine De Royer 142, 143
Durand, Lt Edward 62
Dusard, Col Leo F. 75

Eaker, Lt Gen Ira 109
Echols, Maj Gen 49
Eiche, Raymond E. 130
Eisenhower, Gen Dwight D. 123
Emmons, Lt Gen D.C. 27
Eucker, Bob 130

Fahey, James C. 123
Fay, Charles 127
Ferrying Division 94
Fiedler, 2nd Lt William F. 79
Focke-Wulf Fw 189 58, 85
Focke-Wulf Fw 190 85
Fornoff, Arthur L. 112
French Air Force units
    5th Escadre de Chasse 140
    GC I/3 Corse 98
    GC I/4 Navarre 98, 116
    GC I/5 Champagne 98
    GC I/5 Vende 140, 141, 143, 144
    GC I/9 Limousin 98, 139, 143, 144
    GC II/5 Ile de France 140, 141, 144
    GC II/6 Normandie-Niemen 139, 141, 142, 143, 144
    GC II/6 Travail 98, 117
    GC II/9 Auvergne 98, 139
    GC III/6 Rousillon 98, 141, 142, 144
Fricker, John 54
Fuerza Aerea Hondurena 138

Gardner, Lefty 130
General Electric I-40 126
General Electric I-A 99
Gholson, 1st Lt Grover 65
Giap, Gen Vo Nguyen 144
Gilead, 2nd Lt Michael 65
Glinka, Boris 97, 114
Glinka, Dimitry 97, 114, 119
Gloster E.28/39 101
Golofastov, Capt Vikto Ye 58
Goodlin, Chalmers 'Slick' 125, 127, 129
Green, William 54
Grob, Sous-Lt 143
Grumman F4F Wildcat 20, 61, 69, 72, 86
Grumman F6F Hellcat 76, 86, 144
Grumman F8F Bearcat 135, 143, 144
Grumman TBM Avenger 76
Grumman XF5F-1 Skyrocket 20
Guadalcanal, battle of 69–72
Gunn, 1st Lt George 111
Gunston, Bill 114

Hanson, James R. 43, 49, 53
Hardwick, Jack 145
Harp, James 130
Harriman, Averill 115
Hartmann, Erich 97
Hass, Betty 145
Havens, Larry 130, 138
Hawker Hurricane 11, 34, 36, 58, 96, 114
Haymes, 1st Lt William E. 76
Heaney, Mark 53
Heinkel He 111 58
Heinkel He 178 101
Heinkel He 280V-1 101
Henschel Hs 126 85
Hodgkins, Frank 91
Holloway, Lt Col Bruce 49
Hosler, Russ 130
Huston, John 72

Ilyushin Il-2 Shturmovik 138
Indefatigable, HMS 110
Indo-China, campaign in 139–144
Italian Air Force units
    12th Gruppo 117
    19th Gruppo 117
    9th Gruppo 117
Italy, campaign in 108–110, 116–117, 122–123

Jackson, Lt Red 106
Jodl, Gen Alfred 123
Johnson, Lyndon B. 66
Johnston, A. M. 'Tex' 7, 125, 129, 130
Jones, 1st Lt Curran 'Jack' 66–67
Junkers Ju 87 Stuka 96
Junkers Ju 88 58, 85, 109

Kawasaki Ki-61 'Tony' 76
Kenney, Gen George 71, 104
Khulayev, Grigori 119
Kinkella, Joseph M. 130
Knight, Ken 130
Knoxville News-Sentinel 27
Koga, PO Tadayoshi 63
Koldunov, A. 119
Kozhedub, Ivan N. 119
Krivoysheyev, Lt Ye A. 85
Kuban River, battle of 95–97
Kwajalein, landings at 102

Larcombe, John 130, 155
Lavochkin La-5 107, 54
Lavochkin LaGG-3 96, 98
Lilly, Howard 'Tick' 130
Litvinov, Maxim 93
Livingston, Capt Al 42–43, 49
Lockheed Hudson 67
Lockheed P-38 Lightning 7, 29, 42, 64, 67, 68, 69, 72, 75, 76, 81, 86, 103, 104, 110, 123
Lockheed P-80 Shooting Star 51, 127
Lockheed Ventura 76
Love, 2nd Lt Bob 60
Lovett, 1st Lt Joseph 64
Lynch, 1st Lt Thomas J. 65, 67

Macchi C.202 123
Macchi C.205 123
Magidoff, Robert 55
Mainwaring, 1st Lt Don 63
Mao Tse Tung 139
Marshall, 1st Lt Winton W. 'Bones' 11
Martin B-10 12
Martin B-26 Marauder 53, 76
Martin A-30 Baltimore 117, 123
McDonough, Andrew C. 11
McGee, 2nd Lt Don 'Fibber' 63, 64, 65
McNeese, Lt Col George N. 75
McNickle, Lt M.F. 25
Melton, 2nd Lt William 109
Meng, 1st Lt Lewis 'Bill' 63
Messerchmitt Me 210 58
Messerschmitt Bf 109 9, 11, 12, 18, 24, 34, 57, 58, 64, 69, 96, 97, 112
Messerschmitt Bf 110 68
Messerschmitt Me 262 101, 109
Messerschmitt, Willy 9
Mikoyan-Gurevich MiG-3 58, 96
Miles Master 137
Miller, Maj Wilber G. 72
Missouri, USS 125
Mitchell, Rick 39, 80, 81
Mitsubishi A5M 'Claude' 67
Mitsubishi A6M 'Zero' 9, 11, 17, 18, 24, 39, 57, 58, 62, 63, 64, 65, 66, 67
Mitsubishi G4M 'Betty' 64
Mitsubishi Ki-46 'Dinah' 76

Mitsubishi L4M1 'Topsy' 79
Molotov, Vladimir 115
Morill, Lt Col Phineas K. 72
Morrow, Cole H. 121
Motte, Commandant 141

Nakajima A6M2-N 'Rufe' 73
Nakajima Ki-44 'Oscar' 39
National Advisory Committee for Aeronautics (NACA) 16, 18, 20, 24
New Guinea, defence of 59–68
Newhall, Wilson V. 'Bill' 130
North Africa, campaign in 98–99, 116
North American AT-6 26
North American B-25 Mitchell 67, 76, 93
North American P-51 Mustang 7, 11, 12, 42, 51, 64, 74, 80, 86, 99
North American P-82 Twin Mustang 127
Northrop A-17 12
Northrop P-61 Black Widow 105
Novikov, Gen 37

Odom, Bill 130
Olsmobile T-9 cannon 13
Ortman, Earl 130
Osterberg, W.H. 145

Patton, Sgt James 125
Pearl Harbor, attack on 38, 67
Pemberton, H.L. 130, 134
Perotte, Lt 141
Perrier, Adjutant Leon 142
Pinball, Operation 136
Portugese Air Force 69
Poyer, Harland M. 13
Poykryshkin, Aleksandr I. 94, 96, 112, 114, 118, 119
PQ17 convoy 36
Pratt & Whitney R-2800-23 91
Price, Capt George E. 20

RAAF No.75 Squadron 64
RAF No.601 Squadron 34
Rabaul, battle of 103–104
Ranger SGV-770C-1B 120
Rechkalov, Grigori 96, 114, 119
Republic P-47 Thunderbolt 7, 42, 74, 86, 99, 110, 140
Rhodes, Charles 126
Roberts, Capt Daniel 58
Robinson, Capt James 79
Roosevelt, Franklin D. 68, 91
Royal Aircraft Establishment 137
Rumyantsyev, Feodor 114

Sakai, Saburo 67
Sakhalin Island, battle for 138
Sales, Capitaine 142

Salisbury, F.M. 112
Sandberg, John 130, 155
Savoia-Marchetti S.M.79 123
Savoia-Marchetti S.M.81 123
Scandrett, 1st Lt Harvey 65
Seven Mile Drome 60–62
Seversky P-35 38
Seversky P-36 12
Sheehan, Howard 'Pete' 83
Shomo, 2nd Lt William 79, 80
Singer, Frank 130
Singleton, 'Lucky' Jack 130
Sirotin, Maj V.F. 96
Skoromokhov, N. 119
Slovak, Mira 145
Soviet Air Force Units
   2nd Guards Combined Aviation
      Regiment 37
   9th Guards Fighter Division 53
   16th Guards IAP 53
   19th Guards IAP 37, 85, 96, 98
   30th Guards IAP 85
   104th Guards IAP 96
   17th IAP 96
   45th IAP 96, 97
   57th IAP 114
   78th IAP 37, 96
   153rd IAP 58, 85
   6th ZAB 115
   22nd ZAP 56, 58, 59, 96
   25th ZAP 96
Soviet Naval Air Force 37
Sparks, Brian 19
Spencer, 2nd Lt Roy 109
Sponts, Les 73
Stalin, Josef 34, 36, 93, 96, 138
Stalingrad, battle of 54, 55, 95
Stanley, Bob 48, 49, 53
Stanley, Robert M. 19, 99
Stearman PT-17 26
Stephens, Col Evans G. 26, 29, 39, 41,
   84
Supermarine Spitfire 11, 34, 56, 69, 93,
   96, 114, 117, 123, 140
Suslapatov, Gen Ivan 123
Sutton B-11 harness 15
Swanberg, 2nd Lt 60

Tallichet, David 146
Taylor, Lt James 16, 17
Taylor, Lt Kenneth 38
Thompson, Capt John A. 70
Toubman, 2nd Lt Izzy 63
Tresville, Capt Robert 106

Troxell, Lt Clifton 65
Tucker, Charles 130, 138
Turpin, Sgt-chef 143
Twining, Gen Nathan F. 71

US Army units
   5th Army 108
   82nd Airborne Division 108
   7th Infantry Division 102
   504th Parachute Infantry Regiment
      108
US Army Air Corps units
   5th Air Force 41, 71, 104
   8th Air Force 68
   12th Air Force 69, 75, 105
   13th Air Force 71, 75
   15th Air Force 106
   22nd Bomb Group 65
   97th Bomb Group 68
   5th Fighter Command 60
   8th Fighter Group 58, 59, 60, 63
   15th Fighter Group 77
   18th Fighter Group 72, 77, 103
   23rd Fighter Group 42, 49
   31st Fighter Group 26, 29, 39, 41, 69
   35th Fighter Group 41, 63
   49th Fighter Group 63
   52nd Fighter Group 69
   54th Fighter Group 72, 73
   81st Fighter Group 69, 75
   318th Fighter Group 102
   322nd Fighter Group 105
   332nd Fighter Group 106–110
   347th Fighter Group 71, 75, 77, 79,
      103, 104, 105
   350th Fighter Group 69, 75
   352nd Fighter Group 74
   357th Fighter Group 64
   412th Fighter Group 101
   475th Fighter Group 83
   7th Fighter Squadron 104
   8th Fighter Squadron 104
   12th Fighter Squadron 77, 103
   35th Fighter Squadron 60, 65
   36th Fighter Squadron 60, 63, 64, 65
   39th Fighter Squadron 26, 41, 65, 67
   40th Fighter Squadron 26, 27, 29, 31,
      41, 65, 67
   41st Fighter Squadron 26
   42nd Fighter Squadron 72, 73
   44th Fighter Squadron 77
   46th Fighter Squadron 77, 102
   47th Fighter Squadron 77
   56th Fighter Squadron 72, 73

   57th Fighter Squadron 72, 73
   67th Fighter Squadron 69, 70, 71, 75,
      76
   68th Fighter Squadron 71, 75, 79
   70th Fighter Squadron 71, 75, 77, 79
   72nd Fighter Squadron 102
   80th Fighter Squadron 60, 63, 67
   91st Fighter Squadron 75
   92nd Fighter Squadron 75
   99th Fighter Squadron 109
   100th Fighter Squadron 106
   301st Fighter Squadron 106
   302nd Fighter Squadron 106, 109
   307th Fighter Squadron 69
   308th Fighter Squadron 69
   309th Fighter Squadron 69
   328th Fighter Squadron 74
   339th Fighter Squadron 71, 72, 75
   421st Night Fighter Squadron 105
   68th Observation Group 69
   68th Reconnaissance Group 75
   82nd Tactical Reconnaissance
      Squadron 78, 79, 83, 104, 105
   110th Tactical Reconnaissance
      Squadron 104
   154th Tactical Reconnaissance
      Squadron 75
US Marines 1st Division 70

Vandegrift, Maj Gen Alexander 70
Vandenberg, Gen Hoyt S. 115
Vorozheikin, A. 119

Wagner, Lt Col Boyd 'Buzz' 58, 60, 62,
   63
Washington Times-Herald 27
Weeks, Kermit 146
Welch, 1st Lt George S. 38, 67
Whitehead, Gen Ennis 104
Whiteman, Roy 11
Whiteside, Alfred T. 'Al' 130
Whittle, Frank 99
Wilkins, 1st Lt Lawrence 109
Wittman, Steve 130
Woods, Robert J. 11, 13, 19
Woodson, O.L. 11
Woolams, Jack 120, 125, 127, 129, 132

Yakovlev Yak-3 54, 58, 98, 110
Yakovlev Yak-9 54
Yevstigneev, Kirill A. 119
Yoshino, Satoshi 67

Ziendowski, 1st Lt George A. 13
Zolotov, Yvgeney 114